To Ian
I appreciate your help!
Enjoy the read!   Bill

The Emperor's New Clothes:

An [Un]popular Account of the Origins of Christianity

Bill Johnston

Ian & Rochelle Underhill
19 Doon Dr
London ON N5X 3N9

©2008 William Johnston
All Rights Reserved. No part of this publication may be reproduced, stored in a retrieval system, or transmitted in any form by any means, electronic, mechanical, photocopying, recording or otherwise without written permission from the author. Except for brief quotations embodied in critical articles or reviews.

Thoughtful comments on this work are welcome at
emperors.clothes@yahoo.ca

Printed in Canada
Cover design by Angela Henderson.

ISBN 978-0-9809371-0-7

FIN 09 04 08

Library and Archives Canada Cataloguing in Publication

Johnston, William
    The emperor's new clothes: an [un]popular account of the origins of christianity / William Johnston.

ISBN 978-0-9809371-0-7

    I. Title. Johnston, William. The emperor's new clothes: an [un]popular account of the origins of christianity.

PS8639.H658C75 2008   C813'.6   C2008-901098-1

For Elana, Mike, Jay, Kurt, Mark

PREFACE

This book has had a gestation period of some two decades. It has started, stopped, backed up, changed directions, and generally exhibited a will of its own. One thing that has not changed is my desire to make it accessible to those who are not Biblical scholars. This has meant no footnotes and the avoidance of scholarly language. Occasionally, of course, the reader may want more information on a topic, and I refer him or her to the sourcelist at the back, and recommend reading several of these works. For many people of faith, only by reading several other sources will they be convinced that I am not making this up.

CONTENTS

1. The Intersection of Faith and Knowledge — *1*
2. The Sumerians — *11*
3. The Gift of the Nile — *17*
4. The Greeks: Eleusis, Dionysos, Orpheus — *35*
5. The Romans and Cybele — *47*
6. Mithra the Unconquered — *57*
7. The Mystery Religions Compared — *77*
8. Galilee in the First Century CE — *93*
9. Did Jesus Exist? — *107*
10. Bethlehem — *113*
11. Life and Teachings of Jesus — *123*
12. Passion, Death, Resurrection — *141*
13. The Infant Church — *163*
14. Introduction to the Gospels — *171*
15. The Four Gospels — *181*
16. Paul: The Invention of a New Greek Religion — *197*
17. The Apocrypha and the Gnostics — *213*
18. The Growth of the New Religion — *231*
19. Symbols and Sacraments — *243*
20. Superstition — *253*
21. The Virgin Mary and the Role of Women — *265*
22. The Pagans Strike Back — *279*
23. A Tale of Two Emperors — *291*
24. The Calendar — *305*
25. A Look Ahead — *321*
26. Sourcelist — *327*

1

THE INTERSECTION OF FAITH AND KNOWLEDGE

"The uneducated are always in a majority with us."
Tertullian

"But he has nothing on at all!" said a little child at last.
Hans Christian Andersen

In December 1945, Muhammad Ali Sammar, an Egyptian peasant digging soil for fertilizer, discovered an earthenware jar, broke it open, and found it contained thirteen leather-bound papyrus codices written in the ancient language of Coptic. He took them home, where some of the pages were burned to keep the fire going. The remainder were gradually sold on the black market, and eventually found their way to the Coptic Museum in Cairo. But not until 1955 did scholars realize what they contained—the chief treasure was the only full copy of the *Gospel of Thomas*.

While not as extensive as the celebrated *Dead Sea Scrolls* from the Essene community of Qumran, this find at Nag Hammadi is of more importance to historical Christianity. The *Gospel of Thomas* was at first assumed to be second or third century, but scholars now believe it is very early—probably written in the 40s—a full generation earlier than any of the Four Gospels. The *Gospel of Thomas* is as close as we may ever get to the thoughts and words of Jesus. And the Jesus who is portrayed in *Thomas* is very different indeed from his traditional image in the Biblical Gospels.

The reaction of orthodox Christianity to this new gospel has varied from hostility to a studied indifference. Christianity has its story, and it's sticking with it. But as historical research progresses on a variety of fronts, the church that has been dominant for two millennia will be hard pressed in future to maintain its credibility.

Christianity, among the great religions of the world, is a latecomer. Twenty-first century people, used to thinking in minutes or hours, have difficulty grasping that two thousand years, in the history of ideas, is quite a short time. Basic notions about life and death and the afterlife change very slowly indeed. As the most remarkable religion of a very remarkable age, Christianity quite naturally absorbed beliefs and customs from the thoroughly pagan society that surrounded it.

Unlike some other religions (Hinduism, for example) Christianity is supposed to have been conceived at a definite time, in a definite place, and by a definite person. Christians feel they know a great deal about Jesus and his life, and many have made a close study of his teachings. Huge buildings have been constructed in his honour. Thousands of people make their living explaining the words of Jesus and his friends. At least one billion believers claim to hold fast to the lessons of the *Gospels*.

There is thus little sympathy for the scholar who, in trying to find the truth about some aspect of Jesus or his time, comes across facts that disturb the serene picture that has been created of Christian origins. And yet this happens all the time, because the unarguable fact is that virtually none of what we call Christianity is the product of the life or the mind of Jesus.

Where did it come from then, if not from Jesus? Despite what many Christians have been led to believe, not that much of it was inherited from monotheistic Judaism. As we shall see, Jesus was not a very good mainstream Jew, influenced as he was by Pythagoras, the Nazirites, and by the Greek Cynics. Even more important, most of what we call Christianity was developed not by Jesus, but by his Greekified followers. Forty-five years after his crucifixion, the author of Mark was unaware of most of the details of Jesus' life, but acutely aware of political realities—and that meant legitimizing Christianity by repainting Jesus as a Hebrew prophet. The gaps in his story were filled with convenient pagan legends, and a selective mining of Hebrew Scripture to show what Jesus should have been.

Overwhelmingly, the concepts and practices of Christianity originated in the great pagan religions of the time. Why don't the clergy tell us so? Because they prefer not to look; and if they should look, they prefer not to tell us what they see. How much of modern Christianity is ancient paganism in disguise? That question will take far more than this book to answer, but it has now become clear that virtually all of modern Christian belief has its roots in the worship of the old heathen gods. A person who has only a passing acquaintance with the roots of Christianity, and who takes the *Bible* pretty much at face value, will be surprised and even shocked by the findings of recent scholars.

So an examination of what is currently known about Jesus and his church is like telling the little tykes at the mall that there is no Santa Claus. Of course Santa's real. They can see him…he's right there. And the consequences of Santa being a fake? The nagging doubts that won't go away? The fact that the adults whom you trusted are engaged, willingly or no, in a monstrous deception? And so it is with the origins of the Christian faith. The birth stories of Jesus are demonstrably phony. His life events are completely unknown. Most of his teachings were the product of someone else. The Passion probably didn't happen, nor did the Resurrection. The *Gospels* were written to hide the truth of history, and if he were to return, Jesus would have nothing whatever to do with the Graeco-Roman organization which his followers cobbled together in his name. But let's not tell anybody.

How did theology get into its present fix? How do the great religions of Egypt, Persia, Greece and Rome contribute to modern belief? The last half century's research on the life and times of Jesus and on the organization of the early church has exposed the legendary nature of many Christian claims. As Christianity grew, it became more and more like the gigantic organization which it replaced—the Roman Empire. By the fourth century, the religion of the Galilean prophet was unrecognizable. To see this shift of focus, read first Matthew's version of what a person should believe and do—the Sermon on the Mount—and then read the Nicene Creed of the fourth century. These statements certainly don't appear to be from the same religion.

Much of Western religion is really just undergrowth—the shrubs and weeds of custom, legend, assumption and rationalization that add flavour to the dry gruel of theology. Let's nod our thanks to the Egyptian farmer, the Greek trader, and the Iranian herdsman who, far more than the Galilean carpenter, shaped what we call Christianity.

Historical research and the historical method are the enemies of traditional Christianity. The idea that the past was essentially different from the present began during the Italian Renaissance, and is now deeply ingrained in modern thought.

The writing of history is affected by the daily conditions and concerns of the writer. This is not news. As early as 250 CE the writer Novatian suggested that the image of God reflected not God, but the state of human culture and its ability to understand.

Many devout Christian believers still have a black and white view of religious history: only one interpretation of Jesus and his life can be correct. Their view of all this research is simple: Jesus was good, his church is good, and so historical investigation should confirm what good Christians believe. Many people, including a disturbing number of scholars, believe that Christianity has been triumphant over the past two millennia because that is the will of God. Therefore it should be held unique among religions, and those critical standards that are applied to other belief systems and other ancient personalities should not be applied either to Christ or to his church. Similarly, it has been difficult for the average person to be objective about the great pagan thinkers of the ancient world: for two thousand years they have been portrayed as either precursors of Christianity, or as enemies of the Truth. "Theologians", says G.A. Wells, "are experts at creating fog."

The people who are supposed to know about these things are usually heavily compromised. Seminaries and schools of theology provide (relatively) comfortable livings for church-approved scholars. Too often they use all the apparatus of scholarship to support what their faith has already told them to believe. They are normally well-armed with plenty of Scriptural quotes and references, but we can in no way regard them as objective. On the one hand they claim to be reporting what they find, while at the same time claiming to know the answers before they ask the questions. They are the religious equivalent of advertising copywriters, and they seem to work while looking over their shoulders, for they are well aware of Christianity's tradition of extreme intolerance for wayward theologians.

Of course, to be fair, most of the bias is unintended, the product of a restrictive set of cultural goggles. We are all influenced by what the English historian Sir Herbert Butterfield called the "Whig Interpretation" of history: whatever is, is right; the present is superior to the past; history is the story of progress. The winners rewrite history, minimize the conflict, and claim that the victorious views had always been in the majority. When stated this baldly, the flaws are obvious, but in our day-to-day lives we continue to act as though it were all true. These assumptions are especially and glaringly obvious in our attitudes to religion. Plenty of theologians still believe that human history is the earthly expression of the Will of God.

Christianity has long been an imperialist religion— Romans, Franks, Spaniards, Portuguese, British, and now Americans—all were convinced that their Christian and monotheistic insights ought to apply to all other peoples. The beliefs of others were "myths", but the term "myth" was not to apply to the *Bible*: it was "true", and all too often held to be literally, absolutely, top-to-bottom, you-better-believe-it "true."

But today the Age of Faith is gone, replaced by the Age of Doubt. Literal belief in the *New Testament* stories has largely disappeared from the pews of the great churches. The moral lessons of Jesus are admired, in as far as they are known. The Christmas and Easter narratives still pack an emotional wallop for most believers, but today's Christian is riddled with doubt about the meaning of life, the divinity of Jesus, and the possibilities of the hereafter. Still, a Gallup survey of 1989 showed that 82% of Americans believe that God is working miracles today. This particular statistic is probably a cheap, off-the-cuff response, but it indicates that people dearly want to believe. But mere wanting is not deep faith. The church is hamstrung by its past, and by its insistence on belief in events that didn't happen. The American bishop John Spong claims that given the current psychological state of Western churchgoers, trying to revive traditional Christian belief is "like doing plastic surgery on a corpse."

Nevertheless, Christian churches remain a formidable political pressure group, especially when defending conservative, even trogloditic positions—anti-gay, anti-birth control, anti-feminist, anti-abortion. Since its establishment by the Emperor Constantine as the official religion of the Roman Empire, the church has been both effective and ruthless in attacking its "enemies". As we consider the growth of Christianity, remember that the Christian church is, and probably always has been, a political machine, run by politicians.

Thus there are compelling reasons to have a careful look at Christian origins. If Christian ideas began in first century Palestine, it is legitimate to ask historical questions, and use historical methods to evaluate the data, to try to sort out what really happened. And so we turn to the records.

But the evidence from the early centuries turns out to be very muddy. Not many people of the time could write. Few written documents of the time survive. Important religious documents were fudged, falsified, and intentionally destroyed. The *Gospels*, for example, are not reliable history—as we will see, they are so biased that they should properly be termed propaganda. Still, the *Gospel* stories are so deeply ingrained, so familiar (and to many so comforting), that it is nearly impossible to think clearly about them. Our moral sense, our social sense, key phrases of our language, indeed our very world-view has been shaped by the *New Testament*. Unfortunately, we cannot trust it.

The application of historical-critical thinking to the life of Jesus has rendered most of the Gospel events either untenable, or commonplace. As scholars labour to uncover the Jesus of history, they have increasingly come to a bizarre conclusion—that there is nothing there to uncover. Several theologians have suggested that a biography of Jesus is now impossible—that there was a Christ, but perhaps no historical Jesus behind him. We ordinary folk are left to make what sense we can from that statement.

So there we are. Serious theology cannot continue to ignore history and historians. Historians are increasingly saying we can know nothing certain about Jesus. A lot of people have declared they need him in their lives. Evangelicals are sure we are personally doomed if we reject him. Faced with this dilemma, too many people in the West have opted to ignore both theology and history, to hold fast to an unexamined, irrational, and untenable faith, and to hope for the best—to keep believing in Santa Claus.

Besides providing the vital skill of critical thinking, the Renaissance left Western society with a respect for the past. However, over the last century this respect has steadily declined. Educated people of Shakespeare's time were familiar with Greek and Roman history, and many had studied Latin and Greek. How many people do you know who could translate a simple Latin sentence? Who could tell you a single fact about Alcibialdes? Yet even two generations ago, the classically-trained gentleman was quite a common figure. With the disappearance of the classics and ancient history from the modern mentality, the only connection many people have with the ancient world is the life of Jesus. But if there is nothing to balance it against, or to put it in perspective, then any version of his life could convince the layman. For example, each Christmas, millions of believers ponder over the miracle of Jesus being born to a virgin. The mystery takes on quite a different complexion when you realize it was also seriously claimed for at least eleven other major figures of the ancient world. It cannot logically be true for all of them, but it is vitally important to Christians that it be true for Jesus.

It is very difficult to accept that much of what one believes is "mythology". Myths, even when they are not scientifically verifiable, still fulfill a deep need in believers. In these conflicts between the head and the heart, the heart frequently wins; and the belief, although it may be demonstrably illogical, continues. The author and former churchman Tom Harpur observed:

> "Ancient people did not believe their myths. They believed them in the sense that they believed in the truth beneath the stories."

This requires that we are able to adopt a form of thinking which is quite alien to people of our time… we are not very good at thinking symbolically, and we have a hard time recognizing that. How do you describe a bicycle to a fish? But when we look back into the pagan past, at those beliefs which are no longer held, it becomes easier to accept the mythological nature of religious belief.

So this is a book about faith—what we have believed for about three thousand years. It is also about knowledge—what we know and how we know it. And it is about the intersection of faith and knowledge—how the historical approach using critical thinking has rolled back many of the claims of the Christian faith, but also, and far more difficult, the way in which two thousand years of thinking a certain way has made it very hard to step outside that box and be objective about the life of Jesus of Galilee.

2

THE SUMERIANS

"Don't look behind. Something might be gaining on you."
                                          Satchel Paige

"All gods are only different powers of the sun."
                                          Macrobius

Modern Christianity, like modern society of which it is part, has deep roots in the ancient cities of the Tigris and Euphrates valleys. These early urban centers drew their wealth from the lush countryside around them (since turned to desert), and their peoples organized complex religious and philosophical systems. Their legendary heroes such as Sargon parlayed these cities of the plain into the first great empires. Sargon, incidentally, was condemned at birth (about 3000 BCE) by the local tyrant. In order to save his life, his mother hid him in a basket made of bulrushes and waterproofed with pitch, and then she floated the basket along the edge of the river. Sargon was found there by a daughter of the royal household, and as an adult, overthrew the tyrannical king to lead his oppressed people to freedom. If this story sounds familiar, it is because the same story is told of Cyrus king of Persia (born about 800 BCE), and of Moses (about 1500 BCE), and parts of it appear yet again in Matthew's story of the "Massacre of the Innocents" by the evil king Herod at the time of Jesus' birth. This is typical of the type of problem we will encounter again and again: are the facts true for all of them? None of them? What criteria should we apply to sift out "the truth"?

The religious structure of the early Babylonian civilizations seems enormously confusing to the modern mind. These early cities were subjected to a series of conquering armies, and each new conqueror brought along his new gods which he piled atop the others. No one was particularly offended, except for modern scholars, who try to make sense of it. The priests of the defeated gods tried to make the best of it, claiming that their particular god had intentionally allowed the evil to happen because his people or their leaders were sinful. This claim was made over and over again in the Jewish Scriptures, just as it was in the writings of their pagan contemporaries, and is still being made by Christian clergy today.

In general, the gods of Mesopotamia came in threes- a chief god who lived in the sky (often called Anu or El), an earth-god (Baal or Bel or Saturn), and a god of the underground (such as Mot). Today we have the ironic situation where many Judaeo-Christian names and terms are in fact tributes to the old Mesopotamian sky-god: Abel, Bethel, chapel, Eli, Elizabeth, Emmanuel, Michael, Raphael, and more.

Babylonian religion also had demons in abundance. Sculptural representations of them are probably at the core of the modern image of Satan. The prehistoric battle between Michael the warrior archangel and Lucifer is also from the same ancient pagan source. The dark, gloomy underworld where people went after death was another Babylonian concept: the gods had determined your fate based on how you had behaved on earth (but of course the gods wisely made some allowance for those with high earthly status.)

Sumerian and Babylonian religion also had a variety of other gods and demigods. Inanna, the goddess of love, later became Venus. Her lover Adonis (also called Tammuz and Dumuzi) was killed annually and then miraculously rose from the dead. Gilgamesh was the original Good Shepherd. Enki created humans out of dust. Shamash (or Sol) the sun-god, and his father Sin, the moon-god, also commanded human obedience. Most of these characters seem vaguely familiar to those of us raised in the Christian tradition, because they have appeared and reappeared with different names over the centuries.

Babylonian society was fascinated with and governed by the sky. Colleges of priests studied the stars and planets, gave them names and characteristics, and developed a combination of astrology and astronomy which controlled people's actions. But how did they arrive at the absurd conclusion that the stars and planets controlled human life? At night, the desert stars seem far brighter than they do to modern urbanites. Celestial objects rarely look impressive from the balcony of your high-rise. Moreover, people then, like people now, saw their world as a disturbing and uncertain place. Many of them hoped that somehow, somewhere, Something or Someone was in charge—that there was a Master Plan. If the symbols could be read correctly, maybe the Plan could be decoded, and probably the sky was where the Plan was written.

Both good and bad might come from the desert sky. The sun was essential for the growth of their crops, but was not always the friend that it seems in more temperate climes. Babylonians were not such devout sunworshippers as later, more northerly societies. The sun is nobody's friendly deity on a desert summer afternoon. But the farmers of Mesopotamia understood the basic equation clearly:no sun =

no crops = no food.

Beneath their multitude of gods, though, the Mesopotamian societies were over time moving towards monotheism. Still they persisted in using the old tribal names of the deities, because it emphasized a unique relationship with the gods, and forced them to listen to your prayers. These ancient religions suffered form the same credibility problems as modern ones: bad people prospered, good people went broke, got sick and died. Sometimes the gods responded to prayer, and sometimes they did not. But as time went on, many people in the Mesopotamian valleys came slowly to the realization that nature is unified, and that the variety of gods may in fact be only different names for the same great power.

Customs began in Babylonia which have persisted for centuries. Prayers to Baal frequently led to prophetic frenzies and to speaking in tongues. Well-wishers threw wheat at the womb of a new bride, hoping to make her as fertile as the neighbouring fields. Huge parties and processions, especially at New Year, were held to celebrate the change of the seasons and the return of the sun. Babylonians gave each syllable a number so that every word, every name had its corresponding number. Anu the sky-god's number was 60—he left his mark on every clock. Numerology was born.

But there was a grim side to these religions of the Middle East. To ensure that the crops were adequate, you had to please the earth-god Baal—and sometimes the price was the sacrifice of a male child. The *Old Testament* story of Abraham and Isaac is a vivid reminder of this. So in the custom of killing a male lamb at Passover/Easter. In addition, attractive young women and sometimes young men were expected to serve at the temples of Baal as cult prostitutes. Pious worshippers selected them, tossed them a coin, and then had sex with them. It's a peculiar notion of piety by modern standards, but it was run for the same purposes as the modern church bingo. This "pious" behaviour of their pagan neighbours helps explain why *Old Testament* Hebrews kept backsliding into Baal-worship.

Most Babylonian customs that have survived have done so because Jewish ritual has copied them: Passover, Purim, temple-building, circumcision, strict observance of the Sabbath, and the legends of Adam and Eve are all debts we owe to the men and women of ancient Mesopotamia.

But we don't much care about Mesopotamia. The people are all long dead, the names are alien, and they didn't even have cable. The great difficulty in looking squarely at the past is that we are alive, and we feel infinitely superior to those who aren't. D.H. Lawrence wrote that he hoped his works were useful in "opening a tiny window for the bourgeoisie." We need another Lawrence to open a tiny window for the pagan dead, who deserve more respect than we give them.

3

THE GIFT OF THE NILE

"*A myth is a religion in which no one any longer believes.*"
James Feibleman

"*...everything new is old, and everything old is new, and there has been no entirely new religion since the beginning of the world.*"
Max Muller

While the empires of the Mesopotamian valleys rose, fought, collapsed, and cannibalized each other, the Egyptian empire in the Nile Valley to the west went on and on and on. So did its religion. Prayers were still being said for the Pharaoh Khefren (who died about 2800 BCE) during the Ptolemaic dynasty some 2600 years later, and were still being paid for out of the original bequest. Egypt was the great theological factory of the ancient world. Its citizens were fascinated by religious and ethical ideas. Egyptian religion was generally hopeful and cheerful, not gloomy and terror-ridden like the religions of the Tigris and Euphrates, and for good reason: Egypt was far less likely to be invaded and its cities burned.

Egypt had a multitude of gods, and often used animals to symbolize them. Unlike the Babylonians or Hebrews, they did not sacrifice animals. Typical of their gods were Bes, a dwarf-god of love and the family, and Tauert, a hippopotamus-god who blessed pregnancy and childbirth. While these household gods probably attracted the most attention from ordinary Egyptian men and women, the great national gods of Egypt attracted most of the money. The vagaries of the Nile flood taught Egyptians the value of having extra grain stored for the bad years, and these granaries, and their consequent wealth, were controlled by the priesthoods of the important gods. Temples of the great gods were major employers, with openings for weavers, masons, farmers, craftsmen, brewers, cooks, and so on.

The god of empire, Amon-Re, was the most important state deity. He represented a union of Amon, god of political power, with Re, god of the sun. His importance grew steadily during the period 3000-1000 BCE. Amon-Re's right hand man on earth was the Pharaoh, who like the modern Pope was infallible, and therefore the ultimate judge on questions of faith and morals. The pharaoh had divine approval. The *Pyramid Texts* of approximately 2000 BCE quote the words of Amon-Re at the coronation of the pharaoh, and repeated verbatim in the *Gospel of Matthew*: "He is my beloved Son, with whom I am well pleased." Hymns praising the pharaoh called him "Wonderful Counselor, Almighty God, Everlasting Father, the Prince of Peace", phrases and terms familiar to anyone who knows Handel's great oratorio, *The Messiah*.

Pharaoh's advisors were portrayed circling him as the Big Dipper circles Polaris: they were always available if the divine Pharaoh should need them. These priests formed a powerful and hereditary class who lived very well off the taxes that Egyptian farmers paid to Amon-Re. But few murmurs of popular discontent ever disturbed the political and religious serenity of Egypt.

Life went on, even after death. Bodies buried in the hot desert sand dehydrated quickly. This natural process of mummification soon led to the development of a huge industry, as Egyptian science improved on nature. Internal organs were removed for more efficient preservation—Egyptians held that the heart, not the brain, was the seat of intellect as well as the center of emotion. (Babylonians by contrast, believed emotions came from the liver and bowels; presumably they loved with all their intestines, and hoped the affair would not end with their liver being broken.) Crosses were often placed on the breasts of mummies or perhaps placed in their hands as a symbol of the expected life to come.

If the body persisted after death, so did the spirit. The ka was an invisible replica of the body that came into being when a person was born, and survived as long as the body received adequate care. This ancient Egyptian ka is in fact the modern theory of the soul. But Egyptians also had a ba, a second invisible force that represented the spirit of the dead and it might wander about the world during the day, returning to the tomb at night.

Do all kas and bas fare equally? No, since people are unequal in life, they will be unequal in death. The Egyptians were the first society to develop the notion that there is a judgement after death. Your earthly credentials were important, and your ritual offences would count against you, but by 1500 BCE the theory was quite clear—you were ultimately judged on your moral and ethical behaviour by Osiris, the god of the dead. Your heart was weighed against the Feather of Truth, and there were no magic charms which could help you. If you passed the test, your everlasting lot was one of happiness and light, with plenty of food and drink. If you failed, you went to a place of flames and smoke, where half-human fiends would torture and mutilate you.

Thoughtful and prudent Egyptians who understood what lay ahead of them went to the priests for advice and preparation. These priests were a class of men who (at least in theory) lived quite strict and careful lives. They were always male and always circumcised (the Greek Heroditus wittily remarked that they apparently preferred cleanliness to beauty). In addition, they were averse to all hair, and shaved their entire bodies every three days. They washed five times a day. They wore linen clothes and papyrus sandals, and avoided leather and wool. They refused to eat beans, peas, pork, mutton, garlic, onions, or Nile fish.

Egyptian priests studied for years, and were profoundly learned. They intimidated even the Greeks. As in our society, medical knowledge conferred religious power, and so priests studied the bodily organs which their particular god controlled. Recognizable specialists in anatomy, surgery, pathology, pharmacology, opthamology and gynaecology were available in ancient Egypt. Other branches of knowledge and the arts such as mathematics, magic, acting, literature and law were studied in the libraries of the great temples.

The demonic powers which triggered diseases could be controlled by drugs, magic, or sometimes by the ringing of bells. Demonic dislike of bells is the reason for harness bells on horses and camels, and is the reason why bells toll at funerals even today. Egyptian magician/priests regularly used many of the standard tricks of modern illusionists—they walked on air, handled fire, lived under water, were immune to mutilation, made themselves invisible, read the past, and foretold the future. (And as Moses discovered, turning a walking staff into a serpent was considered a very low-level achievement.) Included in their magical equipment were rosaries—often with a cross on the end—for counting prayers and chants such as "abracadabra."

Egyptian religion was sophisticated, comprehensive, and very very old. We should give considerable weight to these Egyptian priests and their powers as we proceed in our investigation of Christianity. Let us not forget that Jesus lived on the fringe of this society, that according to Matthew he had lived as a child in Egypt, and that he was widely accused by his detractors of being a magician. He too apparently observed taboos of dress and diet. Living where he did and when he did, he could not have been immune to or unaware of the enormous religious influence of the priests of Egypt.

People understand complex issues better when they are done on a human scale. In religion, this means that creator-gods and sky-gods, although powerful and terrifying, are never as interesting to the ordinary believer as a god who becomes man. The god who became human could understand your problems, your weaknesses, your fear of death—because he had shared them. In Egypt, as powerful as Amon-Re became, he was soon eclipsed by the power of Osiris. Just as the stature of Jesus grew over time, so did the powers attributed to Osiris.

Egyptians were as deeply convinced of the reality of Osiris' life as modern Christians are of the life of Jesus, and with about the same degree of credibility. They believed that Osiris had been an early pharaoh of Egypt, certainly earlier than 3000 BCE. His family life was, um, interesting. His wife was also his sister, the goddess Isis. His evil twin brother Seth was his rival, and Seth was married to the goddess Nepthys. Induced by jealousy, Seth and his evil friends built a coffin and persuaded Osiris to climb in. They nailed it shut and threw it into the Nile. It floated downstream to the Mediterranean, along the Palestinian coast, and came to rest at the port of Byblos. A tamarisk tree grew around it. After a long search, Isis and Nepthys found it, opened it, and returned Osiris' body to Egypt.

But Seth wasn't finished so easily. He found the body in the bulrushes where Isis had hidden it, and proceeded to cut Osiris into fourteen pieces which he scattered throughout Egypt. Isis managed to find and reassemble all his parts except the penis. Osiris' penis had been eaten by a fish, or maybe a crab. Therefore Isis made a new one out of clay, or in other variants, of sycamore wood, and as she and Nepthys wept over the body of Osiris, the dead pharaoh came back to life and impregnated Isis. The remainder of his biography is obscure. It is most likely he ascended into heaven, since the name Osiris ("many-eyed") refers to the rays of the sun. How he came to judge the dead is uncertain.

Isis' miraculous pregnancy resulted in the birth of the god Horus. Horus was at first put in the bulrushes (a rather traditional hideout by now), but grew up to avenge his father by defeating and castrating his wicked uncle Seth. Thereafter, Horus ruled as Pharaoh over a prosperous and satisfied Egypt.

This myth, dubious and far-fetched as it may seem to the modern mind, has been of paramount importance in the history of religion, and parts of it appear and reappear in Christianity. Egyptians were convinced that when a pharaoh was conceived, the god Osiris entered his father and thereby impregnated his mother. Every pharaoh thus became Horus, the Son of God. Every dead pharaoh was Osiris, dying and then rising from the dead—like the penis itself, and also like the crops following the flooding of the Nile. However, it is fair to say the images of Horus and that of Osiris are confused, intertwined, and essentially interchangeable.

Isis had made copies of the phallus of Osiris, and they were worshipped in any religious ceremony devoted to him.

Phalluses were also buried in fields to remind Osiris to make the crops plentiful. Portraits of Osiris had him painted a dark green, as befits a vegetation god. Osiris' death and his resurrection was celebrated at the end of October. Many other beliefs have an eerie familiarity. The highlight of the resurrection ritual was the blessing by the priests of small round wheatcakes, each marked with a cross. When these cakes were blessed, they were miraculously transformed into the body of Osiris. Likewise, red wine was transformed into his blood, and drinking it caused the believer to be filled with love for the god. Worshippers ate the cakes to commemorate his death, and pieces of the sacramental bread were reserved to be taken to the sick. These parallels with the Christian communion tradition in both ritual and belief are so powerful that one has to wonder how it has so consistently escaped public attention.

But it doesn't stop there. There were variations upon variations in the story, and many of them are of consequence to later Christian belief. In one, the body of Osiris was washed after death, then wrapped in linen and anointed with spices. He descended into hell, and rose from the dead after three days. Some believers held that he had been crucified. He ascended into heaven, and now sits at the right hand of the Father Re. Osiris was, long before Jesus, commonly referred to as "Our Lord."

As you might expect, Hebrew tradition borrowed heavily from Egyptian paganism. It is easy for scholars who have an acquaintance with prayer texts from the Nile Valley to find Egyptian references in the *Old Testament*. Probably the most glaring example is *Psalm 104*, attributed to the Hebrew king David, which is in fact a wholesale plagiarism of the *Hymn to Aten*, and may be the work of the rebel pharaoh Akhenaten. As the scholars continue to translate more and more

Egyptian texts, the situation has led the author Tom Harpur to remark indignantly:

> "...there is irrefutable proof that not one single doctrine, rite, tenet, or usage of Christianity was in reality a fresh contribution to the world of religion."

The Osiris story is also the origin of the Holy Family: Osiris the divine father, Isis the Mother of God, and the infant Horus, the Son of God. As a result of their devotion to the pharaoh, Egyptians emphasized Osiris in this trinity, but Greek-speaking peoples who later adopted these ideas were more devoted to the infant son, and the Romans in turn were most interested in the Mother of God. The triangle, as symbol of both the family and the three deities, became a persisting religious icon in Egypt, as did the three leaves of the clover, used much later by St. Patrick for the same reasons.

Of course, no ancient religion was without its astronomical side. Osiris, like several other ancient gods, had twelve "apostles" who were in fact the twelve signs of the zodiac. Isis was the bright star Sirius—on the horizon in late October as she searched for her dead husband. Sirius was overhead in August and was useful to sailors—and so Isis became known as Stella Maris, the Star of the Sea—which later became a description of Mary the mother of Jesus.

Particular attention was paid to the calendar because it was important that the Nile flood be timely, and be substantial enough to provide good crops. Religious Egyptians often fasted for forty days before the flood in commemoration of the life and death of Osiris, and to ensure that he provided an adequate supply of water.

Nile water itself was sacred, and had magical properties.

It made those who drank it fertile, and those who had been initiated into the Osirian rites were sprinkled by the priests at major ceremonies. Such people were said to be "born again". These religious symbols have a way of hanging on for a very long time. Nile water (or "holy water") was bottled and exported for drinking as late as the nineteenth century. Modern Catholicism still has its holy water fonts. As a secular parallel, there is a quasi-religious dimension to the health-giving properties of Perrier with a twist of lemon. We will consider water symbolism further when we discuss the question of baptism.

While Osiris' influence on us was profound, it was more indirect that the influence of Seth. Anthropologists see in the Seth-Osiris legends a theological reconstruction of an ancient tribal war. Most experts think Seth had been a native Egyptian god, and the myths are a retelling of his people's defeat at the hands of Osiris-worshipping invaders. Seth may even have been an Egyptian version of Baal. His contribution to history lies in his evil nature, and in the fact that in his battle with Horus, he was unfortunate enough to be hit in the buttocks by Horus' arrow. And since then, the notched and feathered arrow has provided the devil with a forked tail. Other writers suggest that Seth is the dragon/crocodile defeated by St. George/Horus, and that the evil serpent of Eden may in fact be Seth of Egypt.

No such smear blots the image of Horus. After his miraculous and virginal birth, this Son of God was worshipped as a newborn in a crib, shown smiling in his mother's arms, and portrayed atop a cloud with his right hand raised in blessing. His birth was heralded by a star in the East. He was baptized in the Nile. He walked on water, calmed storms, cast out demons, and healed the sick. He went up a mountain and was transfigured. He gave a Sermon on the

Mount. He was crucified between two thieves. He was called KRST, "the Anointed One", "the Good Shepherd", "the Lamb of God", "the Bread of Life", 'the Son of Man", and "the Word". The parallels with Jesus go on and on.

Sometimes he has cute little wings like Eros/Cupid. Horus was also thoughtful enough to create time and the seasons (Horus =hour). In the epic battle with his uncle, he did have his eye plucked out, although it was restored to its rightful place by Thoth the healer god. This evil eye of Horus was capable of enchantment, and Egyptian women wore heavy black eye-shadow to protect themselves. Today the eye of Horus watches us from atop its pyramid on the back of the American one dollar bill. George Washington and a number of other founding fathers, being Freemasons, were far more familiar than we are with Egyptian symbols and lore.

Perhaps we should pause here to reflect for a moment on the numerous parallels between Osiris/Horus and Jesus. Tom Harpur's book *Pagan Christs* raised a storm with its argument that all the Jesus stories were a stale Palestinian reworking of venerable Egyptian myths. Were all these parallels just coincidence? That is hard to accept. Can we agree with the early church Fathers that claims for Jesus are true, but stories of the Egyptian gods were all false, and inspired by the devil? Not any more.

More liberal people take a Hindu approach—any road is good, as long as it leads to the top of the mountain. In this scenario, Jesus and Osiris become merely two facets of some great multi-sided universalist religion of humanity. These two gods would then have to be treated equally, because as we shall see, their stories carry about the same degree of veracity. Christian claims to primacy, to exclusivity, to universalism are all blown apart. Further, this approach implies that humanity gets the religion that it needs at the time. Osiris was fine for

Egypt, Jesus was suited to the Roman Empire, and presumably Islam and particularly Baha'i are better suited to the modern world. Naturally, such claims drive Christian theologians completely crazy.

One of the key myths of the ancient world, then, was that Osiris rose from the dead to impregnate Isis. But other stories said that Isis was hovering over him in the form of a sparrowhawk (or maybe a vulture), and that no intercourse took place. The pregnancy was miraculous, and so Isis was a virgin when she gave birth to Horus. Despite the shortage of real-life virgin births, people identified with Isis the Virgin Mother of God. She was faithful, pure, gentle and good. She had connections to the healing arts since she had reassembled Osiris. She had loved her husband, suffered bereavement, and raised a model child. Who better than Isis to understand the lot of women?

As Egyptian ideas were spread throughout the Mediterranean lands by soldiers, traders, and scholars, the popularity of Isis grew rapidly. There were other female deities of course, but Cybele was too frightening, Diana/Artemis was not at all domestic, Aphrodite/Venus was interested only in sex. Isis, the patroness of family life, had a profound and assertive influence on women of all social classes. For example, in an Isiac wedding service, the husband had to swear obedience to his wife. Modern feminists have good reason to wish that the Virgin Isis had triumphed, rather that the ever-submissive Virgin Mary.

But Isis and Mary are not unique. The world has seen a long parade of mother-goddesses including the Babylonian Ishtar whom we have already mentioned, and Cybele from Asia Minor whom we will discuss below. Many anthropologists have suggested that the original deity—the Earth— was female; indeed no society has been found that uses male words to describe our planet. Palaeolithic female figurines such as the Venus of Willendorf show exaggerated sexual features, and clearly must have had religious connotations. This widespread worship of the Great Goddess was probably overthrown about 10000 BCE by sternly patriarchal herding societies such as the Indo-Europeans who moved out of the grasslands of Asia into the Middle East, India, and Europe. Their patriarchal religions, devoted to male deities symbolized by the sun and the bull, almost completely obliterated any feminine aspects of religion, and incidentally, greatly reduced the status of women generally for the next 12,000 years.

By the first century BCE, the lands around the Mediterranean had been conquered by Greek traders and Greek culture, and were in the process of being subjugated by Roman military might. But these Roman johnny-come-latelys were in awe of the antiquity of Egypt, and so while the Roman legions conquered the Nile, it was Isis, the Egyptian version of the ancient mother-goddess who conquered Rome. She seemed to have far more appeal to Roman sensibilities than did her husband Osiris. The Isiac religion spread along sea trade routes to the Italian port of Ostia, and then inland. Like Christianity, it grew from the bottom up, flourishing first among slaves and the descendants of slaves.

By the time of the Roman writer Apuleius, there were seven major temples of Isis in Rome, each with a high priest and several full time assistants of both sexes. Egyptian customs became all the rage. The emperor Caligula, never known for his restraint, married his sister Drusilla while wearing Pharonic garb, and he was known to consult Egyptian soothsayers. The goddess Isis was thus assimilated by the Romans, and remained a popular figure for centuries. Her features continued to be seen on Roman coins long after the Empire became officially Christian.

A major feature if the worship of Isis was the public procession, commemorating her search for Osiris. Every March 5, a group of worshippers had a procession to the docks and the blessing of a ship, praying that Isis in her role as Stella Maris would provide favourable winds for the upcoming shipping season. The modern Portuguese custom of blessing the fishing fleet is a direct descendant of Isis-worship. Likewise, modern carnivals with their marching bands, flowers, choirs, and grotesque costumes are copies of their Isiac predecessors. If Isis were alive today, she would spend New Year's Day in Pasadena, and Mardi Gras in Rio de Janeiro.

A second major celebration of Isis-worshippers was on August 12—a candlelight procession accompanied by wailing mourners and sad hymns. Non-believers frequently poked fun at the emotional excesses. This procession, like many Catholic ones today, was led by a cross atop a staff—the monogram of Osiris which was soon to be appropriated by Christians. The featured object of veneration was the Ark, a small box (or perhaps a boat or an urn) with an effigy of Osiris (or perhaps just his penis) inside. This ark was somberly carried by a priest who was sheltered by a canopy, and surrounded by acolytes and a choir. The mournful hymns were probably the original Gregorian chants. On their arrival at the temple, worshippers ate blessed cakes, each marked with a cross, to commemorate the event.

Grief, joy and religious devotion were the public face of Isis-worship, but there was an even more compelling private side. There were strict rules of initation into the religion which governed a devotee's behaviour, but did not apparently limit what he or she might believe. The worshipper had to spend money—frequently a good deal of money—to learn the religious secrets of the cult, and to move up in the ranks. The initiation ceremony was preceded by ten days of sexual abstinence, prayer, and ritual bathing. No meat or wine was to be consumed. Sometimes worshippers held all-night vigils in the temple, hoping for dreams and visions from the goddess.

The initiation itself is described in the *Metamophosis* of Apuleius. The hero is required to consecrate his life to Isis before the ritual baptism which admitted him to the cult. This degree of commitment was unknown in the other great pagan religions, but it struck Christians as such a good idea that it soon became a major feature of their new religion. Members of the cult took part in sacred meals. The exact spiritual meaning of the meal to the worshippers is unknown, but they were solemn, emotional affairs, and in some manner they signified that the believers were entitled to eternal life.

The relationship between Isis-worship and modern Freemasonry is also interesting, and cannot be accidental. Both organizations feature brotherhoods, hidden knowledge, solemn oaths, passwords, and rituals involving the passage from darkness into light. Both require considerable expense for temple maintenance, ceremonial robes, and meals. These expenses were not unusual among the pagan cults. By contrast, Christianity was cheap to join. So it may have been the economy of Christianity, rather than its code of ethics, which appealed to converts, and led to its eventual triumph.

The daily rituals at the temples of Isis have a familiar ring to Roman Catholics, or Anglican/Episcopalians. The temple was opened with Matins, and then followed a morning service called the Mass. This Mass included sprinkling of the congregation with holy water, prayers for church and state, choirs singing hymns, and religious images held aloft. Then the priest chanted "Let the people depart!" and the worshippers went off to their daily affairs before reassembling for Vespers in the late afternoon.

   The Isiac cult had strict codes of conduct. Priests were expected to be celibate, and to be frugal in their other appetites. Especially devout members of either sex sometimes joined reclusive organizations that evolved into monasteries and convents. Some Isiac backsliders were required to observe unusual penances which caused non-believers to roll their eyes—crawling naked in public places, and winter bathing in the Tiber were bound to cause some comment. So did the eroticism implicit in a religion which venerated ithyphallic idols and phalluses with prayers inscribed on the backs. So there may have been some truth to the charges made by several Roman writers that the temples of Isis had degenerated into little better than brothels. Nobody's perfect. Altars of Isis were set up on the Capitoline Hill, but they kept being destroyed by Roman traditionalists, making it clear that the Mother Goddess of Egypt wasn't totally welcome in the greatest city of the world.

   What was the major appeal of this religion? Then, as now, people wished for good health. The chief business of any successful religion of that time was healing. Isis, long before the Roman god Mercury, carried the caduceus as a reminder of her healing power. (This symbol—two serpents entwined on a staff—has been adopted in our time by various cancer and medical societies). Isiac priests, as part of their religious medical apprenticeship, carried on the old Egyptian traditions and learned the secret names of diseases. If you knew the secret name of anything, you could control it. Through knowledge, science, and psychological suggestion, Isis helped her followers to overcome misfortune and ill health. An odd modern remnant of this belief is the idea that the ladybug (named after Our Lady Isis) is an omen of good luck.

Religious feelings reflect the spirit of the times and the variations in societies. Osiris-worship, when transferred to the giant Roman Empire, put its heaviest emphasis on Isis. A far more confusing process ensued when the rationalism of Greece encountered the complex (and frankly irrational) theology of Egypt. It occurred to many thinking people then, as now, that all religions were essentially the same. But trying to mesh the human-like gods of Olympus with the animal images of Egypt proved difficult indeed.

One example of this syncretism began under the Greekified Ptolemy dynasty of Egypt about 275 BCE. The reasoning went like this: if Osiris is the sun's rays, and Apis the sacred calf of Memphis is the living image of the sun, then aren't they the same? Presto, a new god, Serapis, was born. His consort Isis remained the same, but the Egyptian Son of God, Horus, was too closely associated with the person and the government of the Pharaoh to be popular among Greeks. So Horus was transfigured to become the child-god Harpocrates.

A new trinity, Isis-Serapis-Harpocrates, was hailed. This grouping was perpetuated on Isiac communion wafers, and the initials IHS may still be seen in many Roman Catholic churches. Catholics may believe that it refers to the cross (In Hic Signum), or to Jesus' role (Iesus Hominem Salvator), but few moderns would care to know they are perpetuating the worship of three (or more properly four) old Egyptian gods.

Serapis went on to become a major figure in the Graeco-Roman pantheon. Like his wife, he had the power of healing and could restore sight. He practiced levitation, and could magically convey others. He became the official god of Roman Egypt. He was addressed as "Our Lord". His portraits show him adorned with Persian boughs, which are easily mistaken for thorns. Oddly, his followers were referred to as

"Christians". The center of his worship was the new and cosmopolitan city of Alexandria.

Not surprisingly, Serapis frequently became confused with other gods. Statues of Serapis have been found in the temples of the Persian god Mithra; he was confused in Roman homes with the household spirits the Lares and Penates, and Mesopotamians might not be able to distinguish him from Saturn. And just as statues of Isis and Harpocrates and Hermes were assimilated by Christians and assumed to be of their own making, so many alleged portraits of Jesus were really those of Serapis, the god invented to help the Ptolemy family maintain political control of Egypt.

We have followed the major outlines of Egyptian religion as it was moulded to fit society while continuing to support the political establishment. In the Graeco-Roman period, the emphasis was on the Holy Family and its healing powers. Isis, Serapis and Harpocrates had the kind of lower middle class appeal of those idealized television families of the 1950s. Since Egyptian religion was a dog's breakfast of ideas, beliefs might be loosely held. Egyptians, with thousands of years of civilization behind them, wisely preferred confusion and illogic to intolerance. The worshippers of the venerable gods of the Nile never held councils to discuss dogma, to excommunicate the unwary, or to burn the unrepentant: only their successors did that.

4

THE GREEKS: ELEUSIS, DIONYSOS, ORPHEUS

"Not to know what happened in the past is to remain forever a child."

Cicero

As the Greeks were intimidated by the Egyptians, so we are impressed by the Greeks. Every schoolchild knows of the humanized gods of Olympus and some of their exploits, but whether these Olympian deities ever really constituted a religious system is doubtful. Certainly the Greeks were religious enough, and left an indelible imprint on our religious thought. It is an unpopular but true observation that Christianity owes far more to the Greeks than to the Hebrews. But Greek theological ideas are even harder to describe than those of Egypt, because the Greeks were also the inventors of logical, critical thought—philosophy. Traditional Greek life and religion centred around the polis, a small independent political unit usually consisting of a city and its surrounding countryside. But this way of life collapsed when first Greece and then the rest of the civilized world were united into one political empire by the Hellenized Macedonian genius, Alexander the Great.

In both Persia and Egypt, Alexander found that the people preferred to think of him as a god-king in the tradition of the pharaoh. Alexander, never troubled by false modesty, promptly agreed that he was indeed a god. This marked the beginning of the tradition in the Western world of great men and heroes being seen as quasi-divine. The Greeks promptly extended this concept—if great men were semi-divine, then were not the gods only divine men? The heroes of Homeric times were declared to be gods, and they were assigned the roles of modern Christian saints: to intercede on behalf of needy believers. In particular, the Greeks felt that a heroic death was evidence of a man's divinity. This idea proved popular with Romans and Jews as well. If you died serving the cause of your persecuted religion, you were destined for glorious immortality. (One has to wonder whether this idea would have been so enthusiastically supported had the ancients seen the modern application of it in the Middle East.)

At the same time as the deification of Alexander was proceeding, so was philosophy altering traditional Greek religion. Greece had no established dogmas and no priestly class. The polis had used traditional social pressures to enforce conformity in religious behaviour. But soon the philosophers were trying to make even polytheism rational. Some myths were abandoned, others were interpreted as explaining a moral. Greek schoolboys were given heavily interpreted versions of Homer and other classics, full of allegory and moralizing. Of course, this same process, using *Bible* verses, provides the mainstay of the modern Sunday sermon. But in Greece, the long range effect of trying to make the gods rational was to destroy belief in the lesser ones in favour of the one god who rules all. To conclude, the twin corrosive powers of Alexander and philosophy produced in the Eastern Mediterranean the germ of a religion which would be rational, moralizing, monotheistic, and would center on a heroic man who had become a god. Things were beginning to fall into place.

In addition to the well-known gods of Olympus, the Greeks had two major "mystery" cults to which the people were devoted: those of the Eleusinians and of Dionysos. The former was the better known at the time—it was almost automatic that every respectable Athenian would be initiated into the rites at a huge temple complex at nearby Eleusis, only a few kilometers to the west. The teacher Demonax was put into a pillory in Athens because he wasn't a cult member. However, Apollonius of Tyana was rejected because of accusations that he was a magician. Clearly the rites could not have been exceptionally demanding, because they were patronized by most of the Roman emperors who followed Augustus. Then, as now, the appearance of piety made good politics.

The cult at Eleusis was devoted to the goddess Kore (or Persephone). She was the daughter of Zeus and of Demeter, the goddess of grain and plant life. Kore carelessly picked a magical narcissus, the earth opened, and the underworld god Hades spirited her away with his horses and chariot. Kore became the queen of the underworld, but she longed for the sky and the grass. Her mother Demeter began a long search for her, and during this search, the plants of the earth withered from her neglect. The good people of Eleusis built a temple for Demeter the sorrowing mother-goddess when she visited there. Eventually Zeus intervened and worked out a compromise. Kore would be returned to earth for six months a year, but each winter she was to return to Hades and his underworld.

The Eleusinian festival occurred each September, as the

seed wheat was being stored away in darkness to be ready for the next spring's planting. The cult had an annual procession by torchlight, a re-enactment of the myth, and the reaping of a symbolic ear of wheat in a great blaze of light. This was followed by the elevation of bread and wine by the celebrant, and a communion meal shared by all those present. It now seems likely that the words of consecration in Christian services were taken directly from the Eleusinian rites. The souls of those initiated were said to have died and been "reborn to a new life in the god". When the service was over, the congregation was dismissed with the words: "The Lord be with you!" These mysteries were carried on here for over eleven hundred years, until the destruction of the Eleusinian sanctuary be fanatical Christian monks in 356 CE.

Common features with other religions jump out at us. The searching, mourning Demeter parallels the image of Isis looking for Osiris, or Cybele weeping over the dead body of Attis. Kore, the earth-mother, appears in other guises as the snake-goddess of Crete, Sophia among Gnostic Christians, as Isis, and eventually as Mary, mother of Jesus. The pre-eminence of two goddesses in the Eleusinian mystery was reflected in the occasional choice of women to the highest offices of the cult. But the greatest and most influential of the Greek mysteries revolved not around Kore, but around her son Dionysos.

As you might expect, Dionysos' beginning was pretty unconventional by our standards: his father was also his grandfather. Zeus became both when he seduced his daughter Kore. Other myths claim that Dionysos' mother was not Kore, but the human Semele. Dionsyos was variously held to be the father, son, spouse and brother of Demeter. We won't worry about this: the Greeks didn't. In any case, the infant Dionysos was kidnapped by the Titans, torn into fourteen parts (a la

Osiris), and his body—except for his heart—was cooked and eaten. The heart was swallowed by Zeus, whereupon Dionysos was reborn. The offending Titans were promptly reduced to ashes, from which, in due course, humans arose. Another version has our hero transformed into a bull and then torn apart by nameless enemies. But the common themes are familiar to us: violent death, dismemberment, and miraculous rebirth.

The adult Dionysos came to be a benefactor to mankind. He was portrayed as a dignified and bearded young man who promoted peace and gave laws to men. Like Jesus, he concealed his divinity while on earth. His principal contribution was the use of the vine. The symbols of his festivals were a wine jar, ivy, a fig basket, a goat and a phallus.

These symbols give us an important clue to the darker, wilder side of the Dionysos cult: he was also the god of excessive drinking, and of goatish, illicit sex. During the Dionysian rituals, female cult members called maenads drank heavily of the sacred wine which probably had some psychotropic additives (maybe a form of ivy) in addition to fermented grape juice and resin. Maenads became "seized by the gods". In a state of uncontrollable ecstasy, they ran shouting through the night woods, and killed goats which they tore apart with their bare hands and ate raw. They believed they were eating the body of their god, and that wine was his blood. This frightening behaviour was obviously too much fun to restrict to women, and as the cult spread throughout the Greek world, Dionysos the god of law and joy also became the god of fear, suffering and death: a god suitable for both men and women. The combination of men, women, wine and religious ecstasy led to more types of scandalous behaviour than just goaticide. Sexual excesses became de rigeur.

The Dionysiac rites (or Bacchanalia) were banned in Rome by shocked patricians as early as 186 BCE, but in vain, because the god's popularity continued to grow. By the time of Jesus, if the number of Roman inscriptions is a reliable index, Dionysos was second in popularity only to Zeus/Jupiter himself among the wealthier people of the empire. We might expect that, by then, the cult had lost some of its frenzied excesses and had become more socially acceptable.

Nevertheless, the worship of Dionysos always retained a good deal of its sensuality and nature-worship. Its mysteries appealed to well-to-do people who enjoyed life's pleasures. It had a positive side. It was one of the few opportunities for Greek women to be outside their homes. It seems likely that the custom of initiating children into the cult led in some unknown degree to a decline in the number of unwanted infants who were killed or exposed. But we cannot argue that the Dionysiac cult as it existed would have led to a widespread revival of imperial morality—one has to think that the people who drank and sang as they carried enormous phalluses in public processions had their minds on somewhat lower instincts.

Fascinating as these nocturnal orgies might be to us, we have to look at other aspects of the cult to see how it has affected modern life. After all, only a minority of us have ever eaten any goatmeat—raw or cooked. And drunken parades featuring those large wooden phalluses crowned with ivy would test the limits of even the most liberal city councillors. But the ivy which the maenads chewed and carried into their homes and temples has susrvived as decoration. So has the tradition of displaying the infant Dionysos as an effigy in a crib. And so has the myth of water becoming wine.

Just as the sun-god turned rain into grapes, so a savior-god could turn water directly into wine. This was one of the specialties of Dionysos and his priests. A spring which gushed wine appeared annually in some locales sacred to him. Every January 6, a fountain in the town of Andros miraculously flowed with wine for the benefit of thirsty worshippers. Coincidentally, January 6 is both the birthday of Dionysos and the Christian celebration of the wedding at Cana. If you recall the story, the miracle of Cana was the first of Jesus' career. Urged on by his mother Mary, he saved his host the embarrassment of running out of wine at a wedding-feast by changing jugs full of water into wine—good wine. The coincidence with the Dionysiac miracles is awfully strong. Even the wording of the Cana story has been traced to a Dionysiac festival at nearby Sidon. Nor is that the only intrusion of Dionysos into the Gospel stories. In the *Gospel of John*, when Jesus says "I am the Vine" (13:1), it would be crystal clear to any first century resident of Palestine that the speaker was Dionysos, not Jesus.

Worshippers of Dionysos were also the first to develop the modern concept of eternal life. Originally they believed that their god rose from the dead. The ancients showed little interest in that possibility for themselves. But by Hellenistic times the cult of Dionysos had become very concerned with the afterlife. Those who died "unsaved" had magical rites performed for them to bring everlasting relief—an exact forerunner of the Latter Day Saints' custom of "sealing" ancestors. Perhaps it was this changing notion of time and the afterlife that led to the great revision of Dionysiac religion sparked by Pythagoras and Orpheus.

Pythagoras, as one of the truly great personages of the ancient world, deserves more attention than we can give him here. He was born in southern Italy in the sixth century BCE, and he traveled widely. He stayed in Egypt for twenty—two years, and was even willing to undergo circumcision in order to be admitted to the priesthood. He probably visited Buddhist monasteries in India. His school became the first of the true mystery cults, with secret doctrines concerning the unity underlying all religion, philosophy, music and mathematics. Regrettably, he was probably not the first to prove the beloved Pythagorean theorem; however, he may have been the first person to understand that the earth is a sphere rather than a flat dish.

Many of his ideas seem to have a distinctly modern ring. He believed that men and women were equal. He believed that possessions were unimportant, and should be shared. He tried to provide a scientific underpinning as to why we like some musical sounds, and dislike others. He thought that mathematics was the key to understanding everything. He preached that animal sacrifice was wrong and unnecessary, that even meat-eating was unacceptable, and that meals should be communal.

But his career had some distinctly non-modern elements. He was several years ahead of Jesus in his miraculous ability to catch a large number of fish. In fact, he predicted the exact number he would catch—153. This was a sacred number for scientific and astronomical use, related to the Golden Section, beloved of classical architects and geometricians. The pentagram was the mystical symbol of the Pythagorean cult. On a regular pentagram, draw a line from one base point to the other, and then draw a perpendicular line from the apex to that line. The relationship between the horizontal line and the vertical line is 100: 153. See how easy that was? We are going no further into the dismal swamp of numerology, where nothing is what it seems, and in the end, everything seems to mean anything, except to point out that according to *John 21:11*, Jesus also miraculously caught exactly 153 fish. This is not a random number. Only someone acquainted with Pythagorean mysticism would know its significance, or care. But the author of *John* did. This alone would imply that there must be some hidden mystical coding as well as strong Pythagorean elements in the Gospel versions of Jesus, as we shall later see. But Christianity was not alone. Because Pythagorean ideas were so widespread and so appealing, evidence of his influence can also be found in the cults of Dionysos, Attis, Adonis, and Mithra.

Pythagoreans were not shy: they proclaimed that they were the most virtuous people in the Mediterranean world. Nor was Pythagoreanism for the faint of heart: initiates took a five-year vow of silence, and rose every day at dawn to face the rising sun. They were puritanical vegetarians, were indifferent to marriage and children (to the point of being celibate), distrusted the world and the senses, and claimed that souls moved from one body to another after death. Of course the theory of rebirth, common in the Orient, is a great comfort to the unhappy person who hopes that his evil neighbour will get his comeuppance next time around. But Pythagoras' theory did not sit well with the rationalist, skeptical Greeks. Nevertheless, the ascetic side of Pythagorean thought influenced both the Eleusinian and Dionysiac cults among the Greeks, and had an even greater impact on the Jewish cult, the Essenes. In addition, Pythagoras had quite an impact on the ideas of Plato, but Plato was not the type to give him credit. Finally, St. Anthony was a former Pythagorean turned Christian who kept most of his teacher's ideas about the ascetic life when he began to found Christian monasteries.

The second reformer of these Greek cults, Orpheus, may or may not have been a historical person. He is said to have refused to honour Dionysos, and so the god had his maenads tear Orpheus apart. Orpheus also was said to have made the obligatory trip to visit the priests of Egypt, and was hailed anachronistically as the founder of the Eleusinian mysteries. Whatever his biography, his teachings certainly resonate with Christian theology. He taught that Zeus the Father and Dionysos the Son were in fact the same divinity. Since our bodies were all originally created from the ashes of the murderous Titans, we humans carry hereditary guilt in the very stuff of our being. We are born with a tendency to evil. Only purification ceremonies can wash away these vile tendencies. It is best to purify children early in life to ensure salvation from an awful fate after death. Certainly efforts at moral purity are essential, but salvation could be made almost certain by following the exact rituals laid down by Orphic teachers.

The result of the Orphic reforms was that the original orgiastic nature of Dionysian religion took on a more somber tone. Good and bad were at war in the world, and that battle is played out within the individual—the divine soul struggling to control the tomb which is the body. Esoteric teachings and elaborate ceremonies could be of great assistance in this war. Orphism also went a long way toward the merging of national and regional belief systems. It gave a dark urgency to religious rituals. It has been convincingly argued that had it not been for the rise of Christianity, the whole of the Graeco-Roman world would evolved into essential religious agreement, praying to Dionysos the Son of God that their eternal souls be spared. We leave it to the reader to determine in the following pages whether the Dionysiac religion didn't completely subvert what we know as Christianity anyway. In any case, there would today be a more optimistic attitude toward life and death had the Greek idea of God's goodness, rather than the fearsome Yahweh of the Hebrews, become the basis for our religious thinking.

Let's summarize the main features of this Greek Dionysiac-Pythagorean-Orphic religion which dominated the Eastern Mediterranean at the time of Jesus. Because of our mixed origins, we humans are a combination of the divine (from Dionysos) and the evil (from the Titans). This was the first expression in Western theology of an irreconcilable dualism in mankind. As with other people who have held this idea, the Orphics gave the divine half but little attention—the overriding concern was that humans had a tendency to evil because of the original sin of our ancestors. Certainly we struggle to be good, but as Epictetus observed, it is "…no equal struggle between a young man beginning philosophy, and a fair young girl." Somehow we must renounce the material world and impose controls on the body which imprisons our soul. Our souls are immortal. We may be reincarnated, or we may not, but in the end we are in desperate need of divine grace for our salvation.

What happens if we die unsaved? Surprisingly, neither Jews nor Romans had a very clear idea of an afterlife—that all dates to the Hellenizing influence of Alexander. The traditional Greek view was that, if there was any afterlife at all, you went to the realm of Hades, a gloomy place in the underworld. This picture was soon fantastically embroidered by the Orphic imagination. The realm of Hades was split into parts: the Elysian Fields for the saintly and deserving, Tartarus for the evil, and regular Hades for ordinary folk who tried to be moral but had not been able to stay aloof from the material world (for example, the young man who tried to have both philosophy and girls). The Elysian Fields were the upper regions, full of light and bliss. Tartarus had fire, sulfurous fumes, and the customary torturing fiends. (For more details here, check with your local televangelist.) Hades then became a temporary stop—a sort of decompression chamber on your way to the Elysian Fields. The Orphics had worked out, well before the time of Jesus, the fate of all Christian souls: Heaven, Hell, or Purgatory.

If that is the afterlife awaiting you, it is best not to die unsaved. It was essential for your soul to be initiated into the Orphic cult, otherwise you were doomed. Orphism became the first modern church, a voluntary organization which claimed exclusive control over who would or would not be saved. The initiate had better recognize his true nature. This was done by a confession of sins, and then a symbolic baptism in which a mark was placed on the candidate's forehead. After baptism, the Orphic had to be present at least once at a sacrifice in which a live animal was torn apart and eaten. Thereafter, Orphics abstained from eggs, meat and sex, and wore only linen. Their memorials of the sacrifice of Dionysos were ritual meals of wheatcakes and barley-wine.

Orphics were secure in their faith. They knew they were saved, and so they could be casually indifferent to other religions, even state religions. They were free to worship any god or goddess or to conform to any imperial decrees. International Orphism is not much talked about today. It could point to few martyrs or giant temples, but it was a set of beliefs that commanded the loyalty of millions of souls in the Graeco-Roman world. Through its profound influence on Paul and others, it came to provide Christianity with some of that faith's most garish doctrines.

5

THE ROMANS AND CYBELE

"To understand the success of the Romans, you must understand their piety."
                    Dionysius of Halicarnassus

The ultimate test of a religion is whether it works. The Romans believed that theirs did. For a thousand years it satisfied people with a wide variety of intellectual and spiritual needs. It was practical, unimaginative, and patriotic. A devout Roman was one who observed his religious obligations to the gods, which included being a good citizen. The model was Cincinnatus, who was plowing his field when the Senate informed him that he had been appointed dictator, and that an enemy army was at the gate of Rome. One version has Cincinnatus wiping his hands, asking his son to hold the oxen, going off and dispatching the enemy, and then returning to find his son and the oxen still waiting, whereupon he resumed plowing.

For these practical farmers, there was no separate code of ethics apart from citizenship. Making people virtuous was not seen as the job of the Roman priests. They worried about the correct ritual, not about sin. Few Romans of the Republican era would be considered dissolute—that charge was never raised until the Imperial period. It seems reasonable to conclude that they were not as committed as we are to luxury and physical pleasure: most Romans would have agreed that happiness in life required some form of self-denial.

As a result, early Romans were very ethical, and considered others less so. But their religion (like a lot of "feel-good" American Christianity) was success-oriented, in the nature of a bilateral contract with the gods. Upper class Romans loved tradition and disliked innovation; enthusiastic religions were for the lower orders. A Roman felt his individual prosperity depended on officers of the state observing the correct rituals, as well as his own correct performance of ancestral customs. In turn, the gods had an obligation to preserve the city and its people. Those such as Christians who refused public worship were directly threatening the well-being of the entire community. This close connection of Roman religion with patriotism was largely responsible for the famous cohesion of the Roman army, and therefore for the rapid spread of the empire. But this same connection made evolution of religious ideas difficult. Contact with foreign gods meant the overlaying of one set of deities on another. The more societies Rome contacted, and the more populations moved about, the more gods were imported, until the whole system of polytheism began to appear dry and lifeless as compared to the monotheism of Jews or Christians.

A phrase such as "Roman religion" is in a sense misleading, because beyond the common rituals, Romans were free to think whatever they wanted. In imperial times, even the state observances varied somewhat, depending of the whim of the emperor. Over time, religious officials such as the pontifex maximus (who was to become the Christian "pontiff"), were increasingly motivated not by high-mindedness, but by political ambition. In the face of this evisceration of public religion, even the private religion of the Roman household declined.

It is useful to think of Rome as a rural village which just happened to get control of the whole world. Roman families of the Republican era had rural concerns: crops, property, the next generation. When a family member died, he or she was buried on the ancestral farm. Usually a large funeral was held in the family graveyard, partly for the living and partly for the dead. It was believed that the souls of dead Romans kept many of their previous needs and feelings, including hunger and thirst. It was a major responsibility of the head of a landowning family to keep the souls of his dead ancestors satisfied. Souls demanded drink—a splash of red wine on the grave would do. Souls demanded food—honey, muffin-like cakes, or burnt meat were preferred. Motivated more by fear than by devotion, Roman men performed this ritual several times a year. Those relatives who had died violent or untimely deaths were likely to become ghosts, and especially needed pacifying. November 1 was the most important day on which to feed the dead, so the most likely time for apparitions to appear and demand food was on late October nights. While modern people may feel this is all outmoded superstition, they also would be reluctant to walk through a graveyard alone on a windy autumn night after dark. Parts of pagan religion are still very much alive in the dark corners of our minds.

The Romans loved spectacle, and Roman religion provided plenty. The Romans, like the Jews, felt that animal sacrifice was the preferred method of influencing the divine. The chosen animal would be sprinkled with water which caused it to shiver, and this, it was believed, was the victim's silent assent to being slaughtered. Only the wealthy could afford a bull—pigs and sheep were more common.

Sometimes the bloodletting got a bit out of hand. The Emperor Caligula, who certainly needed all the divine intervention he could get, celebrated his accession by sacrificing 160,000 cattle over a period of three months on the Capitoline Hill. This kind of industrial-scale slaughter must have created staggering waste disposal problems and world-class smells, especially in the middle of a city of over a million people.

Sacrifice had to be done right. The animal, whether pig, cow, sheep or goat, ought to be a perfect specimen. The throat was to be cut with one motion and the blood flowed over the altar. Internal organs were inspected for abnormalities, and parts (gods were said to prefer the less tasty parts) were earmarked for the deities. If it were for a sky-god, the meat was burned; if a sea-god, it was thrown into the ocean; if an earth-god it was dropped into a chasm. The remainder of the carcass was cooked and eaten by the priests and onlookers, or sold to local butchers. Early Christians had many a scrupulous debate over whether or not to eat the meat of a sacrificial animal. They were often poor, and this was a cheap source of protein. Modern people are far less concerned with the fate of the meat than with the blood, the flies, and the brutality of the whole process. Nevertheless, animal sacrifice in the hands of a skilled priest was evidently a pious and moving experience for Roman believers. Perhaps they had less refined tastes than we do, and more religious devotion.

The gods whom these public ceremonies aimed to please were at first the well-known Roman versions of the Mt. Olympus gang: Jupiter, Juno, Vesta, Apollo, Mercury, Venus, or Saturn. Jupiter always remained the dominant god of the western empire, Saturn was a particular favourite in North Africa, soldiers were devoted to Mars, wives to Juno, virgins to Vesta, thieves and businessmen to Mercury. But even as the

Roman war-machine was leaving the starting blocks, these gods were being supplanted by more exotic Oriental deities.

The gods of Olympus, despite heartfelt entreaties, had been ineffective in getting the Carthaginian general Hannibal out of Italy—his army wandered at will throughout the peninsula for sixteen years without a defeat. So in 204 BCE, the desperate Romans called on an extraordinary source of help: the cult of Cybele the Great Mother was imported from Asia Minor to lend a hand. Apparently it worked, because Hannibal was recalled to Carthage, defeated, and then killed. Oriental deities suddenly became understandably popular, and a swarm of them followed Cybele to Rome: Isis, Osiris, Mithra, Dionysos, Bona Dea, Sabazios, Yaweh, and Christ. These eastern cults appealed particularly to slaves, the working classes, and subversives. Their promises of mystical knowledge, religious certainty, health, and everlasting bliss undermined the corporate state religion that had served the Romans so well and for so long. Never mind the state, the mysteries said, look out for yourself and your salvation.

Traditional Roman religion was doomed. But enough of it survived in ritual, in the calendar, and in festivals to check rampant religious individualism. By the fourth century CE, the heir apparent, Christianity, was able to win out over the other Eastern cults. Numerous ceremonies and ideas of Roman paganism have continued to be preserved by Christians through two millennia.

We use Roman words to describe religious institutions: saint, sacrament, pope, pontiff, piety. The keys of Janus were handed to St. Peter. Janus, as the god of hinges, presumably might still be influencing those "hinges" of Rome, the cardinals. Choirs who had been trained in the worship of Isis learned to sing their hymns to the Christian God. Romans especially favoured choirs of boy sopranos, and these remained a major musical form of expression until about 1900. Roman wedding customs such as the bridal procession, the bridal veil, the form of the marriage ceremony, wedding rings on the left hand, and carrying the bride over the threshold were all apparently swallowed at a gulp by Christianity. On reflection this should not surprise us at all. Christianity was always open to borrowing a good idea. Roman paganism had always been ceremonial and polytheistic, and had assimilated so many new customs and ideas that it took a very long time for anybody to realize that the root of the religion was dead. Now, centuries later, we see Christianity going through the same process as its predecessor, and for the same reasons.

It would be misleading to think that the Romans moved easily from Jupiter to Jesus. There was an intermediate step which began when the Emperor Augustus Caesar, following the pattern set in the east by Alexander the Great, had himself declared to be a god. Just for good measure, Augustus also deified his stepfather Julius. Certainly this alliance of throne and altar was useful to the throne, especially in the Greek speaking parts of the empire. It helped to maintain respect for the imperial power, but it eventually led skeptics to wonder whether perhaps all the other gods had also been created, and if so, who or what was the chief god?

By the third century CE, the answer was in - the sun was the chief god. Sun-worship fitted nicely with the Babylonian idea that heavenly bodies were alive and divine. As late as 274 CE, the Emperor Aurilian built a huge temple to Sol, in a vain and belated attempt to make the sun the dominant god of empire. Many of the trappings of solar worship became associated with the emperors, and with Roman state religion. The emperors began to wear radiating crowns. The eagle, symbol of both sun and emperor, became a common sculptural theme. Solar festivals became (and remain) extremely important annual events. Even dead ancestors got into the act. Iulos, son of Aeneas and founder of the Julian clan, was said to have had "tongues of fire"—the unfailing sign of the sun-god—around his head. Sun-worship, although adopted in part for political reasons, was more sophisticated than other forms of polytheism. When Christian missionaries or artists represented Christ as wearing long hair and a halo, or recounted the story of the tongues of fire at Pentecost, their pagan listeners were justified in drawing the conclusion that here was yet another name for the ancient god of the sun.

Unquestionably the most bizarre cult of the ancient world was not related to the male sky-gods, but was the religion of Cybele, the Queen of Heaven and Mother of the Gods. Her cult began in Phrygia, in modern-day Turkey. She was at first portrayed as accompanied by an earth-serpent, as some statues of the Virgin Mary are today. As Cybele's religion grew, it became more and more complicated. She rode in a chariot pulled by lions, she carried a whip, and she liked wild savage dancing, and the music of tambourines. Her rhythmic music apparently had a powerful effect, and has been compared to modern blues or jazz.

But Cybele would have languished and disappeared had not a silver statue of her been taken to Rome in the war against Hannibal. Many Roman citizens felt her intervention was crucial. Her image was carried in triumph through the streets of the Eternal City. She was hailed with shouts of "Nostra Domina!" (Our Lady!) But these same Romans were far less comfortable with her lover Attis, and downright alarmed by the behaviour of her priests.

The story of Cybele and Attis, like other myths, had a

number of versions. Attis was a shepherd, or perhaps the son of the king of Lydia, and the only mortal ever to have sex with Cybele. But shepherds will be boys, and Attis was seduced by another woman. Predictably Cybele found out, and in a jealous rage, drove Attis mad. Using a broken piece of pottery (or maybe a flint or a knife) Attis castrated himself, and then bled to death beneath a pine tree. Cybele was now full of remorse, and so caused Attis to come back to life. The ancient world found the dramatic re-enactment of these primal human passions to be deeply moving: a combination of love, sex, infidelity, violence, death, pity and horror.

The rites of Attis and Cybele were celebrated annually from March 15-26, and preceded by a period of penance and abstinence. The ritual reached its hysterical peak on March 24, The Day of Blood. An effigy of the dead Attis was publicly displayed and then buried, while believers gashed themselves, and danced in a blood-soaked frenzy to blaring and pounding music. Some especially devout priests were sure to castrate themselves to prove their devotion: such a one was called a fanaticus. Three days later Attis' tomb was found empty—he had risen from the dead. The Hilaria, a carnival of licentiousness and partying then began, in celebration of the resurrection of Attis and the arrival of spring.

In its fully developed form, the cult of Cybele was a late arrival on the imperial scene. There can be no question that it derived a lot of its ideas from other religions, but nobody in the ancient world denied the historical authenticity of either Cybele or Attis. The cymbals, the tambourines, and the dramatic re-enactment had all been used earlier in the orgiastic rites of Dionysos. The flutes and choirs were Egyptian. Other such connections exist with the gods Mithra and Harpocrates. But was there also some cross-fertilization with that other new religion—Christianity? Two Middle Eastern religions, each featuring elaborate mythologies of violent death and miraculous resurrection, each celebrating their rites at the beginning of spring—they would inevitably have adopted ideas and ceremonies from one another, and they would both vehemently deny they had done so. But Cybele's priests and apologists are no longer around to defend her.

Of course even if the priests of Cybele (called galli) were still extant, we would not be favourably disposed toward them. They were the Hare Krishnas of their day. They preferred long yellow robes, and wore lots of rings. Their hair was worn long and bleached and in a feminine style, when not topped by a turban or a tiara. Galli frequently wore makeup. They begged for alms. And of course, some of them were voluntary eunuchs. This was a form of celibacy that meant business. Eunuchs were another Babylonian innovation which the Romans generally found distasteful. But as time passed, other religions adopted the custom. Devout Christian monks of the Montanist sect were expected to castrate themselves, and the prevalence of non-voluntary eunuchs in medieval Islam is well known. Musical friends assure me that spooky-sounding recordings of male castrati choirs still exist, a distant echo of the numerous galli choirs who sang reverent hymns to Cybele, the Mother of the Gods.

The history of Cybele in the Roman Empire is one of mixed success. The Cybele cult was especially strong in southern Italy, where devotion to the Virgin is still vigorous today. Some members of the Roman upper classes could admire her, but scorned Attis and the galli who imitated him. Several attempts were made to ban Cybele and other eastern deities from Rome, but without success. After the reign of the emperor Claudius, the Cybele cult lost most of its eastern flavour and became fully Romanized.

The high priest, or archgallus, now had to be a Roman citizen and so could no longer be a eunuch. As part of the ceremony, he underwent a taurobolium, and after the bull had been slaughtered, it was castrated instead of him. This compromise doubtless pleased both Cybele the Great Mother and the archgallus. He was given a Persian-style tiara studded with precious stones of a type still worn by the Popes today. Moreover, the cult of Cybele owned one of the preferred locations in the city of Rome and they built an impressive sanctuary on Vatican Hill. Even the word "Vatican" is derived from Cybele-worship. This location already had a long history of sanctified use; Pliny claimed the early Etruscans had worshipped under a sacred oak on Vatican Hill even before the Romans arrived. Construction work in the seventeenth century uncovered several altars used by the galli. But for the archgallus himself, his stay on Vatican Hill was short—he was evicted by the high priest of another Eastern deity of consequence—the Persian god Mithra to whom we now turn.

6

MITHRA THE UNCONQUERED

"He who will not eat of my body and drink my blood, so that he will be made one with me and I with him, the same shall not know salvation."

Zoroaster

"...if Christianity had not carried the day, Mithraism would have become the religion of the world."

Renan

From our vantage point a century and a half later, Renan's claim now seems to be an overstatement. Mithraism was not as popular as he believed, but it was certainly the most interesting of the religious rivals to Christianity. Mithra, who still commands a handful of worshippers, is mankind's oldest living god. An inscription found in Turkey dated to the fourteenth century BCE asked Mithra to protect a treaty between the Mitanni and the Hittites. But his worship really took form considerably later.

The sixth century BCE was a period of exceptional religious innovation worldwide. Pythagoras and Orpheus in the Mediterranean, Buddha in India, and Confucius in China all reorganized existing religions into more satisfying philosophic systems. Much the same is true for the great

Persian thinker Zoroaster. By this stage you can probably write much of Zoroaster's early history by yourself. He was miraculously conceived by his mother when she was fifteen. A local prince made an attempt on his life while he was still an infant. He was tempted by the lord of evil, but the spirit of Ahuramazda seized him at the age of thirty and he began his religious life. He made strenuous attempts to reduce the polytheism of the Persian tribes to the worship of his single god, Ahuramazda. In this, Zoroaster failed spectacularly.

The system that grew out of his teachings had not one but two principal gods: Ahuramazda god of light and goodness, and Ahriman god of darkness and evil. Lurking somewhere above them was Zervan the god of time. And as a go-between for good and evil, there was Mithra.

One other group living on the Iranian plateau that deserves notice was the Magi (singular – magus). Magi were probably Medes rather than Persians. They were a class of hereditary priests who were choosy about their social contacts, and commanded a good deal of respect. They acted as tutors to the royal family, and knew a surprising amount about Babylonian, Greek and Jewish ideas. They practiced magic, but were otherwise believed to live austere and righteous lives. They were devoted to Mithra. If you needed impressive witnesses to authenticate a dubious case, Magi would do very nicely.

Like other successful deities of the ancient world, Mithra swallowed up rival cults as he grew in power and popularity. Current thinking is that Mithra had an astronomical origin as the constellation Orion (aka Nimrud and Samson). His early and persisting link with astrology later allowed Mithra to absorb many characters in the Olympic pantheon: he became the sun, the moon, Apollo, Serapis, Jupiter, and many many others. Mithraism mushroomed with remarkable speed.

Christians, seeing the rapid growth of their church, attributed it to divine favour. Perhaps we should ascribe the same causation to Mithraism.

The Mithraic religion had no central temple and suffered from the lack of a clear doctrine. There were in antiquity several elaborate explanations of the religion, but zealous Christians, the Church Militant, have destroyed them all. The sacred writings are also gone; so much of what can be pieced together must be done from a few brief inscriptions in stone, some statuary, and hostile comments from non-believers. It is as though we had to reconstruct the beliefs of modern Lutherans using only medieval cathedrals and a copy of the *Old Testament*. But these old gods don't die easily, and we still see large (and unacknowledged) chunks of Mithraism flourishing in the churches and chapels of the twenty-first century.

Mithra's life abounds in parallels with other gods. He was born to a virgin mother in a cave like Tammuz and Hermes, and on Christmas Day as befits a sun-god. He emerged miraculously from a rock wall wearing a cap and carrying a knife (or a torch). His birth was observed by shepherds who worshipped him and brought him gifts. He made for himself a garment of fig leaves to ward off the winter chill. The infant Mithra was often portrayed in sculpture as holding a globe in his hand; his birth, like that of other ancient heroes, was an event of cosmic importance.

Throughout his life Mithra struggled on behalf of humanity. He created mankind from a single couple. Ahriman the spirit of evil sent a flood, so Mithra inspired one man to build an ark and thereby save his family and his cattle. Ahriman sent a drought, so Mithra (like Moses following him) saved his people by striking a rock and producing water. He worked for peace. Mithra was buried in a rock tomb. He rose from the dead. But his major struggle was with a gigantic white bull, which probably represented the powers of the earth. This battle had the same emotional power for Mithraists that the crucifixion does for Christians. Hundreds of sculptures show the final victory: Mithra pulls back the bull's head and sinks the knife into its throat. Even as he does so, the bull's blood is being transformed into plants and animals, and the spinal cord is becoming an ear of grain. Only by the Mithraic sacrifice of the bull is the earth made fertile. The god is saving the world by the shedding of blood. Some early Persian sources have Mithra himself as the bull; in a familiar theme, the god is sacrificing his own life for the good of humanity.

The relationship between Mithra and Sol the sun-god will probably never be untangled. Mithraists wanted outsiders to believe they worshipped the sun, while in private they taught that Mithra was superior to and the power behind the sun. In any case, after the death of the great bull, Mithra and Sol sat down to a sacred meal of beef, wine, and of course, wheat cakes decorated with crosses. As in the Last Supper, they were joined at the table by Mithra's twelve chief disciples. Then Mithra climbed into Sol's chariot, and Sol drove him up to heaven. Sculptural renditions of this probably inspired both the stories of the Hebrew prophet Elijah, and the ascension of Jesus. When the world ends, says Mithraic doctrine, another bull will appear, Mithra will come down from heaven, people will rise from the dead, and Mithra will slay the new bull. The just will celebrate with bull-fat and wine, and the unjust will perish by fire as Ahuramazda destroys Ahriman and his wicked followers.

This complex and somewhat contradictory myth was really only the surface of Mithraism. It was in its teachings regarding the soul that the Persian religion really intermeshed with the other beliefs of pagan antiquity. Persians were probably the first to believe that human souls were immortal. Moreover, they held that all souls now on earth had pre-existed in heaven. Whenever a soul descended to earth to be infused into a body, it passed from the realm of pure light down through seven spheres; each controlled by a different planet, and in passing the soul picked up qualities of each. This is the origin of modern astrology. The positioning of the planets at the time of your birth is crucial, since that determines the personal qualities your soul will pick up. Thus, it was through Mithraism that Babylonian sky-worship came to permeate the thought of the ancient world, and to infect the gullible today.

Fertile minds went to work constructing fantastic elaborations on these themes. Your moral victories on earth would lighten your soul for a swifter return to the empyrean, the realm of light. Unworthy souls would be blocked by seven metal gates, each guarded by an angel of Ahuramazda. Soon each planet and therefore each day of the week had its own metal, its own animal, its own stone.

The seven spheres of heaven meant that seven became a sacred number in the ancient world. Mithraism's symbol of future glory became the seven-stepped ladder. You had to be a truly exceptional Mithraist to be carried up, as the Evangelist John claimed to be, to the seventh heaven. The wise and the clever studied the movement of the planets with considerable insight into astronomy; the foolish and the credulous accepted their findings as astrological determinism.

The sun, the moon, and the five visible planets had had their own days of the week since Sumerian times. Sunday was Mithra's day. It was "The Lord's Day", and Mithra was "The Lord" long before the coming of Christianity. As mediator between Ahuramazda and Ahriman, Mithra had the seventh month dedicated to him, and the midpoint of each month (the 16th) was his day. Annual festivals celebrated his birth on (you guessed it) December 25, and his victory over the great bull on March 21. Perpetual fires commemorated his victories in his Asian temples, and kept alive human hopes that Mithra The Interceder would plead our case with the unknowable god Ahuramazda.

Mithra traveled with the Persian armies into the Tigris and Euphrates valleys in 538 BCE. It was here that the powerful alloy of Persian dualism and Babylonian astrology was first struck. The ideas of the Persians also had a great impact on those Jews who had previously been take captive to Babylon. When the Persians defeated Babylon and allowed those Hebrews who wished it to return to Palestine, they carried with them valuable Persian theological ideas. Heaven, hell, angels, devils, and the personal struggle between good and evil were all transmitted through Judaism to the modern world from its contact with the Persians. Both Mithraism and Christianity, the former directly and the latter indirectly, derived numerous customs and beliefs from the priests of Babylon. Neither religion seemed to be aware of its own background, and when they encountered one another in the West in the second and third centuries CE, they savagely attacked one another as plagiarizing devils. The irony was, of course, that both religions were shamelessly stealing good ideas from any other cult they encountered and that was the very reason for their successes.

When Alexander the Great crushed the Persian Empire in the fourth century BCE, these Persian ideas became available on a broad scale throughout the eastern Mediterranean world. Alexander began a mania for things Persian: he married Persian wives; encouraged his officers to do the same, dressed in Persian robes, and worshipped Persian divinities. Mithraism became extremely popular among the Greek-influenced population of Asia Minor, although curiously not within Greece itself. Part of its popularity in Anatolia may have been that Mithra was co-opted into the native cult of Cybele. The myth says that Mithra offended the all-powerful goddess, and so she transformed him into a fir tree. (Much later, the survival of this Mithraic tradition in Germany probably led to the custom of the Christmas tree.)

The cult of Mithra first spread to the West in 67 BCE when Pompey the Great took back to Italy as slaves a nest of Anatolian pirates who were also devout Mithraists. Although Pompey's victory secured the coast for Rome, the inland areas of Anatolia remained unsubdued and unrepentant for another century. One of these inland cities, Tarsus, was a hotbed of Mithraism. This environment left a deep impression on its most famous native son, Paul. As a staunch Jew, Paul would not have had intimate knowledge of the secret Mithraic ceremonies, but his writings are bursting with Mithraic assumptions. We will explore this further when we turn to Paul and his accomplishments.

While Mithra was well-known and popular in the east (there was an entire dynasty of Parthian kings named Mithridates), the god's success in the western part of the empire came considerably later. For example, there are no evidences of Mithraism in Pompeii (destroyed 78 CE), although the Emperor Augustus had been initiated into the cult a full century earlier. The *Aeneid*, the masterpiece of Augustus' favourite writer Virgil, has been recently interpreted in a rather far-fetched essay as the history of he Mithraic cult in Italy.

The boom period of the religion can be closely tied to the great population shifts of the second and third centuries CE.

The three groups most likely to move (willingly or unwillingly) were soldiers, slaves, and merchants. Mithraism appealed to all three, but was exceptionally strong among army officers. Roman military policy required the regular transfer of centurions, and frequently whole legions. Moreover, Rome had trouble getting enough Italian-born soldiers, and began to enlist recruits from Asia Minor. Mithra moved west with his followers.

Mithra became a soldier's god. He soon eclipsed Mars and Hercules, two macho deities who had long been favourites of the Roman army. Most of the archaeological evidence of Mithraism comes from the frontiers of the empire where the army was stationed; both northern France and the Danube—Rhine areas have yielded numerous Mithraic sanctuaries.

These sanctuaries were usually small and unimpressive, and many were underground. Perhaps the worshippers in the garrisons expected to be moved, or perhaps the lack of decoration was a result of an exclusively male congregation, or there may have been theological reasons, now lost through time. Unsurprisingly, Mithraists seem to have been social conservatives, especially in the third and fourth centuries when the religion was at its zenith. Moreover, Mithraism had no public ceremonies, and generally kept a low profile, when compared to the excessive emotionalism of the cults of Cybele or Dionysos.

Because of the factors we have been discussing, the extent of Mithraism in the Roman Empire has excited considerable debate. While it flourished well before Jesus in the Eastern Mediterranean, its spread in the West can be traced only by non-literary sources. The city of Rome has no fewer than 100 former sanctuaries. In some ways its late arrival in the West was a boon: it was never persecuted as was the cult of Isis, and it benefited from its connection with the previously established religion of Cybele. Where it has been intensively studied, as in the Italian port city of Ostia, the power of Mithraism provides a clear indication that the traditional religious system of Rome was bankrupt, and that one complex Eastern religion or another would be its successor.

Because Mithra was born in a cave, an underground vault was the preferred place of worship. If a natural cave were not available, some type of underground structure was built. These turned out to be ideal for archaeological preservation. The grottos were built on an east-west axis so the rays of the rising sun would fall on the rear wall and on the image portrayed there of Mithra and the great bull. Stone benches stood at right angles like the choir stalls of a medieval chancel. We might ask why a sun-god would be worshipped in a dark underground room. The answer seems to be that it made a great impression on the worshippers. The small congregation, no more than twenty or thirty, would have known one another, and the underground always evoked notions of death and the spirit world among the ancients. Most Graeco-Roman religions had people pray while standing with upturned hands and faces. How much more terrifying to worship while kneeling in an underground chamber, lit only by a shaft of sunlight and a few candles. Asian temples to Mithra show evidence that a perpetual altar fire was kept burning, but no proof of this exists in the West.

The Mithraic priest, as an intermediary between god and man, was responsible for rites at dawn, noon and dusk. Ceremonies involved unveiling a representation of Mithra, accompanied by the ringing of a small bell. The priest, always addressed as Father, was Mithra's deputy. He wore a ring that believers kissed, and carried a staff which symbolized his authority. His robes were derived from the costumes of the Magi. The Pater Patrum, or bishop, was distinguished by his mitre, modeled after the tiara worn by the Persian king.

Of course, the priesthood was all male. In fact, one of the fatal limitations of Mithra's cult was that women could not join. Many of the major religions of antiquity, such as those of Isis, Kore, Dionysos and Cybele, admitted both sexes. Others were more restrictive. The cult of Bona Dea, for example, consisted only of women. The Mithraic refusal to admit women to full membership did not mean they were rejected totally. They might dedicate themselves to the god and join strict prayer groups if they were virgins. This kind of sexism was reflected almost exactly in Paul's admonition to Christian women that they might attend services, but only if they were inconspicuous. However, the wives of Mithraists commonly joined the cult of Cybele, where they doubtless felt more welcome.

As with other cults we have discussed, Mithraism was organized somewhat like a modern fraternal lodge in which secrecy and esoteric knowledge played a big part. The hierarchy was complex, with four stages, each with three steps: a total of twelve degrees in all. These grades had evocative titles such as Bride, Raven, Soldier and Lion. The Bride was mystically married to Mithra in the same sense that a nun is the bride of Christ. The twelfth grade was the high priest Pater Patrum, the Father of Fathers. Officeholders might wear costumes such as masks or animal skins to denote their degree. A candidate for admission to the cult had to undergo twelve trials—The Tortures: fire, hunger, cold, bleeding, etc. There was some sort of ceremony involving a sword stained with the blood of a man who had died violently. Applicants to join the Mithraic brotherhood were not to participate in any other mystery cults, but it is doubtful if this rule could have been enforced, considering the degree of syncretism among the religions of the late empire. A more effective oath required complete secrecy about rites and doctrine: the success of this injunction may be measured by how little we know about this fascinating religion some two millennia later.

However, we do know a bit. No one was admitted to the cult without a long initiation period. The initiation oath required to join the cult was called the "sacramentum". It was a form of baptism which forgave all the sins of one's past life. A Mithraist was "reborn" when he joined the cult. The ceremony normally took place in early spring. One form involved the candidate being sprinkled with holy water, and the tracing of a cross on his forehead by a priest. The initiate was expected to be tattooed, sometimes on the hands, but in several portraits of the time the tattoo is visible on the forehead of the believer. A second type of baptism, more familiar to us, required bodily immersion in water. A third type, which must have been rare, involved immersion in the blood of a bull.

If you find the idea of a bloodbath revolting, you aren't alone—so did most of the ancients. The baptism of blood (known as the Taurobolium) had a naked believer stand in a pit covered with planks. A sacrificial bull wearing a crown was led onto the planks, its throat was cut, and the blood gushed over the man beneath. Presumably it was an old Oriental rite, since it was practiced in connection with both the worship of Mithra and Cybele. It was unknown in Rome until 134 CE, and it most often occurred near the religious sanctuaries on Vatican Hill. Taurobolia seemed to increase in numbers until the fourth century.

Since the underground crypts were small and access to them was difficult, the Taurobolium must have been an open-air ceremony and would have attracted the notice of a large number of unbelievers. But this was the Rome of "bread and circuses", and a taurobolium would have been only slightly more interesting that other animal sacrifices on the Capitoline Hill, or the day's adventures at Circus Maximus. But for the wealthy man who underwent it, the "Baptism of Blood" meant that he was reborn for all eternity, or at least that his earthly life would be extended. If the believer couldn't afford a bull, a Mithraist might have the same ritual with a ram (the criobolium), or even a lamb. This certainly puts a grotesque twist on such Christian phrases as "the redeeming blood of Christ", or the old hymn *"Washed in the Blood of the Lamb."*

To an archaelologist, a garbage dump is better than a gold mine. The refuse-pits of Mithraic shrines have given us tangible evidence of their communion feasts. The remains of not only cattle, but pigs, sheep and fowl have been found. Perhaps these other animals were substituted for bulls for reasons of economy. A particularly interesting find was a Mithraeum in which the expenses were scratched on the wall. Predictably, the chief costs were for bread, meat and wine.

Sacred meals were common to many of the religious communities of the time, as we have already discovered. Even the terminology was the same: the term "mass" used to describe the Christian ritual may have been derived from the Mithraic "mizd" (sacred cake), or from the Dionysiac "maza" (a cake of barley and honey), or may even have been of Egyptian origin. Preaching from the holy texts (none of which survive) was followed by the consecration of bread (usually thin wafers, marked with a cross) and wine, and the sharing of communion with those initiates present.

The communion ritual has been such a key one in the Christian tradition that usually the scholars, in discussing the parallels, prefer not to offend and to take a conservative stance on the meaning which Mithraists attributed to their ceremony. Kane, for example, says he does not believe that

Mithraists thought that eating flesh or drinking blood had any sacramental importance. He says it was a relaxed, social-religious activity. Vermaseren, on the other hand, thinks that they believed the meal had magical properties: that it brought sustenance to the body and salvation to the soul. Common sense sides with Vermaseren. Because they were kept secret, we don't know the exact words of the ceremony, but they were probably those first spoken by Zoroaster, and made familiar to millions of Christians:

> "He who will not eat of my body and drink of my blood, so that he will be made one with me and I with him, the same shall not know salvation."

Mithraism, like early Christianity, sometimes varied the exact food and drink provided. Romans were not great meat eaters, and bread was far more economical than sacrificial meat. Some authorities claim Mithraism used water as a sacred drink, and there is evidence that in some places in the second century, under Mithraic influence, that Christianity replaced its use of wine with water. In later centuries, both religions mixed some of each as their sacred drink. The sources seem agreed that Mithraic bread was baked with a cross on it, and that it was distributed only to those who had attained a certain level in the hierarchy. Through all this, we need to remember that Mithraism was a shamelessly eclectic religion, and may well have stolen a number of these rites from Christianity. On the other side, the Mithraic rites were indisputably older, and Christians were as quick as anyone to adopt an appealing ceremony or symbol. For us, this "chicken and egg" puzzle is part of the mystery of these religions.

There can be no question, however, that the Mithraic code of day-to-day conduct was very high. There were far fewer accusations of impropriety against them than were leveled against the Christians. Every Mithraist was a soldier in the war against evil. Chastity was a source of physical strength, so women ought to be avoided wherever possible. A Mithraist did not eat certain foods, kept himself clean, spoke only the truth. Morality was the basis of goodness. Mutual aid and charity toward the needy were important virtues. Even the wealthy were to wear simple and austere clothing while attending religious ceremonies. Mithra himself was always portrayed as solemn, earnest, full of the spirit of goodness. This was a religion of unswerving nobility: it had no Judas, no Mary Magdalen, no tax collectors, no thieves, and definitely no crucifixion by the political authorities.

Mithraism also left its mark on the art and iconography of its Christian rival. For example, the Mithraic symbol of a lamb carrying a cross with its forefoot was astrological in origin, but was adopted by Christians for their own Lamb. As late as the seventh century, however, Christian councils were still vetoing the portrayal of Jesus as the Lamb of God—it was just too glaringly pagan. But the authorities lost, because the connection in the popular mind between the Savior and the Lamb ran too deep. The Mithraic halo—identified with the sun-god—soon made its appearance in Christian art, and could be found atop representations of the Holy Family, angels and saints. Artisans produced plenty of cheap and shoddy Mithraic sculpture for home use, and Christians were bound to appropriate and appreciate a good deal of it, without being aware of its origin. Perhaps a more dramatic example is this: Mithra the sun-god, surrounded by the twelve signs of the zodiac, became transmuted in the hands of early Christians into the belief that Jesus had twelve special "apostles."

Many other aspects of this ancient creed survive in magic

and esoteric cult knowledge. Mithra had secret names including Abraxis and Abracadabra. Calling out the secret name was believed to compel the god to do your bidding. Abracadabra is probably Egyptian in origin. The believer kept saying it over and over, dropping syllables until only "Ra" the sun-god remained. Tarot cards are also Mithraic. Mithra's secret numbers, predictably for a sun-god, were 7 and 365. It would be a mistake to underestimate the appeal this kind of mystical nonsense has had over the human mind of the last two millennia. In fact, it may not be far off the mark to say that most major secret societies of the West have been based on Mithra-worship: the Persian Sufis, the medieval Knights Templar, the Rosicrucians, and the Scottish Rite Freemasons—as well as Dan Brown's bestselling potboiler, *The Da Vinci Code*.

If Fortune, in the person of the sun-god, controlled individual fates, then the head of state would attract particular interest. This notion that the king is different, and must have divine approval, is an early statement of the divine right of kings, a philosophy that was to lead to a great deal of European bloodshed between the eleventh and eighteenth centuries.

The Mithraic priesthood was well-established in Rome, so when the Pater Patrum took up residence on Vatican Hill, close by the Archgallus of Cybele, the real estate of that small knoll became inextricably linked with both the past and the future of the world's religions. Perhaps we should jump ahead in our story just a bit here to note that a) legends of St. Peter visiting Rome and founding a church on Vatican Hill are certainly false; and b) it is absurd to believe that devout Christians would have buried Peter (the "rock") on a hill sacred to The God From the Rock, despite what many Christians would like to believe. These foolish notions are perpetuated in our time by the absolute ignorance of people about ancient paganism. They arose as pious inventions at the time when Christianity overthrew Mithraism. The Pater Patrum of Mithraism was simply replaced by the Pope, who took over both his religious and military authority. In fact, one historian claims the very pontifical throne itself has pagan carvings on it, and is probably Mithraic in origin.

Mithraism peaked in popularity about 250 CE. It seems to have taken advantage of its position to support the persecution of Christians. A half-century later, Mithra the Unconquered Sun-God was proclaimed Protector of the Empire. He enjoyed his position a mere twenty years before Christ replaced him. Now the tables were turned. By about 370 CE, the violence of Christianity against Mithraism was massive. All across the empire, Mithraic shrines were burned and looted while officials turned a blind eye. The stone statues and bas-reliefs were pounded into gravel as Christians destroyed all traces of the demons.

At Saarburg in the Rhineland, a grotto was discovered which contained a grisly spectacle—the charred bones of a male approximately thirty-five years of age, his hands chained behind him and lying on his face—the body of a Mithraic priest left to die in the fire that destroyed his temple. Leaving a murdered priest in his sanctuary to profane it may have happened more than once, but here we can go no further.

We simply do not know any real details of the persecution because no Christian would record it, and no Mithraic records survive. We can only say that in a spectacularly short time, Mithraism was totally annihilated as a religion in the West. How many died, how many forcibly converted, how many willingly converted, and how many disappeared, cannot even be speculated upon. On the one hand, Mithraists were closely tied to the government and the army; maybe many of them were the type who used religion to curry favour, and so were able to adjust when the wind blew hard from another direction. Nevertheless, if we had the sources, I suspect we could write a Mithraic version of the *Lives of the Saints*, full of prejudice, torture and death suffered by good men in the name of Mithra The Saviour of Mankind.

By now the reader may wonder where Mithra went wrong. If the religion was so profound and noble, why wasn't it the ultimate victor? Some authors have made the argument that Mithraism did in fact win out—that Christianity swallowed so much of the Persian religion that the two became indistinguishable. (Usually these authors conclude their works with a call to return to the "true" principles of Jesus, but as we shall see, this is easier said than done.) In any case, most twenty-first century people have never heard of Mithra, while they certainly have heard a good deal about Christ, so the question deserves an answer.

First let us review their major similarities. Both Christianity and Mithraism were oriental faiths with widespread popularity among the people of both eastern and western parts of the Roman Empire. They each had complex mythologies of sacrifice and atonement, but their major appeal was to emotion. Their practices were nearly identical: baptism, a eucharistic meal, the liturgy, brotherly love, the priesthood. Their beliefs about the soul were too similar to be dismissed as coincidence: immortality, a last judgement, heaven as a shining mansion, good versus evil, and the resurrection of the dead through the mediation of the Son of the Most High.

The point is that the wide gulf that modern people often perceive between Christianity and its rivals simply did not exist. Some Greek philosophers in the third century CE compared Mithraism and Christianity, admitted there was very little to distinguish between them, but came down in favour of the former. They did not see the life of Mithra as any more or any less believable than the life of Jesus.

But the religion that became Christianity did enjoy several advantages. Its admission of women was crucial. This seems to have humanized the character of Jesus, while at the same time women made great contributions to the pageantry of the public rituals. Although we can't prove it statistically, the impression is that women of the late empire were perhaps more prone than men to ecstatic conversions. Christianity specialized and encouraged these conversions, while Mithraism avoided them.

Mithraism began as a religion of the poor and the humble, but its theory remained difficult, and its believers were socially and economically above average. Christianity appealed to the lowest strata of society. The late Roman Empire was not a very edifying time, and so the victory of the religion of the slave over the religion of the soldier may be seen as one more example of this decay. Christianity adapted to this new state of affairs, and unlike other cults, ceased to emphasize the allegorical nature of its teachings. The stories of Jesus and his friends were declared to be literally true. Miracles and a strict belief in the *Bible* replaced Greek rationality. Meanwhile, the political, social and religious institutions of the ancient world staggered as Germanic tribes drifted across imperial borders, burning cities, disrupting trade, and making civilized life a wistful dream of the past. Plague and starvation stalked the great cities. It was not a time for speculating about the structure of the seven gates of heaven.

The story of a poor carpenter with miraculous powers was immediate and concrete. His teachings seemed clear and hopeful as they were explained by the missionaries of the fourth and fifth centuries. But the *New Testament* contains much that is not clear. The lessons of the parables are not obvious. The *Epistles* of Paul are difficult, even for educated people. Christianity had wrestled with these problems and had managed to control most of the wild speculation by means of a strong central authority. Perhaps because of its Jewish roots, Christianity also had resisted emperor-worship and developed a far stronger sense of cohesion than Mithraism ever did. This group loyalty was all the more remarkable considering the essential Greek-ness of the *New Testament*, and the philosophic bent of the Hellenistic mind. Mithraism had never adapted to the Greek mindset. That fact alone would have doomed the Persian religion in the long run.

By the late fourth century, then, Christianity had proven its resourcefulness. Like the anaconda, it had proven it could swallow entities apparently bigger than itself, and digest them with difficulty. The great historian Edward Gibbon enumerated the reasons for the Christian victory some two hundred years ago: 1) the enthusiasm of its believers, 2) its belief in immortality, 3) the preaching of miracles, 4) its high code of ethics and 5) its disciplined organization. To this we might add the comment of Arthur Weigall a half century ago—Mithraism collapsed because its doctrines and rites had been so thoroughly adopted by the cult of the Palestinian carpenter.

7

THE MYSTERY RELIGIONS COMPARED

*"The history of religion is a long attempt to...
find a sound theory for absurd practices."*

Sir James Frazier

We have been examining the major religious systems of late antiquity. Certainly by the zenith of the Roman Empire the attraction of the state cults, that of Zeus/Jupiter and his fellow Olympians, was still present although in gradual decline. Likewise the religion of the Roman household seems to have been eclipsed as the empire became more cosmopolitan. But as the size of the political unit grew, so did the remoteness of its gods, and by the first century CE, many people were feeling a clear need for a more personal relationship with a deity. The result was a supermarket of religious ideas contending for the individual's loyalty, all offering salvation as a reward.

Especially in the eastern empire, the stew of peoples, cultures and languages, and the rapid growth of great cities, made the eclectic combination of religious ideas the norm. And there was no shortage of cults: for birth, death, sexual potency, prosperity, crops, health—some for men, some for women, some for both. If the official state religion was intended for social cohesion, then these mystery cults were for the individual's spiritual growth. They all claimed a special revelation, secret knowledge, personal immortality, arcane symbols, powerful rituals, and a claim of universal brotherhood. All these ideas had enormous appeal to the huge underclasses in the great cities of the Roman Empire. Christianity, as one of this jostling crowd of creeds, was the best positioned. A religion that preached acceptance of the present order, meekness in the face of power, and poverty as a blessing would enjoy rapid growth.

Then, as now, the triumph of evil over good was part of the daily experience of most people. Shabby ideas, shoddy goods, and shady ladies all could be bought as easily under the Pax Romana as under the Pax Americana. The moral person needs faith that some day the righteous will get even, and so a religion of salvation is tailor-made for a civilization in decline.

Any successful religion expands by capitalizing on the problems of its age, and moving toward a realization of its ideals. The demand in the first century was for mystery, redemption, and a savior. The ancient world had been built on certain assumptions upon which most people agreed—that the inward life was more important than outward display, that wisdom was preferable to jewels, that a good man was happy whatever happened, that material wealth was good, but not essential. These widespread views meant, for example, that even well-to-do Athenians of the classical age were willing to live in what we would today consider appalling privation. By the first century BCE, this had changed. New material and psychological conditions called for a religion with a high degree of certainty.

Life in the three hundred years between Alexander and Jesus had produced a sense of political and ethical turmoil. Greek philosophy had conquered the region, but had left in its wake the interminable disputes that philosophers (but few others) love. Greek and semi-Greek princes had struggled for control of the great cities and their taxes. And then came the Romans. Palestine was the frontier, a potential battleground between the two superpowers of the day—Rome to the west, and Parthia to the east. Military skirmishing between the two had already begun.

It isn't surprising that thoughtful people took a gloomy turn of mind. Pessimism, mysticism and a deep sense of sin coloured all the religious thinking of the region. A deep spiritual yearning affected Egyptian, Jew and Greek alike. Reaction to the rampant materialism of the time led to godseeking on an enormous scale, and literally thousands of schools and creeds competed for the loyalty of souls. So it was that from Antioch and Alexandria, where men wrote learned and reflective books, to Galilee where simple fishermen experienced instant conversion, virtually the whole eastern empire was looking for certainty. All religions became missionary religions in this most devout of centuries. Each believer had an obligation to increase the size and the prestige of his cult.

As might be expected, the tenor of the times was reshaping the older religions as well. Historians comment on the increasing standards of morality expected from the worshippers of Isis, Dionysos and Mithra during the first three centuries of our era. Regulations on who might take communion became stricter. Orgies were discouraged. The conviction spread that the deities preferred moral behaviour to animal sacrifice. A widespread ethical reformation was underway from the bottom up, as the cults discovered that asceticism and moral purity drew and kept new members. And Christianity was riding the crest of this new wave of morality.

This was the origin of the celebrated Christian sense of ethics. Born in an era of tolerant and enlightened paganism, Christianity reflects back the noblest parts of Hellenistic civilization. The ethics of Jesus included nothing that would seem particularly remarkable to a morally educated person of that unusual century.

For although moral behaviour was a driving force, the mystery religions of the time succeeded or failed on emotional grounds. Whether called Adonis, Attis, Jesus, or some other name, the saviour god was not passionless or abstract. The god-man had experienced and shared our human suffering. He retained a personal involvement in each believer's well-being. It was easy to feel warm and affectionate toward this god. He had struggled and died, true, but he rose gloriously from this apparent defeat. He was a god of hope, a friend of the masses. The annual festival of his passion and death was designed to build up great emotion among the believers: long preparations, abstinence from food and sex, silence, darkness, then music, light, pageantry, dancing, and frequently frenzy and behavioural excess. Christianity was probably the most successful at condemning the sexual vices, but on Good Friday and Easter it employed all the common techniques used at the other mystery-festivals, and there is no reason to think that Christians were superior to the others in their day-to-day morality.

Unfortunately for us, the mystery religions were just that: they tried—and often succeeded—in keeping secret their essential doctrines and rites. Besides that, they have been extinct for nearly two thousand years. It is not possible to reconstruct their extent or the power they had over the internal lives of their believers. We know, for example, that Athenians of the classical period felt enormous emotional involvement when they attended the works of Sophocles or

Euripides at their great dramatic festivals. Today, these same plays leave most modern theatergoers emotionally unmoved. The novelist John Fowles, in *The French Lieutenant's Woman*, suggests that emotions, like living beings, can evolve and even become extinct. So perhaps the closest we moderns can come to the mystery religions is the emotional excesses brought on by a really effective fundamentalist preacher. The sermon which flows and ebbs, increasing in tension and vividness of imagery, the urgency of conversion to achieve salvation, all are carried directly from the mystery-religions to us. As Aristides described it in the fourth century, an ecstatic conversion to a religious cult involved a mixture of tears, joy and a near-trance, impossible to describe, but

"...anyone who has been initiated will recognize it from experience..."

If you know any evangelical Christians, you will recognize this emotional crisis, whether the god be Aesculapius, Jesus, or Dionysos.

A further point—whether ancient or modern, these religions appealed to people and to cultures that had lost their self-confidence. Engagement with the world was now in question. Virtually the whole range of tactics used by medieval ascetics came from the mysteries. First to be restricted were the chief demons—sex and money. Sex was restricted to marriage, and then it was even discouraged within marriage. And not everyone should marry. As we have seen, many of the galli of Cybele were willing to put a permanent end to their reproductive possibilities. Other mystery-religions, especially in Egypt, encouraged the devout to withdraw into communities of the same sex, or move alone into the desert as hermits. Likewise, material goods were evil;

best give them to the priests. Some groups, such as the Jewish Essenes and the early Christians, practiced a sort of semi-communism. Other forms of penance and self-abasement were widespread: self-torture, public humiliation, pilgrimages, public confessions, and so on. Government attempts to control these excesses were deemed persecution and produced more saints and martyrs; believers who were willing to take upon themselves some of the sufferings endured by their particular god.

From another viewpoint, these mystery-religions that flourished during the latter part of the Roman Empire were specific versions of that great world-religion that much of humanity has embraced since we began to live in large groups. The religious person at the time of Jesus, looking to choose one among the many cults, would tend to select, as a modern person would, on the basis of class, nationality, geographic region, and religious psychology. Many of the larger cults could point to an extraordinary history. The Eleusinian Mysteries survived for 1,100 years, the Orphics for 1,200, the Gnostics for 500. The worship of Cybele flourished for 600 years in Italy and for a thousand years before that in Asia Minor. As for the Blessed Mother Isis, she was 3,000 years old at the time of Jesus and had never been more popular. Moreover, Egyptian traders who were in contact with India returned with stories and traditions whose antiquity intimidated even the priests of Alexandria. For the thinkers of the Roman Empire, whose respect for age and tradition was far greater than ours, these time spans must have seemed very impressive indeed. It all serves to remind us that two thousand years, while a very long time, may not yet be decisive in the field of religion.

All these mystery-religions offered salvation through a saviour-god, and promised an afterlife of blessedness for those who had been initiated. They all stressed salvation for the individual and showed little interest in the well-being of the state. All had rituals and rites that had to be performed correctly to bring down the expected benefits. These rituals which triggered divine grace, called sacraments, were seen as symbolic. But symbolic of what? Let us consider only one example we are familiar with, the goddess Isis. She was seen as the symbol of mother, wife, lover, virgin, whore, healer, scientist, the star Sirius, sisterly loyalty, Mother of God, spirit of the earth, guardian of the dead, and patroness of pet owners. Furthermore, she was all of these at the same time. We cannot hope to fathom the allegorical nature of symbols used by the mysteries. What we can say is that for the mind of that era, any symbol that seemed to work would be appropriated, including any useful ideas which might have been first held by rival cults.

A quick survey of some common elements of these religions might surprise us with the degree of mutual borrowing. A whole raft of potential saviours—Adonis, Apollo, Baal, Dionysos, Hercules, Horus, Jesus, Krishna, Mithra and Osiris—were all

- born on Christmas Day in a cave or underground
- born to a virgin mother
- lived a life of toil on behalf of humanity
- died, and then rose from the dead
- founded a religious organization
- were commemorated by their devotees with a eucharist.

The dove, symbol of the sky-god's approval, circled the heads of Astarte, Buddha, Cybele, Isis, Juno and Mary. The fast of forty days and forty nights had a Hebrew origin and was undertaken by Elijah, Jesus, St. Joachim (father of the Virgin Mary), and Moses. The road to hell and back was an expressway: Adonis, Dionysos, Hercules, Horus, Jesus, Krishna, Mercury, Orpheus, Osiris and Zoroaster all remained there for three days and nights before they rose to life again. The end of the world will feature war, pestilence, and the triumphant return of Buddha, Dionysos, Jesus, Krishna and Mithra. And the judgment of the dead will presumably be a jury decision by Ahuramazda, Buddha, Jesus, Krishna, and Osiris.

We have by no means exhausted the parallels, but the point is clear. Try then to be sympathetic with those Hellenistic men and women, desperate for certainty, who encountered this confusion and eclecticism at every turn. No wonder they opted in the end for a religion that promised (and perhaps only promised) monotheism, simplicity, and authority.

To be sure, not all those who espoused mystery-religions did so because they sought knowledge of the divine. People being what they are, we might expect a healthy amount of baser motivation. Recent studies of surviving pagan inscriptions indicate that most were requests for good health, not eternal life. We certainly should expect that a good number of people joined for the fellowship, perhaps even for the quality of the food and drink at the communion meals. The cities of the empire were huge and impersonal places, with far less security for the man or family plagued by injury or illness than the modern city dweller of the West enjoys. Numerous clubs and associations known as "collegia" helped to fill this gap for those not in the upper classes. These collegia might have a religious or an occupational basis, and had banquets on a regular schedule or on occasions of importance to an individual member.

Most of us concede the importance of this type of celebration in our own lives, and we cannot deny that for many ancient pagans, the appeal of the mysteries lay no deeper than this. In fact, a major regulation at cult eucharists and at the collegia banquets was that a member who drank so much wine that he vomited should be expelled from the organization. We would be on strong grounds in suspecting that the modern Christmas or Thanksgiving dinner—gluttony under the veneer of religion—is not really dissimilar to the eucharistic feasts of many of the mysteries.

There are other reasons to believe that the mysteries were not all they appeared to be. It was a common complaint of Greek husbands that their wives were never at home, because they were off at the Orphic or Eleusinian temple engaged in cult activities. From our egalitarian perspective, we might observe that there were precious few other places a Greek wife might go without causing scandalous comment. And of course there were numerous claims that this cult or that consisted of magicians, or charlatans, or conjurors, or even practiced ritual murder or cannibalism during the celebrations of the mysteries. Christianity seems to have drawn more than its share of these accusations, but they all seemed suspicious to outsiders.

On balance, however, the mystery religions were clearly a force for the side of goodness and light in the later Roman Empire. People did take them seriously. Even Christian writers assumed that these rival saviours were quite real: the Church Father Clement of Alexandria was typical in claiming that they were mere men, but he did not consider denying their existence. Even those mysteries which were quasi-public commanded a lot of respect. Virtually every Athenian had been initiated into the Eleusinian Mysteries.

Nevertheless, Diagoras the Atheist incurred the wrath of the public for having publicized the secrets of the cult, and thus "...making them seem futile".

But then, any hostile description of a religion causes it to look trivial and silly, no matter how profound its hold upon the human heart. We should judge neither the pagan mysteries nor Christianity by their fallen examples, for they have done much good. In the days before any type of psychotherapy, the insane were left to wander the streets of the great cities. Healers and preachers of many types could draw a crowd, and might be efficacious for at least some of their listeners. Whether devoted to Isis or Cybele or Jesus, who could deny the poor and outcast their only real source of hope?

A wider gap existed then between the beliefs of the educated and the uneducated than is the case today. Then, only the learned doubted. Today everyone is racked with doubt, and the religious differences in our time arise from how we come to terms with it. The thinkers of the Roman Empire knew that idol-worship was silly. They knew that gods could not be persuaded by cutting the throat of an innocent animal. They knew that an eternal god could not be born, die, or cavort around as the Olympians did. Gods did not need men at all, and cult behaviour was at best useless, and at worst insulting.

The popular belief was that there were three destinations in the afterlife—the upper sphere where you rejoiced with the deity, the intermediate sphere where you suffered until you were purified, and the pit in the depths of the earth where the wicked suffer eternally. Both Cicero and Seneca scoffed: only old women were foolish enough to believe these stories. But Cicero and Seneca's view was widely rejected in their own time, and it is widely rejected now. Few minds of any era can maintain an attitude of religious skepticism without sliding off into complete materialism. For many of the men and the women of the first century (and probably for ours), it was exactly materialism that they were fleeing, and if that meant the occasional acceptance of nonsense, or of magical divisions in the afterlife, so be it.

The increasing reliance on astrology, magic and the occult during the second and third centuries CE marks not only the rejection of logic and skepticism, but is a certain sign that the traditional religion was worn out. The Romans began to borrow words and phrases from dead and foreign religions in the hope of influencing the powers of the universe. This same pattern was to recur in Reformation Germany, and again in seventeenth century Massachusetts. The modern observer, surveying the contemporary religious scene, is entitled to wonder whether we may see another massive religious upheaval in the near future.

Since hindsight is always perfect, let us take advantage of that fact to review what we might expect of a new world-religion evolving in the first century CE. Any successful religion would have to promise future happiness in another world. In such a cosmopolitan and impersonal society, the emphasis would be on the relationship between the individual and God; it would not talk of public duty. It would draw on the common doctrines of its time: sin, salvation, a saviour who suffered, a eucharistic feast. The religion would be dominated by a powerful male priesthood which stressed sexual denial in their own lives and that of their followers. Finally, the religion should be (at least superficially) monotheistic, the religion of a powerful father-god who would sweep away the dozens of deities across the Mediterranean world.

The Hellenistic civilization of the Greeks and the Romans

had arrived at a cultural level in which awareness of time, or the temporary nature of being, was acute. Here came a religion which preached a Saviour who lived at a certain time, and in a certain place, a new religion that fitted better with the linear notion of time which the world was developing. Certainly there was much that was old in the story of Jesus—as old as Osiris himself—but the details and the framework were new.

Christianity drew from the same common stock of ideas as did the other mystery religions. It had the same cultural apparatus. It took words, symbols and ideas from the others, and it almost always employed these things in exactly the same way. It will not do to argue, as John Henry Newman did a century ago, that

> "...these things are in Christianity; therefore they are not heathen...from the beginning the Moral Governor of the World has scattered the seeds of truth far and wide over its extent; that these have variously taken root...wild plants indeed but living..."

A more recent and more astonishing comment is that of Fr. Hugo Rahner:

> "Christianity is a thing that is wholly sui generis. It is something unique and not a derivative from any cult or other human institution, nor has its essential character been changed or touched by any such influence."

This conclusion is so wrong, so wildly wrong, that it might be tempting to dismiss Rahner as a crank, or a member of the Flat Earth Society. But he was neither – he was a respectable theologian, and this is just the sort of thing respectable theologians have been writing for years without serious challenge. As we turn to the particular aspects of Christianity, it will become even clearer that a large part of Christian theology involves this type of whistling past the graveyard, and of flatly denying the true origins of the Christian faith.

Before we attempt to summarize Palestinian life and thought at the time of Jesus, we will turn for a moment to a fascinating and little-known contemporary of Christ, one Apollonius of Tyana. Apollonius shows in his life what we might expect of a brilliant religious teacher of the first century. His career and achievements were so impressive that even the most dogged of Christian apologists had to work very hard indeed to make a case against him as a false prophet. One certainly gets the feeling that everything about him makes Christian theologians very uncomfortable, and thus his career has been almost competely ignored.

Apollonius and Jesus were almost exact contemporaries- he was born in Tyana, Cappadocia, in what is now southern Turkey, during the reign of Tiberius Caesar. There is no question of his existence, since during his life he met so many famous people, including the Emperor Domitian himself. Some parts of his writings still survive. So his life is far better attested than that of Jesus. Our main source is a biography produced about 220 CE by the Roman Philostratus, who may have been urged to write it by Julia Domna, the wife of the Emperor Septimus Severus. Another biography by a writer called Sidonius has been lost except for its conclusion:

> "...perhaps no historian will find in ancient times a philosopher whose life is equal to that of Apollonius."

He got off to a good start. He was raised in a prosperous Greek family, but, of course, he may have been the son of a god. As a youth, he was remarkable: precocious, gentle, modest, compassionate, rarely indignant. In physique, he was strong, well-formed, handsome. But his good looks did not prevent him from being rejected by his native city of Tyana when his miraculous cures disturbed some people. His family then sent him to the local center of learning, Tarsus, to study rhetoric. He did not remain there long. He began a life of travel, and he adopted Pythagorean customs. Apollonius became a vegetarian, abstained from alcohol, went barefoot, let his hair grow, and wore only linen. As time went by he moved beyond Pythagorean beliefs, for he considered himself a citizen of the world, and a priest of the universal religion. Many considered him to be a "divine man", a god in human disguise.

His travels took him to every part of the known world, and to some parts that weren't known. His itinerary would be remarkable even in our time. He visited Babylon to study with the Magi. He was in Asia Minor, Greece, Syria, Spain, Rome, Egypt, Ethiopia, North Africa, Persia, Media, the Khyber Pass, the Indus Valley, the Ganges Valley and even the remote Buddhist monasteries of Nepal. Moreover, Apollonius seemed welcome wherever he went. As a seeker of ultimate truth, he apparently was freely admitted into the inner sanctums since he clearly knew more than the resident priests. He was falsely accused of treason, and so he voluntarily went to Rome to answer the charges in person. He met the Emperor Domitian who promptly acquitted him according to one story, but according to another Apollonius magically vanished from the courtroom and was transported back to Greece.

However, it was in his beliefs that Apollonius seemed most subtle. He prayed at dawn, noon and sunset facing the sun. His prayers were never an attempt to change the future, but only that all people should accept the truth. In his sermons, he tried to persuade people to return to their ancient gods and to restore the original and uncorrupted forms of worship. His attempt to reform the cult of Serapis at Alexandria was rebuffed by the local high priest, who asked haughtily, "Who is wise enough to reform the religion of the Egyptians?" Apollonius had his answer ready, "Any sage who comes from India!"

To Apollonius, all cults or religions were acceptable, providing they were driven by the right spirit. For example, he opposed animal sacrifice as not arising out of the right spirit toward other beings. He preached that we should practice love and charity toward all people, charity to the point of sharing all worldly goods in common. He believed that only one God lay behind the facades of the pagan temples, and like Pythagoras and the Buddhist teachers, he was convinced of the reality of reincarnation.

First century observers may have been impressed by Apollonius' ideas but they were downright astonished by his powers. He cast out demons, raised a girl from the dead, and displayed a range of psychic powers such as clairvoyance and precognition. The most celebrated case was when he stopped in mid sermon in the Greek city of Ephesus in 96 CE to announce that he had just seen the Emperor Domitian assassinated in Rome. The event and his report, it turned out, were simultaneous. He attracted a good deal of both attention and opposition, but generally was successful in refuting claims that he was a magician or that he trafficked in demons. He was less successful at controlling the myth-making of his followers: they were to claim that he had a miraculous birth, that he was the Son of God, that he rose bodily from the dead, and that he would ascend bodily into heaven. Apollonius claimed none of these things for himself.

Certainly Apollonius was a remarkably holy and powerful healer. Many of his cures were of the same stock types as we find Jesus performing, and so carry about the same degree of credibility. He did not have as many, though—the Gospels list nearly 200, Moses had 124, but Apollonius was credited with only 107. Christian opponents, perhaps realizing their position was vulnerable, refrained from challenging the reality of these miracles, instead they attributed them to demonic intervention. However, Apollonius passed the acid test of legitimacy: he performed good works, the good lasted, and he avoided making money from his preaching. He wrote a number of letters, and summarized his beliefs in a sort of will. The style is brief, and has a kind of witty irony.

How much of this is believable? Fr. John Meier, in his huge opus *A Marginal Jew: Rethinking the Historical Jesus* is predictably negative: the sources for Apollonius are "skimpy", contemporaries dismissed him as "a fraud", and most of his adventures are "a conflation of pagan myths". Meier significantly does not apply these same standards to the sources or the stories about Jesus, and he apparently thinks that Paul's version of Jesus is historically reliable. A reasonably objective reader might conclude that had Apollonius attracted a biographer with the enthusiasm of Paul, the religious history of Europe and the world might have been very different.

8

GALILEE IN THE FIRST CENTURY CE

"Nazareth? Can anything good come from Nazareth?"

John 7:14

Galilee in the first century of our era was one of the three areas of the old Hebrew heartland. (Samaria, the second, is today that sad land known as the West Bank.) Judaea, the third, lay further south in higher, drier, more difficult land around Jerusalem. Nevertheless, Judaeans looked down their noses at Galileans, and barely acknowledged Samaritans at all.

Galilee was densely populated, with about three million people living in an area roughly 75 km by 40 km. It has recently been the center of intensive investigations by a learned army of researchers: anthropologists, archaeologists, linguists, sociologists and historians have been assembling a portrait of Hellenistic society there. For example, there is a list of 204 first century towns and villages—and Nazareth is not one of them.

Galilee was a crossroads for trade between Egypt and Mesopotamia, and a fertile farming area, and so had long since been controlled and commercialized by Hellenistic Greeks: the Aramaic speaking Jews had been reduced to a rural minority. And now the Romans were moving east. They had discovered that the East was militarily weak and economically strong – rich pickings for the tax farmers (the "publicans"). Taxes were in fact brutally high, and the legions were always nearby, to ensure the locals paid them. New Graeco-Roman towns were popping up, and Jewish peasants were being dispossessed from their lands by the rapid pace of social and economic change.

Contrary to the impression given in the Gospels, Greek language, culture and religion were dominant. So the Sadducees and other conservatives in Jerusalem were rightly suspicious of the orthodoxy of Galileans, who showed signs of being infected with both Greek and Persian ideas. In short, the northern area was much further along in the process of economic and social integration into the Graeco-Roman world.

Did Jesus speak some Greek? Probably yes, because many Jews in the area needed it for employment reasons. Could he read and write? As a Jewish peasant from a rural village, probably not. Literacy rates in the area at the time are estimated at about 3%. The story in the *Gospel of Luke* of Jesus teaching in the Temple of Jerusalem is undoubtedly fraudulent. Even Meier admits grudgingly that the three brief references in the *New Testament* to Jesus reading are probably fabricated, and inserted long after his death.

However, Jesus had received some training in the Hebrew traditions and would have memorized large sections of Hebrew Scripture from the oral culture. We routinely underestimate the power of human memory in illiterate people. Homer's *Iliad* and *Odyssey* were memorized and preserved for hundreds of years before being written down. Recent studies of the megalithic structure at Callanish in Scotland has led one commentator to estimate that the builders, long before the invention of writing, must have memorized a staggering 100 000 mathematical calculations in order to build it. So Jesus' references to the Scriptures and to numerology should not surprise us, but they do not prove that he was literate.

His village would have had a synagogue, possibly a school, plus a lot of unhappy tenant farmers, beggars, and bandits. Jewish Galilean peasants were notoriously discontent with the political state of affairs. Peasant revolt was never far from the surface, and the immense popularity of miracle workers such as Hanina ben Dosa and Jesus suggest a population in a permanent state of psychic crisis.

Based on the archaeology of bodies from the time, life in these peasant villages was very harsh. Half of those born died in childhood. The average adult lived to 30. Food was scarce, unappealing, and low in protein: mostly bread, olive oil and wine. Malnutrition and famine were a constant threat—there was no good way to store or to transport food. Large numbers of people died of those old foes of humankind: malaria, tuberculosis, and pneumonia.

The first century existence of the village of Nazareth, as hinted above, has not been demonstrated—it was never mentioned in Jewish or Roman texts until the fourth century. The name may have been attached much later to a convenient Galilean town in order to attract Christian pilgrims and their money. Or it may have had another origin.

As we have mentioned, Galilean Judaism in the first century had a rough and rugged face. The combination of political fanaticism and creeping Hellenism made the Jewish authorities of Jerusalem suspicious—they looked on all Galileans as unsophisticated wildmen. Included in these wildmen were a group called the Nazirites. They were an old ascetic cult that claimed to trace its origin to Samson, but really owed most of their ideas to the Greek philosopher Pythagoras. They didn't shave, marry, drink alcohol, eat meat, swear oaths, or tell lies. It now appears to a lot of scholars that both John the Baptist and Jesus' brother James the Just were Nazirites.

What about Jesus? It seems more accurate now that the term "Jesus the Nazarene" ought to be translated as "Jesus the Nazirite" and not "Jesus of Nazareth". This would account for the fact that in a culture which measured the worth of a man by his male children, neither Jesus nor James apparently married. Nazirite avoidance of wine also means that if Jesus was a member of this cult, the miraculous conversion of water into wine at Cana was emphatically not his doing, but instead was stolen by early Christians from the rites of Dionysos. A final, tantalizing verse from the *Dead Sea Scroll* entitled *The Essene Gospel of Peace* quotes Jesus the pacifist-vegetarian:

> "For I tell you truly, he who kills, kills himself, and whosoever eats the flesh of slain beasts eats the body of death."

No imperial religion worth its salt could abide this kind of idea. It would have to be edited out of Christianity, and so it was.

Nevertheless, Jesus, if he existed, had to come from somewhere, so let us assume for the moment that his home village was situated near the modern location of Nazareth. It would have had a synagogue and a school, and probably only one carpentry shop. Politically it would have walked a tenuous line between peasant conservatism (reflected by Jesus' brother James the Just) and the anger and rebellion just below the surface in first century Galilee. Every village in Galilee was within a day's walk of a Greek city—Nazareth was located about an hour from Sepporis, a brand-new and sizeable city of approximately 20 000 people.

Astoundingly, Sepporis is never mentioned in the Gospels. But the construction of the temples of Demeter and Apollo, the theatres, the baths, and other public (and therefore pagan) works would have provided jobs for many otherwise unemployed Jewish labourers. But that doesn't mean they liked it. It was clear that many rural peasants hated both the Graeco-Roman cities, and the exchange economy for which they stood. Jesus, his family, and his friends would have been profoundly affected by Sepporis and the cultural tensions which it provoked. A lot of men from Nazareth worked on those construction projects, and Jesus would have known them well. This is all pointedly absent from the *New Testament*. So maybe the whole Nazareth scenario is also imaginary.

Political control of Galilee during Jesus' adulthood was in the hands of Herod Antipas, whom Jesus described as "that fox". Antipas needed to be a fox. He had to please the Romans, whose client he was, and they wanted stability and regular remittance of the taxes. On the other side, Antipas tried not to offend the Jews, who were exceptionally prickly about religious issues, and who seemed to use religion as a lightning rod for what was often resentment at economic exploitation. So the Roman army was always nearby, and Galilee had a bad reputation.

Throughout the first century the tension continued to grow. Sometime after Herod Antipas executed John the Baptist, Jesus moved from Galilee south to Judaea—maybe to avoid persecution, maybe to act on a bigger stage. And perhaps he didn't realize that the political situation in Judaea was in fact worse—it was directly administered by Rome, and Pontius Pilate, the Roman governor in Jerusalem, had even less time or patience for agitators than Herod Antipas. Life in Jerusalem was dominated by conservative Sadducees, and the

Sadducees were acutely aware of the dangers of provoking the occupying Romans.

But they weren't wary enough. As relations between the Romans and the Jews deteriorated, it became harder to remain neutral. Herod the Great, for all his notoriety, had been able to keep a lid on the pressure cooker, but his death in 4 BCE was followed by a violent encounter at Passover. Three thousand Jews were killed by the Roman legionaries. The following Pentecost was worse: 2,000 rebels crucified, and 30,000 sold into slavery. Most of these seemed to be Galileans, followers of Judas of Gamala, known as Judas the Great. Jesus would have been an impressionable young boy at the time his neighbours were fighting against the Romans. No whisper of this emerges in the *New Testament*.

A generation later, Florus, the Roman procurator of Judaea, infuriated the hypersensitive Jews by taking money from the Temple treasury. The riots that followed led to 3,600 deaths. Interspersed with the violence were at least six huge non-violent protests. The final act began a generation after Jesus' death. In 66 CE there were riots in Jerusalem, followed by armed resistance against the legions, the destruction of the city in 70 CE, and finally the fall of the fortress of Masada in 73 CE.

Even by the standards already set, this war was exceptionally vicious and bloody. The Jewish historian Josephus estimated the death toll at a staggering 1,200,000 with 100,000 sent into slavery. The Roman Tacitus, who was probably not as well informed, estimated 600,000 dead and 100,000 enslaved. Even if these numbers are unreliable, we are talking about an extraordinarily violent popular uprising of a magnitude unknown in modern times.

A well- known example of this bitterness was the struggle for the Roman fortress of Masada. When the Roman garrison surrendered to the Jewish militants, they were put to death one and all. When it became obvious three years later that the legions were about to recapture the fort, the 900-odd defenders committed mass suicide.

And still the rebellion persisted. Anti-Roman uprisings by the Jews in North African cities in 115 CE led to the deaths of 500,000 more, and the massive rebellion under the messianic Simon Bar Cochba in 130 CE had an estimated 1,000,000 fatalities. Finally the Romans totally destroyed the entire city of Jerusalem, and the struggle was over. Besides the devastating impact on the lives of Jewish people, these rebellions ensured that Judaism would have a terrible reputation within the Empire and was never going to win many pagan converts. Clearly, if Christianity were to prosper in the future, it had to make it very clear that it was not merely a modified version of the Hebrew religion.

This was the background against which Jesus preached in Galilee, and briefly, in Judaea. His followers were frequently the dispossessed and the angry, looking either to rebuild their shattered lives, or forward toward the apocalypse. In any case, the Gospel image of Jesus as a meek preacher offering abstract parables and a non-political message is untenable. The atmosphere was too tense and too volatile for pacifism.

The Jews of Palestine also had deep philosophical divisions based on their political stance. The Sadducees tended to be wealthier and more socially conservative, and used their authority from the Temple of Jerusalem to counsel peace and accommodation with the Roman occupiers. Jesus disliked them, and the feeling was mutual. Their allies were the scribes, who were the legal experts.

The Pharisees had a larger presence in Galilee, where they frequently controlled the local synagogues and taught Hebrew Scripture using oral traditions. Jesus would have received instruction from some of them as a young man. Many of their illiterate students were probably better educated and more knowledgeable about Scripture than those few who were lucky enough to be literate. Pharisees urged fellow Jews to aim for the perfect life under the Law, and to observe the rituals carefully: tithing, fasting, the Sabbath, washing foods, and charity. Jesus tended to ignore a number of these admonitions.

The third major group of Palestinian Jews, the Essenes, preferred withdrawal from the contaminated world by establishing desert communities, often with strict codes of behaviour. Their life was a war on evil, and the Roman occupation of the Holy Land demonstrated the earthly power of that evil. They were austere, devout and celibate, and they called themselves "The Sons of Light". They probably had Pythagorean influences, and Jesus may have known them well. In addition, their writings, principally the *Dead Sea Scrolls*, have made them better known.

The fourth group also had strong association with Jesus, since they made up many of his inner circle. Zealots were revolutionary activists (or in modern military-speak, insurgents) and they urged resistance to the Roman occupation. The *Gospels* are extremely cagey here, often not explaining the terms or nicknames of the disciples: Simon Zelotes (The Zealot), Simon Bar-Jonah (The Terrorist), Judas Iscariot (The Sicarii, or urban assassin), James and John (Sons of Thunder), and the two "thieves" at the crucifixion (Lestai, or terrorists). There was good reason for the Roman authorities to have misgivings about the crowd from Galilee.

Estimates of Zealot numbers are hopeless, but there may have been 5000 Pharisees, 5000 Essenes, and 2000 Sadducees. All Palestine was alive with these saintly eccentrics, deeply distressed by the threat the Romans posed to their traditions, and susceptible to being roused to fury. Each of these four groups represented an option chosen by some Jews who believed it was the best way to repel Greek culture and Roman imperialism.

As if all this is not confusing enough, we can now mix in an Egyptian group known as the Therapeutae. This sect was described by the writer Philo of Alexandria as existing near his native city about 5-15 CE. They were Jews who observed the Sabbath and Pentecost, but otherwise showed a lot of the characteristics of pre-Jesus Christians. They dressed in white, shared all their goods, admitted women as equals, believed that Hebrew Scripture was all allegorical, and were deeply influenced by Pythagoras, Dionysos, and maybe the Buddha. In short, they were very much like many early Christians, but they existed before Jesus began his public teaching. Future scholars may want to investigate whether Jesus may have had some contact with them.

Finally, there were the Jews of the Diaspora. At the height of the Empire, trade was well developed, and many Palestinian Jews had left their homeland and moved to the great imperial cities to make a living. They greatly outnumbered those still in Palestine. Jews were quite numerous and widespread, and constituted a significant minority among the business class. They were urbane, cohesive, and they jealously guarded their special privileges. Most of them saw the hegemony of Rome as a fact of life, if not the will of God, and frequently were embarrassed at the violence back home in Galilee and Judaea. From their vantage points far from Jerusalem, they generally recognized the uprising against the Roman army for what it was—military and cultural suicide. Some may have agreed with the Roman historian Tacitus who wondered whether the Jews of Palestine were motivated by bitter enmity against the whole human race.

The Jews presented the Romans with a ticklish problem. On the one hand, the Jewish religion was full of disagreeable ideas and superstitions, but on the other hand every enlightened pagan had to admire its antiquity. And so the Romans compromised: they exempted all Jews from emperor-worship, allowed the use of special coins in Judaea, and licensed synagogues wherever the Jewish population was sufficient. Diaspora Jews responded by engaging in fervent missionary work among their pagan neighbours. Their high ethical standards, their monotheism, and their lack of animal sacrifice (they were too far from the Temple) helped to prepare the way for the Christian missionaries who followed a generation or two later.

Of all these Jewish religious groups, the Essenes were the most creative, and had the largest impact on Christianity. Between 168 BCE and 135 CE an enormous outpouring of Essene-influenced literature savaged the Greek way of life, and warned of the apocalypse to come. Essenes avoided the animal sacrifice of the Great Temple of Jerusalem in favour of the ascetic life. Essenes shared their goods with their fellows, lived on the results of manual labour, and practiced sobriety and restraint in speech. Essenes were not to trade, not to own weapons, not to own slaves. Their aim was purity of body and purity of thought.

Curiously, this pacifism and quietism in the long run seemed to instigate political revolt, and the Essenes became the instruments of the Zealots and other radical groups. Numerous Jews of the period have been perceived as being Essene in outlook—principally John the Baptist and Jesus. For example, a majority of scholars would now agree that most of the Sermon on the Mount—the epitome of the Christian message—was taken directly from the ideas of the pre-Christian Essene master known only as the Teacher of Righteousness.

Whole libraries have been written on the state of Judaism at the time of Jesus. It certainly was at a key point in its history. The great Judaic scholar Hillel's equally famous grandson, Gamaliel, presided over the Sanhedrin, the highest Jewish court. The Great Temple, begun by Herod, was finished in Jesus' lifetime. Within another generation the Romans would reach the end of their patience and destroy the Temple and most of the city. The Jews were on the verge of becoming a permanent minority in every land.

All Jews were of course monotheists, but they were monotheists of a modified type: most believed in angels, demons, aeons and spirits, all of which could be bought off, or at least persuaded. Monotheism of this type is virtually indistinguishable from polytheism. Jews of the time were, like their pagan neighbours, susceptible to magic, astrology and rank superstition. The "simple Galilean fishermen" of the Gospels were simple only if you don't think about it. They had no science, no mathematics, and no geography. But they did understand messianic Judaism, one of the world's most complex religions, very well.

One of the figures thrown up by this maelstrom of conflict in the first century was the man known as John the Baptist. We know little about him, and our ignorance about the Baptist makes it difficult to assess just how unique Jesus was. The historian Josephus seemed to be acquainted with his career, and he called him a good man—which means at least that he had no obvious Zealot connections—and furthermore, we can assume he existed. However, many of the details of his life are mythological. His birthday on June 24 was a pagan celebration of midsummer devoted to water (water, baptist...get it?) His quote "He must increase, I must decrease" probably defines John as being associated with the sun-god. The tradition that he was Jesus' maternal cousin is just a pious invention.

Josephus devoted a good deal of attention to John and the other charismatic figures in Palestine at the time. Josephus does not give similar attention to the career of Jesus—either he never heard of Jesus, or Jesus was not important, or all the comments about Jesus were edited out. Moreover, the only sources that link Jesus with the career of John are the *Gospels*—even Paul makes no mention of the Baptist.

The alleged baptism of Jesus by John has caused no end of problems for the Christian church, for the baptism of Jesus was nearly as embarrassing as his death. John the Baptist, after all, was a wild and uncouth figure. His image was shaped by the *Old Testament* prophet Elijah. John was said to have dressed in camel skins, reputedly lived on an unappealing diet of locusts and wild honey, and preached an Essene-influenced message of sin and repentance. A man such as this would not have impressed the cultured people of the empire.

Worse, why did Jesus, if he were the Son of God, consent to being baptized by John? Was John in some way superior? Did Jesus consider himself a sinner? Was it the ritual of baptism which caused Jesus to be "born of the Holy Ghost", and develop spiritual enlightenment? This particular idea was condemned as heresy, but as late as 450 CE Pope Leo was still fighting it among the bishops and priests of Sicily. The details of Jesus' baptism – the opening of the heavens, a great voice, the words "This is my beloved son, in whom I am well-pleased" all are derived directly from the Egyptian papyri connected to the coronation of a new pharaoh. (Incidentally, two other *Gospels* don't agree that this is what the voice said.)

After John was executed by Herod Antipas, his followers expected the apocalypse. It didn't happen. But there must have been more to the story. Why did Antipas arrest John but not Jesus? Both were undermining the authority of the

Temple, and both were perceived as subversive by the authorities. We don't know. However, it is apparent that the careers of both John and Jesus have been considerably embroidered and even falsified by the expectations of the behaviours associated with a holy man of the time. The influence of the Baptist over the god-seekers of his time may have been considerable, but his contribution to the subsequent development of Christianity has been negligible. In the long run, the Baptist was just too Jewish, and not Greek enough.

Although Greek religion was not welcomed into the Jewish heartland, Greek philosophical ideas did, as modern pundits say, gain more traction. The Hebrew tradition of Yahweh was that of a crabby, wrathful deity, prone to inexplicable outbursts, and with a notoriously dim view of humanity. But in the new Hellenistic world, Jews became minor players in a very big world, and their local god also was dwarfed. God became more distant, more unknowable, more spiritual, less human. It occurred to people that this distant God of spirit and light must find it distasteful to deal with the material world and its corruptions. Probably he used a mediator—the Logos—to interact with his creation. Maybe other, demonic forces played a role in the affairs of the universe. Plato, for example, had made the influential suggestion that matter is evil, stubborn, intractable, against which our higher nature must struggle.

The Stoic school of thought took the high road: they believed in the brotherhood of man under the fatherhood of God. They tried to react to evil and viciousness in the world with pity, with gentle resignation, and with dignity. They represented virtue and rationality, so naturally their ideas had no chance at all. No saviour? No miracles? No grace? No supernatural aids to overcome our weak and evil nature? This was not the basis of a mass movement, in their century or in ours.

The Cynics took the low road. They were critical of conventional behaviour and of government. They went out of their way to be irritating. They were today's homeless, but with a cutting edge. They dressed badly—very badly. They wandered, begged, harangued passersby, and were known to defecate and have sex in public. They loved aphorisms, and attacked hypocrisy where they found it...which was everywhere. Beneath their dirt and abusiveness, however, Cynics were trying in their own way to conquer the world and their human nature with a sort of studied indifference.

Was Jesus in fact a Galilean Cynic? The parallels between the Hellenistic Cynics and the ministry of Jesus are very, very strong. His band of followers traveled Galilee staying where they could, eating what they were given, and hectoring the smug and the powerful with wit, aphorisms, and parables. Like other Cynics, Jesus put no hope in political reform until individuals changed. The elites of Rome and Jerusalem all looked the same to him.

This was the main, and perhaps the only, message of the historical Jesus. Within a few decades this message had been overlayered by other messages from other sources—the apocalyptic threats, the passion story, the resurrection—all loaded on later and coming from somewhere else. To you and me, the uninitiated, it's astonishing. As the *New Testament* experts work at unraveling and unpacking these layers encoded in the *Gospel* messages, the image of Jesus which appears there is increasingly strange, and increasingly Greek.

9

DID JESUS EXIST?

> *"The trouble with Oakland is, that when you get there, there's no there there."*
>
> Gertrude Stein

Did Jesus exist? To most people this is among the silliest of questions. For them, his existence has the same degree of reality as Vitamin C or the city of Nairobi. There may have been as many as 60 000 biographies of Jesus written in the nineteenth century alone. But more skeptical people, including a lot of Biblical scholars, have very serious doubts. Nor is it new—it was the first question Napoleon asked the German scholar Wieland when they met in 1808. Our brief discussions of the rivals of Christianity have suggested that the life of Jesus, as portrayed in the *Gospels*, is full of the stock elements of paganism: a virgin mother, a mystical conception, miracles, twelve apostles, suffering, death, resurrection after three days, etc., etc. The existence of these legends does not automatically guarantee a kernel of truth beneath them. William Tell, the Swiss hero, did not exist, despite the believable nature of the stories about him. Moreover, certainty of belief is no reliable guide either. Millions of people lived and died absolutely convinced of the historical reality of Dionysos and Osiris, just as it was a universal belief in the Middle Ages that the sun moved around a flat earth. Universal agreement sometimes just means universal error.

But surely the existence of such a great person is verifiable from non-Christian sources? Well, yes and no. Both pagan and Jewish references to Jesus up to 150 CE are rare, unsatisfying, and unconvincing. The historian Justin of Tiberias, a Jewish writer living in Galilee at the time of Jesus never mentions him. Likewise Jesus is never mentioned in the *Dead Sea Scrolls*. The first non-Christian mention is by the Jewish historian Josephus in 93 CE. He refers to him twice, and in a rare burst of unanimity, modern scholars agree that both the references were too laudatory to have been written by a conservative and orthodox Jew such as Josephus. In short, the passages are fakes, inserted by later Christian copyists to make up for Josephus' supposed oversight. In addition, at least one historian has suggested that a whole chapter of Josephus' *The Jewish War* dealing with the trial of Jesus has been omitted. Josephus put first century Palestine under a microscope, recording every disturbance, every political upheaval, every unjust act of Pontius Pilate, but he has no account of Jesus' trial or death. Clearly Jesus was not the major messiah-figure the *Gospels* claim he was.

The first pagan references to the new religion come from the well-known Roman Pliny the Younger, who in 110 CE wrote to the emperor Trajan asking how to treat Christians in his bailiwick in northern Asia Minor. Written shortly thereafter was the passage of the historian Tacitus (dated 115 CE) discussing Nero's persecution of Christians some fifty years before in 64 CE. These sections in Pliny and Tacitus are accepted as genuine, but the existence of a group of "Christians" is regrettably not proof of the previous existence of Jesus.

Christianity is a revealed religion that is alleged to have begun at a certain time and place. The historical existence of

Jesus is absolutely crucial to any claim the religion may have to universal truth. Christian believers traditionally dismiss the parallels with Osiris or Mithra on the grounds that those figures are mythological, whereas, they argue, the person of Jesus was historically concrete. The difficulty is that the historically concrete Jesus melts into air when details of his life are examined. Albert Schweitzer is said to have remarked that there is nothing more negative than the critical study of the life of Jesus. Nor can we turn away by arguing that the historicity of Jesus is immaterial. This would mean that a beneficent God is teaching us his divine truths by false statements about his son who didn't exist. In this impasse, it should come as no surprise that the theological writing of the last century has become increasingly desperate: can we know anything at all about Jesus?

One area that we have established is that his life has been mythologized and embroidered in the same fashion as the lives of other heroes. If we examine the career of Orpheus or Zoroaster, virtually nothing of their personality survives—it is all mythical. Why should Jesus be any different? Christianity was astoundingly successful; this led to the erroneous conclusion that it must have been founded by a remarkable man who did remarkable things. The world was desperate for a saviour, and it remains a moot point whether the Jesus of the *Gospels* was real, or a cleverly imagined portrait of what a saviour should be.

For those of us who are not specialists, it is best to keep an open mind and apply the same standards of probability to the past that we do to our own time. For example, we accept that Alexander the Great was a real person, yet we emphatically reject as legend the stories that he stopped the sun, or that his grandfather was Zeus in the form of a snake. So with Jesus: we can't accept it all, but it seems on balance that some religious reformer lived in Palestine whose life and ideas somehow inspired the founding of the greatest religious organization of the past two millennia.

No doubt all this seems far too skeptical for most readers, but there is a reason for it. For one thing first century Palestine was a period of many revolutionary leaders, and only a few given names. Is it possible, for example, that Jesus Christ was the same as a Jesus Barabbas who was crucified? Could Jesus have been confused with Judas the Great who came out of Galilee twenty years earlier and was also crucified? What of the story in the Jewish *Talmud* of Jesus ben Pandera who was crucified by the Romans on the eve of Passover about 100 BCE? This Jesus ben Pandera was the result of a liason between a Roman soldier and a peasant girl who, to avoid scandal, married an elderly carpenter.

The writers of the time, whether out of tradition or motive, give us insufficient clues to the personal traits of life and character that might help us distinguish one of these men from another. By the early second century, when the *Gospels* were being given their final shaping, nobody was alive who remembered the events. Jesus Christ was perceived as a personage of the first third of the first century whose career was tied into that of Pontius Pilate, who was exactly the kind of hardened bureaucrat who might have crucified the Son of God.

It would be improper, however, to argue that Jesus was a complete fabrication of the Judaeo-Greek mind. The *Gospels* do contain a good deal of information that locates his career in time and place. Nobody in antiquity denied the existence of Jesus. (Of course, nobody denied the existence of Osiris or Dionysos either.) Recent commentators have not always been so accommodating. J.M. Roberson asserted that the life of Jesus was what remains of a lost Palestinian saviour-myth.

John Allegro speculated that Jesus was a code name for a species of hallucinogenic mushroom. G.A. Wells has decided that Jesus didn't exist by a closely argued analysis of *New Testament* sources. Tom Harpur declared that Jesus was nonexistent, and that the *Gospel* stories were a stale reworking of Osiris-Horus legends from Egypt. The same general conclusion was reached by Timothy Freke and Peter Gandy in *The Jesus Mysteries: Was the 'Original Jesus' A Pagan God?* These may sound like lunatic conclusions to those unfamiliar with the field, but the power of their arguments makes distressing reading for any believers who actually might read them.

The reigning heavyweight champion of this branch of theology remains the great German scholar Rudolf Bultmann. Bultmann's approach, known as "Form Criticism" argues that when the first evangelist, Mark, went to write his *Gospel*, he had no prior idea of the chronology of Jesus' life. He did his best to make sense of the disconnected moral stories and miraculous events that were floating around the Christian communities. In such a situation, it was unavoidable that a good deal of pious invention crept into the *Gospels*. Thus, the *Gospels* are accurate reflectors of the beliefs of early Christians, but inaccurate records of the history of Jesus' life. In fact, says Bultmann, there is not a single sentence attributed to Jesus which we can confidently regard as having been said by him. Just as a modern preacher chooses texts which he understands and avoids those he doesn't understand or like, so did the early evangelists unintentionally shape the life of Jesus into something that reflected their own concerns. However, a text or a parable ignored by a modern cleric may be taken up by another generation with a different world-view, but one ignored by the four Evangelists has probably been lost forever.

In 1925, W.R. Halliday offered the opinion that the more we came to know about Jesus, the more revolutionary he would seem in Graeco-Roman life. Regrettably for Halliday, exactly the opposite seems to be the case. Jesus' life has merged so thoroughly with the background of his time that we cannot extricate him at all. Theologian after theologian points out, in books intended to be read largely by other theologians, that it is no longer possible to write a serious biography of Jesus. The task has become hopeless.

This strikes most casual readers as truly incredible. The image of Jesus is so clear in our culture, he plays such a large part in our history and mythology, he dominates our calendar, he provides hope in an age that is critically short of hope, he fulfills so many profound psychological needs that if he did not exist, it's best not to think about it. When the wife of an Oxford don left the celebrated debate between T.H. Huxley and Bishop Wilberforce on the subject of Darwinian evolution in 1870, she is reported to have remarked,

> "Let us pray that it is not true. And if it is true, let us hope that it not become generally known."

Christians of our time understand her dilemma. We are left to choose between a Christianity with no founder at all, or one founded by a person whose life is a total mystery, who might or might not have been crucified, and whose religion of messianic Judaism and Greek Cynicism would be so alien to us that we would reject it out of hand. No wonder attendance in the great liberal churches of North America and Europe has declined. No wonder, too, that the evangelical denominations, with their resolute rejection of historical-critical thinking, are enjoying a great revival.

10

BETHLEHEM

"We do not destroy religion by destroying superstition."
                                                              Cicero

Twenty-first century Westerners are remarkable among the cultures of the world for our indifference to kinship ties and ancestry. For people of the Hellenistic civilizations, a person's genealogy was important—it helped to define who he was and the traditions for which he stood. A great man needed great ancestors, so the birth and childhood of famous people was frequently derived backward from their adult status, and so it was with Jesus. Even his name has been changed. It should be Yeshu'a, but that apparently worked out to a bad number according to the numerologists. So it was clumsily translated into Greek as Iesous, which has a much luckier number of 888.

Jesus' background, as recounted in the *Gospels*, is both impressive and confused. To look at the four *Gospels* does little to help. Mark wisely skips his birth and childhood altogether, Matthew offers a long list of ancestors to Joseph, Luke gives us the story of the virgin birth, and John begins with what was probably a Mithraic poem. As a pagan hero, Jesus was the Son of God. As a Jew, he was the Messiah, the descendant of David. This is the basis of the considerable disagreement between the genealogies offered by Matthew and Luke. Naturally, he was claimed to be of "royal descent", as was Aesculapius, Buddha, Confucius, Dionysos, Heracles, Horus, Krishna, Perseus and Rama. Matthew's account of Jesus' ancestry from King David down to Joseph becomes spectacularly irrelevant if we accept Luke's story of the Virgin Birth. But both Luke 3:23 and Paul in Romans 1:3 give us broad hints that the Virgin Birth story was not widely believed, and Mark strikes closest to the target when he calls Jesus "the son of Mary": the absence of a father's name suggesting that the parentage was uncertain. Poor old Joseph, in fact, looks like a late and rather lame addition to the *Gospel* story.

While the identity of a child's father may have been debatable in the days before DNA testing, human parentage cannot be denied in the case of the mother. "Mother" is a powerful word to adult men, and so is "virgin". "Virgin" literally meant "young woman" in Hebrew. Presumably it was unthinkable that the latter might not be the former. Jane Schaberg in *The Illegitimacy of Jesus* explored several ancient stories, including the one that attributed Jesus' parentage to a Roman soldier who raped Mary. The reaction to her book was scandalous, both from the Catholic clergy who chastised her and threatened her employment, to the citizens of Detroit, one of whom torched her car. While it is not intellectually ethical to claim special privileges for the Jesus stories while denying these same privileges to pagan deities, this nicety is lost on some modern believers.

Nevertheless, in the broader culture of the Hellenistic Eastern Mediterranean, "virgin mothers" became remarkably common. The list of heroes whose mothers were impregnated by sky-gods included both historical and mythical figures: Aesculapius, Apollonius, Buddha, Confucius, Cyrus,

Krishna, Octavian, Perseus, Plato, Pythagoras, Simon Magus, and Zoroaster. Even Julius Caesar and Alexander claimed their fathers were gods, although neither attempted to retroactively restore their mother's virginity. So many young Greek girls blamed their unplanned pregnancies on a god that the practice was outlawed as being insulting to the deities. In the typical scenario, the clueless husband was frequently warned in a dream of the impending arrival of a young Buddha or Confucius or Jesus or Plato. Thus was scandal avoided.

If we need further evidence that the virgin birth of Jesus was unlikely, consider the incident related in Mark 3 in which Mary and her other sons express their doubts about Jesus' sanity. Who would for a moment doubt the mental faculties of a person whose conception was miraculous and whom you knew to be the Son of God? But unlikely or not, the Virgin Birth became the official doctrine of Christianity, and books that denied it were burned during the second and third centuries. Among these otherwise reliable books was the *Gospel of James the Less*, which related that Joseph, an elderly widower with children, had been pressured by the high priests to wed Mary, by whom he had several children, with Jesus being the eldest.

Just as the ancestry of Jesus is fabulous, so too are the other elements of the Nativity. The illogical elements of the Bethlehem story are common knowledge, yet it is so deeply rooted in our culture that even non-believers frequently find themselves being caught up at Christmas by the emotional power of the traditional narrative. Luke's account is both powerful and deeply sentimental, and it strikes deep resonances, even among total non-believers.

The reason given for Mary and Joseph being on a journey—to go to Joseph's ancestral home for a census—

must have struck the Evangelist Luke as a handy if illogical explanation. We know that Roman census and tax rolls listed people where they lived and worked. Forcing Jewish people back to their hometowns would have been imperial insanity, for they were living all over the Mediterranean. And the last thing the Roman authorities would have wanted was more disgruntled Jews wandering around Palestine. Moreover, if Joseph were from Nazareth, Roman orders would not have applied there anyway since it was in Galilee and outside the sphere of direct Roman rule. Finally, despite the very best efforts of Christian researchers, no trace of an imperial census can be found near the time of Jesus' birth. The closest one would have been when Jesus was about 13 years old.

What was the real source of the Bethlehem story? As usual, look for a confluence of Jewish and pagan legends. The mothers of Apollo, Buddha, Krishna, Lao-Tse and Pythagoras were also on journeys, usually to pay their taxes, when their heroic sons were born. The Hebrew prophet Micah had claimed the Messiah was to be born in Bethlehem. The patriarch Jacob had just come home to Bethlehem when his wife Rachel gave birth to Benjamin. Both Matthew and Luke would have known these *Old Testament* references, both were convinced that Jesus was the Messiah, and neither one, writing almost a century after the event, would had had any evidence that Jesus had been born anywhere else. This is the first example of events in the life of Jesus being fudged to fit "prophecies" from the Hebrew Scriptures—and it was certainly not to be the last.

Fudging is one way to shade the truth. Here is another, courtesy of Fr. John Meier, writing in 1991:

> "Historical-critical research simply does not have the sources and tools available to reach a final

decision on the historicity of the virginal conception..."

Yes, it does have the tools. But nobody can provide the courage to a theologian to contradict what his tradition tells him to believe.

The American scholar John Dominic Crossan points out that the Roman writer Suetonius records, presumably with a straight face, that Octavian, the future Emperor Augustus, was conceived when his mother Atia was impregnated by Apollo in the form of a serpent. Nobody believes that for a moment. Thus, Crossan says, it is hypocritical to argue that my hero's miracle birth is true, and all others are false. But we should not assume that the Evangelists are nothing but cheats and liars. The tradition of the time was that building on previous stories was a legitimate way to write history. We will continue to see this as we look at other aspects of the Bethlehem story.

The *Gospel of Luke* does not directly claim that Jesus was born in a stable, however, it does suggest it by saying that he was laid in a manger, but this detail was soon overwhelmed by legend. (Matthew by contrast, does not mention a stable, and has three wise men come to visit the newborn in a house.) Abraham, Adonis, Apollo, Dionysos and Mithra were all born in caves, not stables. Within a century of the Evangelists, Christian writers such as Justin Martyr and Origen were claiming that Jesus' birth had been in a cave. The rock grotto so beloved of tourists beneath the Church of the Nativity in Bethlehem was originally a rock shrine to the god Adonis who was born there, in legend at least, on a Christmas morning long ago.

Given the dominance of astrology over first century minds, it is predictable that a celestial oddity would accompany the Nativity. After all, unusual stars had also announced the arrival of Abraham, Ali, Buddha, Julius Caesar, Krishna, Lao-Tse, Moses, Rama, and even the Jewish rebel leader Simon Bar Cochba. The attempt to date the birth of Jesus exactly has used up a lot of paper and ink. The date we use, Christmas Day of the year 1 CE, was calculated by Dionysius Exiguus in 525 CE. Current scholarship holds that the chronology of Dionysius was a bit off, and that Jesus' birth was probably in 7 BCE.

It was a strange year for sky-watchers. In early 7 BCE, Jupiter the planet of kings, and Saturn, the special planet of the Jews, were prominent in the sky over Judaea. On May 7 of that year, Jupiter and Saturn were in conjunction in the constellation Pisces. This was followed by both planets going into retrograde motion in July: because of the position of their orbits relative to Earth, they appeared to be going backward. They had a retrograde conjunction on October 9, and after they had resumed their normal direction, had yet a third conjunction in Pisces on December 1.

This bizarre combination of events was made more significant by the fact that a new star-age had just begun. Because of a slight wobble in the rotation of the earth, the constellation that appears on the eastern horizon at dawn on the first day of spring changes approximately every 2,200 years. In 8 BCE, Pisces had just displaced Aries, and a new star-age had begun. To the celestially wise, that meant that a new world religion whose symbol was the fish, would replace the religion of ram-sacrifice (Aries), which had in turn replaced Taurus. In summary, astrologers believed that the events in the sky of 7 BCE meant that a king (Jupiter) of the Jews (Saturn) was about to found a religion for the new age, symbolized by the fish. This Age of Pisces is now passé, because even Broadway realizes we have entered the Age of Aquarius.

Astrology was widespread, so it should be no surprise that the birth of Jesus would be accompanied by other supernatural oddities. Choirs sang in the heavens as they had for Apollo, Buddha and Krishna. Voices from the clouds announced his birth as they had those of Apollonius, Confucius and Osiris. A Greek hymn devoted to the child-god Hermes described the pagan infant as "a child wrapped in swaddling clothes and lying in a manger". Christians cheerfully appropriated the image, and even the words. The ox and ass in the stable were originally present as representatives of the high god Ahuramazda at the birth of Mithra. As befits the birth of a sun-god, the infant Jesus was frequently portrayed with a nimbus of light around his head, and the entire stable was bathed in brightness, as were the birthplaces of Aesculapus, Apollo, Buddha, Dionysos, Krishna, Moses, and Zoroaster.

The "three kings" are the three bright stars immediately to the right of Sirius in the belt of Orion. You may recall that the Persian Magi identified Orion with the sun-god. And by now the Magi were seasoned greeters of famous infants. They had visited Egypt for the birth of Moses. They were in India to give gifts to the newborn Krishna. The infant Buddha had to be content with the visit of unidentified "wise men". Mithra and Socrates, like Jesus, got the full treatment: each was visited by three Magi bearing gifts of gold, frankincense and myrrh.

The Massacre of the Innocents, allegedly ordered by Herod the Great to eliminate the infant Jesus as a potential rival, is also a common and well-worn myth—the attempted murder of the child sun-god. It has exact parallels in the birth-stories of Abraham, Aesculapius, Buddha, Cyrus, Dionysos, Heracles, Horus, Krishna, Moses, Oedipus, Perseus and Zoroaster. Its historical authenticity is exactly nil. Herod was extremely unpopular with the historian Josephus and with Roman writers. Josephus devotes 37 chapters to a minute examination of Herod's evil deeds; had any massacre of children occurred such as Matthew describes (a reasonable estimate would be 14,000 deaths), Josephus would have reported it with glee. So why is the story there? Matthew probably included it, as he did so many other events, to provide historical legitimacy by recalling an *Old Testament* prophecy (in this case from Hosea). We can also disregard the veracity of the Flight into Egypt—the portrait of an old man leading a donkey which carried a woman and her baby had its origin in Isis-worship.

An alternative view of the birth stories is offered by Freke and Gandy in *The Jesus Mysteries*. They suggest that perhaps early Christians saw the entire divine birth as a metaphor: God the father, the divine spirit, impregnated matter to create life. Virginal matter alone is not enough. We have no real idea whether early Christians would have thought so symbolically, but it may well have been the case.

What did Jesus look like? A version of Josephus written in Old Slavonic (rather than in the usual Greek) has been found in a Russian monastery and reconstructed. It described Jesus as very short, homely, and hunchbacked. His face was "not handsome" (meaning non-Aryan): dark-skinned, with heavy eyebrows, a long nose, and with his hair parted in the middle. The suspicion is that this description may have come from the original Roman records to which Josephus was given access. The pagan Celsus concurred; he described Jesus' body "...as they say, small and ugly and undistinguished". We cannot say. Some early Christians thought he would have intentionally chosen to be ugly. Moreover, anti-Jesus factions existed, and were certainly capable of libel. What we can say is that by 200 CE, images of Jesus have begun to show the influence on Hellenistic myth-making: his portraits show him as the serene and handsome shepherd, or in the role of wise philosopher, and these artistic conventions have continued until the present day. The fair blue-eyed Nordic Jesus of my childhood has come to seem symbolic of how far Christian tradition has wandered away from objective reality.

11

LIFE AND TEACHINGS OF JESUS

"I'm a Muslim, but I think Jesus would have a drink with me. He would be cool. He would talk to me."

Mike Tyson

Jesus' life, seen in the context of other saviour-gods and heroes of the time, reveals nothing unique. There was not a miracle, a legend, or a story told of Jesus that had not been floating around Hellenistic Palestine decades before his birth. This is not easy to accept. We grow up with so much folklore about Jesus, and so much resistance to applying standard methods of criticism, that we honour without question unverified claims that Christianity is unparalleled and that Jesus' life was without precedent. A better acquaintance with the history and ethics of ancient paganism would reveal that claims of this kind are without foundation. Nevertheless, the combination of ideas we call Christianity has the power to stir humanity to its depths. This fortunate combination may well be in part an individual effort by the person we call Jesus. Or not.

Let us turn again to the work of Rudolf Bultmann to see where theology stands, and then examine in more detail some of the miracles, the teachings, and the death of Jesus. As existential philosophers, Bultmann and his followers have broken up the gospel stories into classifications—parables, miracle-stories, disputations and so on—and then compared these with non-Christian literature of the period. The result has not been pretty, for it has removed the uniqueness of Jesus' life. Bultmann reluctantly declares the *Gospels* to be "myth"; and he rejects the possibility of knowing anything about the "historical Jesus". However, Bultmann the Christian says the "historical Jesus" whom we cannot know must be distinguished from the "risen Christ". This Christ is the real Christ, who by his death and resurrection has the power to save mankind.

Bultmann's position is understandable, and a common one among contemporary theologians. In his case, he had to be a "confessing Christian" to hold a professorship of Christian theology at a German university. But it's all very confusing to most of us. We have been taught to relate to the legendary person known as Jesus. In our humdrum lives we all look for the exceptional, the wondrous, the mysterious. If we strip away the birth-stories, the miracles, and the resurrection, much of the religious fervour disappears too. And it is precisely these areas of his life which historical inquiry has melted away. The Jesus who remains is historical all right, but the known facts about him approach zero, as we shall shortly see.

It was Jesus the miracle-worker that first attracted attention in Galilee; indeed, miracles by Jesus or his disciples were probably the main cause of conversion to early Christianity. (Although there are no miracles mentioned in the *Epistles* of Paul.) For the people of his time, his superhuman powers were a lot more interesting than his teachings. Any religious teacher in the first century also needed to be a healer. Jesus was typical of his time—he did not distinguish between physical and spiritual problems—he treated them all as cases of demonic possession. It was a remarkably tense time and place, and there probably was an extraordinary degree of mental illness. People were looking for cures, and when a healer appeared, he was mobbed. Given both high expectations and the degree of psychic excitement, some cures were bound to occur.

Were these exorcisms permanent or temporary? We don't know. But it matters. A childhood acquaintance of mine was plagued by poor eyesight, and went to a faith-healing service. He was caught up in the enthusiasm, had hands laid upon him, and his eyesight was miraculously cured. He threw away his thick glasses, climbed onto his bicycle, and rode homeward, but ran into a tree which he didn't see and broke his arm. Not all healing is worthy of the term.

Although the miracles are presented (especially by Mark) as the key part of his ministry, we get the feeling that they were not Jesus' major interest. He was unable to work miracles near his home, because everybody knew him and they were skeptical of his powers. He frequently showed reluctance and even parochialism—he at first refused to cure a Caananite girl because she was not Jewish. Most of his healings were by touch: touching lepers (if leprosy it was), using his saliva, or having the sick touch him.

Moreover, we have a right to be skeptical of the miracle stories. They are of two major types: healing (both physical and mental) and interfering with natural events (calming the storm, withering the fig tree). Names, places and times are too often missing. Many of the nature miracles of Jesus had been previously attributed to Horus, the Egyptian Son of God—walking on water, for example. Harpur claims that John's account of Jesus' most spectacular miracle—the raising of Lazarus from the dead—is a rewrite of an ancient tale of Horus raising Osiris, and that the weeping sisters Martha and

Mary were really the Egyptian goddess sisters Nepthys and Isis (also known as Meri).

The celebrated story of the loaves and fishes is clearly derived from the story of the prophet Elisha feeding 100 people with 20 loaves, as found in *2 Kings Chapter 4*. I was always impressed with the story of Jesus driving the demons into the herd of swine in Gadara, whereupon the pigs then raced off to drown themselves in the Sea of Galilee. My innocence was rudely shattered when I discovered that Gadara was eight kilometers from the sea. I grew up on a farm, and I knew that most pigs will not run even eight meters. Good story, but I don't believe it.

People in the first century did not share my views—they were all to ready to believe in miracles; today we are all too ready to disbelieve. Miracle cures were everywhere. The Emperor Vespasian, although never admired as a role model, was urged to try healing. He was understandably doubtful and at first refused, but then he tried it, and he successfully cured a boy who was blind and a man with a maimed foot. Do you believe that?

Christian theologians regularly refer to Jesus as a miracle worker, but are deeply offended when he is described as a magician. The term "magic" is never used to describe events in your own religion; it seems lower class, subversive, demeaning. But Jesus' family didn't object—they apparently saw his ability to cure as an economic opportunity: they wanted him to come home and set up shop as a healer and they would all benefit. Jesus refused.

The *Gospel of Mark* has as its main focus the image of Jesus as wonder-worker, and the evangelist tries hard to publicize the miracles without opening his hero up to the charge of magic. In this, Mark failed. Virtually every pagan commentator accused Jesus of practicing magic. This was because most of Jesus' miracles were part of the standard repertoire of any competent Egyptian magician—exorcism, walking on water, controlling the weather, disappearing without warning. Matthew's story that Jesus had spent time in Egypt as a boy caused doubters to look for Egyptian models, and to find them. The pagan critic Celsus claimed Jesus had ties to the priests of Isis.

Was Jesus practicing magic? An old rabbinical tradition within Judaism accepted as a commonplace that Jesus had magical spells tattooed on his body. Perhaps this was not that unusual: Paul in *Galatians 6:17* seems to admit to having magical (albeit Christian) tattoos. Finally, the Vatican library has a fourth century gold glass plate of Christian manufacture showing Jesus in the costume of a magician, complete with magic wand. All in all, then, signs, wonders and miracles were the stock in trade of first century holy men. The crowds expected those things, and, if we can trust the *Gospel of Mark*, Jesus obliged. Two millennia later, we are less impressed with the wonder-working than with the ideas he espoused. After all, a world full of miracles, in which a pliable God changes course on a whim, is not a very reassuring place.

What of the teaching of Jesus? It's all so confusing and contradictory when we wish it were clear. Was he peaceful or violent? Jew or Christian? Taxpayer or subversive? Did he observe the Jewish Law? The confusion on so many fronts suggests that the version we received from the Evangelists has been heavily edited, and a lot left out. Jesus may not have been at all what we were taught—and maybe was not someone you would like to have lunch with. For one thing, his sermons were so inflammatory that his own family tried to have him declared insane. Predictably, he lashed out at them with anti-family pronouncements. He was abusive to his critics: they were "vipers", "whitewashed tombs... (full of) bones and all kinds of filth". Non-Jews were "swine" and "dogs", and he had no intention of giving them the benefit of his wisdom. His contempt is palpable.

His social relations left a bit to be desired. He admitted he had a reputation as a glutton and a drunkard. These seem to be calumnies triggered by his refusal to fast, and his disconcerting habit of eating with, and socializing with, just about anybody. (If he were a Nazirite, the drunkard accusation must have been particularly galling.) In any case, his life was a direct attack on social class and convention, then and now. Had he no honour? No shame?

Was Jesus married? There is no mention of a wife in the Gospels. It would have been normal for a Jew of the time to be married, except for those who were Essenes or Nazirites. Jesus advised his disciples to leave their wives behind. He did have friendships and associations with women, which led to gossip, and probably to the slanderous accusations against Mary Magdalen. It does seem that his relationship with her was a close one. In the Gnostic *Gospel of Philip*, the other disciples are annoyed at Jesus' habit of kissing Mary Magdalen, presumably on the lips. Moreover, he apparently did not make negative comments about women, or female sexuality, as his followers were to do. Centuries of anti-female bias has reduced the importance of women in both the contemporary church, and the imagined past. In summary, however, Jesus was probably single, maybe as a result of his contact with the Essene movement, but more likely because he was a member of the Nazirite sect.

He urged his listeners to give what they had to the poor—of whom he was one. He and his followers, like the Greek Cynics who influenced them, were wandering beggars who preached, healed, and ate whatever was given to them. Jesus' disdain for wealth was unmistakable. Turn the other cheek to evil, he advised. Begging, voluntary poverty and total pacifism are teachings which, if broadly applied by society, make sense only if the world is about to end. If the world and society are to be ongoing, more practical approaches are needed. The fact that these sayings were preserved would suggest that the Evangelists and other Christians of the late first century expected the world to end shortly.

The attitude to the Jewish Law was the same—contradictory. One day it was obsolete, the next day "every jot and tittle" of the Law was permanent. Obviously one of these is true, and the other was put into his mouth. It begs the question: what did he really say? What should we believe? Bultmann, after a lifetime of study, said we could believe virtually nothing. The Jesus Seminar, a collection of liberal scholars who assembled annually, looked very closely at his words in the *Gospels*, and estimated 18% of the *Gospel* sayings were real, others were "possible", still more were "unlikely". And of course there has been a backlash from those who were horrified at the inappropriateness of "grading" the sayings of Jesus.

The salient point on Jewish Law is this: Jesus never abandoned Jewish beliefs and practices, although he clearly wished to reform them. Generations later, Christian writers would deny this position. His religious disagreements with the Pharisee party over the Law were serious but not deadly; but his political criticism of the Sadducees cost him his life.

The parables are probably mostly genuine. Burton Mack describes them as "pungent, slightly unnerving, mildly humorous", but certainly they are also strange and difficult. Matthew's account of the wedding banquet is a good example. When the invited guests spurned the banquet, the king's servants invited anyone they met in the street to attend. But one poor soul showed up without a wedding robe, and so the king tied him up and threw him out. Maybe this story made sense to someone in the first century, but not today. The parables were clearly important to his teachings, but they are opaque to modern readers, as they were to most of his followers. The conclusion must be that these allegories represented secret teachings, but in the drive to make the Gospels literally believable, early Christians seem to have lost the key to the code. We really have no idea what Jesus meant.

On the other hand, the Lord's Prayer is straightforward, and is probably not the product of Jesus, although it is very early. His opposition to divorce may have been real, given that it ran contrary to Jewish, Greek and Roman practices. The "Give unto Caesar the things that are Caesar's" quote is clearly not legitimate, and has served to make the Christian Church politically reactionary. Like the issue of the parables, it also points up a serious problem—early Christians (like us, I suppose) understood only part of Jesus' teachings. He may have invented the phrase "The Kingdom of God", since it is not found in earlier sources. At least, say the experts, this is "credible". But that is of little solace, since many statements of the fictional Huckleberry Finn are also "credible."

Among the powerful ideas set loose by early Christianity was the duality of the world—the existence of Satan, the perpetual struggle between good and evil, and the coming battle to decide the fate of the cosmos. As mentioned previously, these were originally Persian ideas which were finding fertile ground in the Mediterranean world.

Dualism is useful in explaining the existence of evil in the world. If there is no Devil to inspire evil, then in some sense it must come from (or be allowed by) an otherwise good God. The more favourably we think of God, the more necessary is the existence of the Devil. (Conversely, in our time, a disbelief in the Devil has led a to disbelief in the goodness of God.) We have been taught to think of Christianity as monotheistic, but in the first century, everybody conceded the existence of invisible supernatural creatures: angels, demons, spirits, demiurges and many other entities, mostly evil.

Palestinians of the time went further and attributed all kinds of evils to demonic forces. These evil forces predated the world, and whole armies of angels had fought pitched battles with armies of demons. Despite their prehistoric defeat, these evil beings were said to dominate the world to a shocking degree. They caused mental and physical illness: blindness, disability, epilepsy, insanity and more. They controlled political affairs. They interfered constantly in daily life so that every human soul was a battleground. Demons had corrupted and defiled the world so badly that it must shortly be destroyed. Neutrality was impossible. Good Jews were aware of the struggle, and looked forward to the final decisive battle in which good would vanquish evil forever. Most pagans, by contrast, thought all this was childish nonsense. They did not subscribe to the idea of Satan, or of an afterlife, or of Hell. The Greeks had no "devil". Gods could certainly be harmful, but none were totally malignant. Instead, the Greek world believed in Fate—but Fate did not have a personality.

The career of Jesus reflected this upheaval. His temptation in the wilderness made it plain that the Devil ruled the world—after all, Satan had the power to offer him control of "all the kingdoms of the earth". Jesus performed exorcisms as part of this cosmic war, helping to subdue this demonic rebellion against God. He looked forward to the destruction of the forces of evil at the end of the world, and he believed that it would be soon.

If we accept the Gospel version, Jesus, like so many visionaries of the time, including his mentor John the Baptist, was certain that the world was about to end. It was this apocalyptic view that gave his message such power and urgency. As just one of many possible examples, in Mark 9:1 he says:

> "There are some of those standing here who shall not taste death until the Kingdom of God be come with power."

This was not vague—it was very precise, and of course it was dead wrong. We have waited two thousand years. It has caused world-class squirming by twenty centuries of Christian apologists—the Dance of the Embarrassed Theologians. Meier, for example, cannot admit that Jesus was wrong, so he attributes the apocalyptic predictions to "early Christians". (Of course, he refuses to consider that these same "early Christians" might be responsible for most of Jesus' other quotes too.) Was Jesus deluded? Was he not divine? Were these words inserted into the Gospels by a later generation? Was the Christian Church founded on a whopping mistake? At the very least, it is clear that a major part of Jesus' teaching had to be widely ignored—it was inappropriate for ordinary people in ordinary circumstances.

Not only do Jesus' apocalyptic views cause intellectual difficulties, they also pose certain practical roadblocks. If the world is about to end, why do any long-term planning? Why not give away all your possessions? Rather than the prosaic virtues of home, family and responsible behaviour, the focus is on eternal glory, and this may lead to violent and confrontational political activities. Religiously-inspired horrors such as Waco, Jonestown, the Saints of Munster, and Masada all begin to make sense. Mainstream people find these millenarian movements distasteful, so we prefer a more sanitized image of Jesus as cultural critic. Nevertheless, the tradition of the marginalized and disenfranchised of society falsely expecting an immediate apocalypse is a deeply-rooted tradition in Christian societies, and may go back to Jesus himself. However, some recent scholars, poring over the *Gospel of Thomas* and the mysterious document called Q, have suggested that most of these apocalyptic predictions were not original to Jesus at all, but were quotes put in his mouth by the Evangelists.

Did Jesus see himself as the Messiah? Did he see himself as the Son of God? Modern scholarship is divided over the former. It is well known that most Jews of the day expected the Messiah to be a triumphant military leader, and so Jesus attracted more than his share of the Zealot party. But the term Messiah also carried other implications. For example, a tradition dating back to the prophet Isaiah in the eighth century BCE was that the Messiah would not be involved in political life, but would be a despised and rejected Servant of Yaweh who by his suffering would redeem the world. He would be meek and humble, yet confident, but he would meet a shameful death as a common criminal. This "Suffering Servant" role was well understood at the time, and would have had a huge impact on Jesus' self-image, such that Isaiah's predictions would have influenced Jesus' behaviour. In summary, it is more likely that Jesus saw himself as this "Suffering Servant" than as someone who would drive the Roman legions out of Israel. Moreover, even if this did not influence Jesus' behavior, it undoubtedly influenced the image of him held by early Christians. After a generation, they knew virtually nothing of his life, but they would have expected Messiah-like behaviours from him, and these undoubtedly crept into *New Testament* accounts.

The most common way Jesus apparently referred to himself was as the "Son of Man", a phrase he used some seventy times. Like everything else in our story, this term also is the subject of venomous debate among the theological set. The expression seems to date back to the *Book of Enoch*, probably written by several authors from 170 BCE–66 BCE. Interestingly, Paul never used the term in his references to Jesus. The translators of the King James Version capitalized it in an attempt to make Jesus seem more impressive. Many traditionalists see it as the equivalent of "Son of God". Modern linguists try to downgrade the term, saying it should not be capitalized, and that in Aramaic it has a self-deprecating quality to it. So "Son of Man" might mean something such as "a guy such as me", or "a man in my position", or even "a human being."

Far more than Messiah or Son of Man, the term his followers have used to describe Jesus is the Greek term "Christ". In modern usage, "Jesus" is used to describe the historical person, and "Christ" refers to the divine eternal Son of God. The term "Christ" had wide pagan use long before Jesus; it was used to describe Horus, Mithra, Serapis, and even Cyrus king of Persia. Thus it is vital to understand that it was not "Jesus" the Jewish prophet who conquered the world, it was "Christ" the Hellenistic Son of God. The religion of Jesus became victorious when he was adopted by a Greek theology he would have abhorred.

Was Jesus divine? There are three possibilities: he was, and he knew it; he was, but he didn't know it; or he was only a human. The scholars generally agree that Jesus never thought of himself as divine…in fact, given the atmosphere of the time and place, such a claim by anyone would have led to immediate death by stoning from devout Jews in the crowd.

As we have seen, there was a venerable tradition of pagan gods and heroes being called "the first and only-begotten Son of God". In the synoptic *Gospels* (Mark, Matthew, and Luke) Jesus never makes a clear statement to the effect that he was the Son of God, or that he came from God. These types of statement do appear in profusion in the *Gospel of John*, but it was written a generation later, and its reliability is deeply suspect.

Virtually every statement in the *New Testament* where Jesus is or is not called divine is a battleground for contending theologians. In general, we can say that Jesus prayed to God as to a father, and usually didn't act as though he knew he was divine. For example, *Mark 10:18* has Jesus say:

> "Why do you call me good? No one is good but God alone."

As his career developed, however, he may have gradually convinced himself that he was a divine emissary. But even though Jesus may have been uncertain of his nature, his followers weren't. For pagans, divinity was often widely diffused among men—for example, emperors were divine—but this pagan subtlety escaped most mainstream Christians, for whom it was a black or white affair. Christian Gnostics took up the idea of diffused divinity, but by the fourth century they were defeated. The Incarnation became the official doctrine of the new church, a doctrine which was unknown to Jesus. That early Christian statement of belief, the Apostles' Creed, says:

> "I believe in one God, the Father Almighty, and in Jesus Christ His only Son..."

By 325 CE, the Nicene Creed is far more detailed and difficult:

> "I believe in... one lord Jesus Christ the Son of God, begotten of the Father, of one substance with the Father, God from God, Light from Light, true God from true God, begotten, not made..."

Jesus was now clearly and unequivocally God, and his own doubts about himself were forgotten.

As Jesus travelled about Galilee the crowds grew larger, and he would have begun to see himself as a player on a larger stage. In particular, to one of his messianic bent and traditional training, he would begin to be more and more convinced that he was the Suffering Servant whose arrival had been predicted in the Hebrew Scriptures. And, whether consciously or not, his behaviour and choice of actions would have reflected this growing conviction. His entry into Jerusalem was carefully orchestrated to reflect these *Old Testament* prophecies: the mare and foal, the palm branches and the scripted crowd reaction to his arrival all suggest a rather blatant and fruitless attempt to manipulate public opinion in Jerusalem. But the Saducee-dominated population of that city clearly saw Jesus as big trouble, and stood aside as the Roman officials dealt with the threat.

However, these *Old Testament* parallels had occurred to more than just Jesus. When the Evangelists later set out to write their accounts of his life and work, they laced their *Gospels* with references to the Hebrew Scriptures...more than 400 direct quotes by one count. Generally it does not impress the modern reader, but it probably did impress people of the time. They lived in a culture with a deep respect for and both antiquity and oracles. And the gospel authors were desperate to show that the new religion of Jesus had an honourable and familiar past—that in fact, Jesus was the true heir of Moses.

According to John Dominic Crossan, the evangelists were really in the dark—they knew almost nothing about Jesus except that he had been crucified. But they were deeply steeped in Hebrew Scripture, and so over time Christian writers constructed a story with more and more detail, and more and more reflections of "prophetic" *Old Testament* writings. What we are reading in the Gospels is not history, certainly not memoirs, but attempts well after the fact to express powerful religious experiences in politically correct ways.

One of the weirdest examples of this need to retrofit events to ancient traditions was the notion of the twelve apostles. Twelve had long been a powerful number to both the Hebrews and their pagan neighbours. Moses had gone up on the mountain and named twelve tribes, then he sent twelve spies into Canaan. Likewise Jesus went up on the mountain and called twelve disciples, just as the Egyptian sun-god Horus had done. And just like Horus, Jesus had come of age at twelve. Most importantly of all, Mithra had twelve disciples and so did Dionysos—it would have been churlish for the Evangelists to have attributed a lesser number of key followers to Jesus. One has to conclude that there was no defined in-group, that twelve was a mystical number which was taken without much thought from the pagan background of the times, and the claim of twelve chosen disciples existed only to put Jesus on an equal footing with his rivals.

Clearly the number twelve counted for more than the names, since the *Gospels* don't even agree on who was included. Christian tradition even gives membership to Paul, who never even met Jesus. But if we grant that Jesus existed, he would have had followers, and we might make a few observations about some of them. First, they were an unlikely collection: some fishermen, a tax collector, and at least two terrorists. It must have made for strange conversations when Jesus was not around—they could have had very little to say to one another. They left wives, families and jobs to follow an itinerant healer, who over and over made it plain that they were clueless about his message to the world. Very odd. And imagine the reception, says Crossan, when thirteen of these scruffy beggars arrived in a Galilean village begging for food while all the men were at work in the fields.

All in all, the behavior of the "Apostles" was not exemplary. When things looked threatening, they ran. After the Resurrection, most of the so-called Apostles played no defined part in leading the infant church—that fell to Peter and someone named "James". James was the brother of Jesus, and as such he would have wielded considerable authority, but he seems to have been parachuted in to take charge, since The Twelve did not exist. The final indignity was that the *New Testament* book known as *The Acts of the Apostles*, which should have recounted their exploits pretty much ignores them, has Peter disappear after chapter 15, and the balance is mainly about Paul.

The chief Apostle, Simon Peter, was in fact a major beneficiary of the Christian whitewash machine. Simon and his brother Andrew were fishermen, and were casting their nets into the Sea of Galilee when Jesus called on them to follow him. Later in Matthew 16:18, Jesus gave him his nickname:

> "And I tell you, you are 'Peter', and on this rock I will build my church, and the gates of Hades will not prevail against it. I will give you the keys of

the kingdom of Heaven, and whatever you bind on earth will be bound in Heaven…"

Jesus would have said nothing of the sort: it is an example of words being put into his mouth by a much later generation of apologists trying to provide authenticity for their particular claims. The tradition arose that Peter was a solid, reliable successor to Jesus who then went on to become the first Pope. He was no such thing. His nickname should be translated not as "the Rock," but probably as "Rocky." Like the movie character Rocky Balboa, he was both thick and violent. Only four verses after giving Peter the keys, Jesus calls him Satan and a stumbling block. He never seems to get Jesus' message. In the Garden of Gethsemane, Peter attacks the servant of the high priest with a sword. When Jesus is arrested, Peter flees, but then returns and thoughtlessly gives himself away to the crowd as a Galilean. After the death of Jesus, he effectively concedes the leadership of the infant church to Jesus' brother James. Peter is hornswoggled by the fast-talking Paul into agreeing with him on the question of converting pagans until James angrily sets them straight. Peter is responsible, directly or indirectly, for the mysterious deaths of Ananias and Sapphira in *Acts*. And finally, the story that he went to Rome and was crucified upside down there is yet more pious fraud.

12

PASSION, DEATH, RESURRECTION

"Extraordinary claims require extraordinary evidence."
                                        Carl Sagan

Great empires are not run by stupid people. Modern American officials are pleasant, educated and persuasive. Nineteenth century British bureaucrats were certain, but always civilized. So too, the Romans who ran their Empire were not given to rash or inflammatory acts. So when the Romans executed Jesus, they must have had evidence that he represented a definite political danger.

The whole story of Jesus' arrest, trial and death is awash in serious and insoluble contradictions. For centuries, scholars within the Christian community have laboured to resolve the legal, chronological and historical issues without much success. The reason for this failure is now becoming obvious—most of it simply didn't happen, and the few parts which did happen have been fudged and irreversibly distorted by the Evangelists. Again and again we need to remind ourselves that the *Gospel* accounts are not history, but propaganda—inspired, spiritual, brilliantly composed—but propaganda nonetheless.

For two thousand years, commentators have had good reason to wonder whether Jesus was a political activist.

Evidence linking Jesus to the Zealot party is strong, but circumstantial. He was surrounded by men with Zealot connections. The movement was founded in Galilee by Judas the Great, whom Jesus may have remembered from childhood. He and his family would certainly have known insurgents involved in Judas' failed rebellion. One of Jesus' disciples was Simon Zelotes. ("Zelotes" is left in the Greek, rather than being translated as "The Zealot": is this failure to translate significant?) Jesus' most notorious follower, Judas Iscariot, got his nickname from his organization, the Sicarii, or "knife-men", who were pledged to assassinate disloyal Jews. Jesus suffered crucifixion, the usual punishment for Zealots, and he died between two "lestai"—the usual term for Zealots. At least one of his disciples was willing to offer armed resistance when the Romans came to arrest Jesus. Finally, in some confusing way, Jesus' fate is entwined with the fate of another "lestai", Barabbas. Unfortunately several scholars now suggest Barabbas was not a real person—that this was a code word for the lower/base side of the personality, while Jesus was the higher/spiritual side. The name is rich with suggestion: Bar meant son, and Abba was the term Jesus used to describe God. Does this make Barabbas the Son of God? If any of this is true, this is of no help in untangling what really happened.

Obviously, Jesus' message did not sit well with imperial officials. He had a low opinion of the ruling classes of the world, and consistently cast his lot with the poor and the disaffected. The rich, he was fond of pointing out, were unlikely to be welcomed into the kingdom of Heaven. Under questioning, he temporized, but eventually public pressure forced him to confront the major issue of the day—how to resist the Romans - and Jesus disliked not only the Romans, but also the whole tide of Hellenization which they represented.

On the other side, Jesus could not count on wholehearted support from the Jewish elites. They did not like his attitude to the Law. His behavior was anti-social. His neighbourhood was infamous for its bandits. His friends were working class or worse, but his parables seemed to be appealing to the petty bourgeoisie of Palestine: people who had servants, owned vineyards, and gave big wedding feasts. His liberal attitudes to women would have been noticeable departures from Judaic tradition. When the crisis came, the crowds and followers melted away, and those with power were all aligned against him.

Most of Jesus' life and preaching was in the small towns and villages of Galilee, and the teachings and miracles of the Galilee years are only tangentially connected to the passion/resurrection stories which centre on Jerusalem. For most people, the most significant (and contentious) period of Jesus' life began with his visit to Jerusalem. (The *Gospels* disagree on the timing of this visit, but it seems most likely that John erred and that the timing recounted in the other three *Gospels* is correct—it occurred just before the crucifixion.)

The Roman writer Pliny the Elder, an urbane and objective observer, claimed that Jerusalem at the time was the jewel of the eastern Mediterranean. It had all the attractions of a great Roman metropolis: palaces, aqueducts, a hippodrome, an amphitheatre, the Antonia Fortress, and above all, the Great Temple—the very heart of Judaism. Herod's Temple had been years in the making and was nearly finished, its architecture dominated the skyline, and its size amazed visitors to the city. It drew sightseers from all over the Roman world. For country boys from Galilee, the first visit to Herod's Temple must have been an overwhelming shock.

The Temple was the only place where Jews could offer sacrifice, and only a priest could do it. Only a Jew could enter, and in fact even Roman money was unwelcome within the sacred precincts. Because of its size and the constant flow of Jewish pilgrims, the daily operation of the Great Temple must have meant slaughtering animals on a massive scale. Many of these animals, especially the smaller birds favoured by the poor, could be bought on the precincts—but certainly not with idolatrous Roman currency. So moneychangers set up tables in the outer court where a devout Jew could exchange his Roman coinage for Jewish money, and then buy birds and other small animals to be sacrificed by the priests. It was all legal, it was necessary, and it probably worked pretty well to solve the problem of Jewish religious scrupulosity in a major city where most of the business was transacted with Roman coinage.

So what set Jesus off? Why did he attack the moneychangers and upend their tables? Their location? The rate of exchange? Maybe he saw the whole truck and trade, and the modus vivendi with the nearby Roman garrison as inherently corrupt. Maybe he took the Hebrew prophet Zechariah's overheated comments on the Lord of Hosts slaughtering sheep and sheep traders a little too seriously. Maybe it was his first visit to the big city, and he expected something different. Maybe his message that the blood sacrifices of the Temple were outmoded (why would a disembodied God want a dead pigeon?) which had found some favour up north in Galilee, seemed even more necessary as he stood and looked at this giant market. We don't know. But it is clear that his attack on the moneychangers was very ill-advised, for it would have been seen as an attack on the organization of the Temple, and thus an affront to all Jews.

What are we to make of this outburst? If Jesus was seen as unbalanced and self-destructive, no wonder his disciples "fell away" from him when matters became serious. Surely any attack on the Temple was meant to provoke anti-Roman riots. The British historian S.G. Brandon speculated that Jesus' offensive against the Temple was carefully orchestrated to coincide with an attack on the Roman garrison on the other side of the city, led by (who else?) Barabbas. This makes Jesus very political indeed. An opposite view was offered by J.M. Robertson, who believed that the whole incident was invented: that the story arose from an attempt to Christianize and mythologize a common Egyptian sculpture of our old friend Osiris carrying what looked like a scourge, but was actually a grain flail.

On balance, it seems unlikely that Jesus was deeply involved in the Zealot movement. That was entirely political, and he was probably more interested in theology and social reform. Unquestionably, he had a lot of Zealot contacts, but we cannot make that the basis of his whole career. Given the acrimonious political atmosphere, both Jewish and Roman authorities were interested in preventing another massacre of Jews by the Roman army, and so they agreed that meant putting an end to the naive Galilean preacher.

However, any cursory check of his background would have uncovered his parable of the wicked servants. These foolish minions had murdered the son of the landowner when he came to collect his rents, and so the property owner had promptly killed the servants. This was one parable whose meaning would have been crystal clear to the Jerusalem elites, and they responded to the threat. Official reprisal against Jesus, with extreme prejudice, was now unavoidable.

As the authorities were preparing to close in, Jesus and his followers rented a room for what has come to be called The Last Supper. The timing and sequence of these few days has been much studied, but again it is hopelessly confused. If the Galileans were in Jerusalem as part of the feast of

Passover, then was the Last Supper a proper Jewish Seder? That seems doubtful, because as Bishop Spong has demonstrated, the entry into Jerusalem was probably part of the autumn festival of Sukkot, and did not occur at Passover. In all probability, the entire "Palm Sunday" story is pure invention, spun out of an *Old Testament* story found in *Zechariah*. The Last Supper, on the other hand, traces its origin to the Eleusinian Greek cult rituals, and its historical reality is equally false.

In any case, the real issue with the Last Supper is the set of words Jesus was said to pronounce over bread and wine. Again, the *Gospel* writers have significant differences over the exact wording—a familiar problem. But given the strictness of the kosher laws concerning blood, it is ridiculous to think that Jesus or anyone in his circle would ask believers to drink his blood. It was not Jewish—it had to be pagan—and the most likely source was Paul's Mithraic influences. But this ritual which disgusted Jews had a strange appeal to Hellenistic Greeks, and soon this belief and liturgy became a key part of the new religion. Within only a few generations the Christian writer Justin Martyr felt confident enough to claim that all those earlier pagan rituals of bread and wine and sacred meals were demonically inspired attempts to deceive the human race.

But demons have no monopoly on deception, and the accounts of the passion and crucifixion are so full of implausibilities, cover-ups, and downright untruths that after two thousand years we can be confident only in the fact that we will never know the truth. For example, Christian tradition holds that the Last Supper fell on the Thursday before Passover, and that the Crucifixion was the following day. That would mean that the Last Supper, the long evening in the garden of Gethsemane, the arrest by a squad of soldiers, and two or maybe three trials—at least one of them a public spectacle—all happened in one night. It defies logic.

Three incidents in the Garden of Gethsemane deserve comment. According to Mark, when the Roman soldiers arrived, Jesus was conferring with a young man dressed only in a linen cloth. He evaded the soldiers by slipping off the cloth and running away naked. This odd little episode coming on the evening of the Last Supper suggests some sort of initiation rite into a cult. But if it happened, (and it's weird enough to have the ring of truth) we should suspect that there may have been a lot more which the Evangelists knew, but tried to keep hidden from us outsiders.

Second, Judas kissed Jesus to identify him for the benefit of the Roman soldiers. We have to assume then that Jesus was not well-known enough that he could be identified by any Roman, and so this was a low-level arrest. Again, Jesus could not have been the major figure that the *Gospels* pretend. Moreover, only Jesus seems to have been arrested. Had the Galilean gang been perceived as a serious or widespread security threat, there would have been a lot more soldiers, and a lot more arrests.

One of the arrests that apparently didn't happen was that of Simon Peter. According to Mark, "one of the bystanders" drew a sword in defence of Jesus, and cut off the ear of the slave of the high priest. Matthew narrowed it to "one of those with Jesus", Luke agreed: "one of those with Jesus", and John identifies the perpetrator as Simon Peter. Jesus' admonition to put away the weapon seems quite weak: was this the first time the Prince of Peace noticed that his deputy was carrying a sword? Was his intervention merely an attempt to minimize bloodshed? Why were there no consequences for Peter? The whole incident seems extremely implausible, and yet something happened, or it would not have been mentioned in all four *Gospels*.

Trying to sort out the trial situation is hopeless. The *Gospel of Peter* has one trial, John has one and a half, Matthew and Mark have two, and Luke has three. There are credibility problems with all of them. For example, a trial in front of Herod Antipas, the Roman puppet in Galilee, would have required either moving the prisoner to and from Galilee, or that Herod tried him illegally (the legal term would be ultra vires) in Jerusalem. The Romans weren't that dumb. The *Gospels* make a desperate attempt to convince us that Jesus was tried for blasphemy, but he was clearly condemned to death either as a political agitator or as a rebel. Any evidence for this has long since been expunged, but significantly, none of the Evangelists protested that the Crucifixion was a miscarriage of justice. Whatever charges the Romans brought against Jesus, common sense says that he was at least partially guilty. This part of Jesus' career was explosive and damaging, and the Evangelists were fully engaged in covering up—with falsification, fudging, and a blizzard of *Old Testament* references.

What of a trial by the Sanhedrin? This Jewish high court certainly had the power to execute by stoning those convicted of serious religious crimes. In fact, Jesus' brother James was later to be the victim of just such a trumped-up charge by the high priest Ananus in 64 CE. But Jesus was crucified, not stoned, so his condemnation came from the Romans, not the Jewish authorities. Had such a trial by the Sanhedrin occurred, it would have been the talk of the city. Josephus, the Jewish historian would have reported every detail. Instead there is silence. At the same time, Paul was a rabbinical student in the city. Again, there is silence.

In a crushingly convincing book *The Court Martial of Jesus* that ought to put an end to the controversy, Weddig Fricke, a German lawyer, debunks even the possibility of a trial by the Sanhedrin. It is, he says, so full of illogicalities and illegalities that we can only regard it as a total invention. So why is it there in the *New Testament*? First, in the supercharged political atmosphere in which the Gospels were written, it was absolutely vital not to exacerbate the situation by blaming the Romans for the death of the Son of God. Likewise, it was just as vital, in the struggle for the hearts and minds of Palestine, that the blame for Jesus' death be put squarely on the shoulders of the Jews who had rejected him. Over the years, the *Gospel* comments on the Jews of Jerusalem grew into full-blown anti-Semitism, an unimaginably ugly result of a falsified history.

The trial in front of Pontius Pilate probably happened. It would have been a short, no-nonsense condemnation of a public nuisance. Pilate the historical figure is reasonably well known from the writings of both the Jewish historian Josephus, and the Jewish philosopher Philo of Alexandria. What they have to say about Pilate is unflattering. His superiors expected him to be tough. He was in charge of one of the most unstable parts of the Roman Empire, and he certainly didn't much like Jews. Violence, treachery, brutality, and "endless cruelties" were his stock in trade. In turn, the locals detested him for his disrespect of their ancient religion, and his affronts to the Temple precincts.

However, the Gospel details of the trial are pure invention—after all, Jesus' supporters had fled for their lives at Gethsemane, and would certainly not have been admitted to any hasty drumhead proceeding. So there were no sympathetic eyewitnesses. But the Evangelists tried their level best to shift blame away from the Romans, and that meant giving a degree of exoneration to Pilate. Would he ever have released someone such as Barabbas? Never. Would he ever have admitted a crowd of Jews to the trial, and then asked for their input? Never. Would he have agonized over the guilt of a peasant agitator with a Galilean accent? Never.

But the whitewash brush was in full swing, and we are given the image of Pilate being admonished by his wife, publicly washing his hands, then transferring responsibility to the Jews. In reality, Pilate would have ordered the crucifixion without batting an eye. Centuries later, Pilate's wife was canonized as a saint, presumably for her vain (and imaginary) protest. It was the Jews who were to take the blame for the death of Jesus, and the prejudice lasted for generations. (From our modern perspective, it makes about as much sense to blame the descendants of the Romans—namely the Italians.)

But is there any historical evidence of the trial at all? Not much. An ancient copy of the Jewish *Talmud* from Babylon recounts that on the eve of the Passover, someone named Yeshu was hanged for sorcery. For 40 days before the execution, a herald went through the streets of Jerusalem asking for someone to plead on his behalf, but no one did. But if there had been a trial of Jesus, there would have been official government reports at the time, and they would have been sent back to Rome. The Romans were excellent record-keepers, and this was capital punishment. Rupert Furneaux reported a story that the imperial archives did indeed contain documents on the trial of Jesus as late as the second century. The very existence of such records roused Christian writers to fury—they claimed, unsurprisingly, that the documents had been forged. Equally unsurprisingly, these records have long since disappeared. They did not survive the Christianization of the Empire.

On the other side, an increasing number of scholars claim the passion narrative did not happen at all, that it was all invented. Crossan says it was created by Christian apologists digging through Hebrew scripture, and he dates it very early, probably 40-60 CE. What we are reading, he says, is propaganda—it is *Old Testament* prophecy dressed up to look like history. Spong agrees. He maintains that it was created out of Psalm 22 by the Evangelists, or their friends, who were seeking to encourage the tiny Christian community. Or was it the remnant of a lost pagan Palestinian ritual, or perhaps the Roman Saturnalia, reflected in the mockery, the crown of thorns, and the jeering title "King of the Jews"? The evangelical American scholar Ben Witherington, seeking to distance Jesus from the Zealots, asked why the other Galileans weren't rounded up, and why Jesus' brother James was allowed by the Sadducees to live as a public figure in Jerusalem. The answer may not be to Mr. Witherington's liking: there is a good chance that the Passion didn't happen at all.

Still, the Passion narrative is an extraordinary and powerful one. Like the narrative of Attis and Cybele, it involved a gripping story of primal human emotions: nobility, betrayal, torture, death, hope and triumph. Especially torture—Mel Gibson's recent movie *The Passion of the Christ* provides a powerful reminder that graphic suffering and religious enthusiasm has always been a winning combination. And we can be assured that, had a decent translation of Attis' death and resurrection survived, it too would have been graphic and deeply moving.

We are on more solid ground with the Crucifixion. The first god claimed to be crucified was Orpheus in the third century BCE. The punishment was occasionally used, even by Jewish courts, shortly thereafter. But it took the Romans to exploit crucifixion on an assembly-line scale. The benchmark had been set by Crassus, who in 72 BCE crucified 6,600 of Spartacus' rebellious slaves along the Appian Way stretching hundreds of miles from Rome to Brundisium. Long after they were dead, the rotting bodies were left hanging by the roadside as an object lesson to others. The Romans did not fool around.

Romans claimed to reserve crucifixion for the poor and for political criminals, but the application of this policy in Palestine was appalling in its scope. Varus allegedly crucified 2,000 Jews in 4 BCE, an additional 3,600 died under the hand of Florus in 66 CE, and an unimaginable 500 a day were crucified in Jerusalem by the Roman general Titus in 70 CE. Military squads were given special training so it could be done more quickly and efficiently. Archaeologists have found only one partial body out of that immense number, largely because the policy was to leave the bodies for dogs and vultures, and there was usually nothing much left to bury. We are appalled at the suffering and inhumanity, but the ancients, always leery of ghosts, were just as alarmed at the inability of the victim's family to provide a proper burial. We can hardly imagine the depth of a family's horror and dishonour when one of their members was crucified.

The Crucifixion of Jesus was said to have occurred at Passover, and the ancient fertility rite of Passover had involved human sacrifice. Later this was modified from the death of a human to the death of a lamb, but oral traditions kept alive the notion that "the Son of the King" was the preferred victim. Other crucified mythological heroes had included Cyrus of Persia, Prometheus of Greece, and Odin of Scandinavia. Jesus fit the pattern. J.M. Robertson, in the preface to the second edition of *Pagan Christs*, wondered at the reaction, or lack of it, to his scholarship:

> "The Gospel story of the Last Supper, the Agony, the Betrayal, the Crucifixion, and the Resurrection is demonstrably not originally a narrative, but a mystery-drama, ...inferrably an

evolution from a Palestinian rite of human sacrifice in which the annual victim was 'Jesus the Son of the Father'. Against this twofold position I have seen not a single detailed argument. Writers who confidently and angrily undertake to expose error in another section of the book pass this with at most a defiant shot."

Some things, for theologians, are just too horrible to contemplate.

Crucifixion was the common punishment for those who fell seriously afoul of Roman authority. The usual process was that after a period on the cross, the legs were broken so that the body weight fell on the wrists, and this caused the internal organs such as the lungs to be constricted. The death which followed was slow and agonizing. Pilate expressed surprise that Jesus had died after only six hours, and he required the centurion's assurance that he was in fact dead.

Was the crucifixion as we imagine it to be? In *Acts*, Jesus is described as being hung on a tree. In Galatians, Paul says he was hung on a tree. The god Adonis was hung on a tree. The Babylonian *Talmud* describes one Yeshu being hung on a tree on the eve of Passover for sorcery. The *Gospel* version has him executed on the hill of Golgotha flanked by two "lestai." These lestai have traditionally been rendered in English as "thieves", but the term lestai was usually employed to describe Zealot terrorists. But who knows? They may have been the two torchbearers who always accompany the saviour-god Mithra. Or they may be the mythological Greek twins Castor and Pollux who, incidentally, were also called "The Sons of Thunder", just like the apostles James and John.

A legendary feature that has been attributed to the Crucifixion is that it was accompanied by three hours of darkness at midday. This darkness was remarkably common: it also accompanied the deaths of Aesculapius, Alexander, Julius Caesar, Heracles, Krishna, Osiris, Prometheus and Romulus. Some Christian apologists have tried to suggest a timely eclipse, but a moment's thought would dispel that notion, if the crucifixion occurred at Passover. A solar eclipse involves the moon passing between the sun and the earth, and that would be impossible during Passover, which is timed to the first full moon of spring.

So we know virtually nothing of his death. But a few things are clear. It was the Romans who executed him, and any Gospel stories that the Jews had influence over the course of events are just nonsense. It is certain that his friends deserted him, and no sympathetic eye witnessed his passing. The Roman records no longer exist. His final words from the cross are all imaginary.

The story that Jesus was taken reverently down from the cross and buried with dignity in a rock tomb is yet more pious invention. The Romans would never have allowed it. To do it without authority would have required a huge bribe for the guards—and given the social background and the panic among Jesus' friends, that was unthinkable. Mark and Matthew give credit to one Joseph of Arimathea, described variously as a member of the Sanhedrin and as a follower of Jesus, who used his own tomb to provide a burial place for Jesus. If this Joseph were an observant Jew, it is not credible that he would bury Jesus, and ignore the two Zealots with whom Jesus was crucified. Indeed, what convicted felon would be given an upscale burial?

Let us go so far as to accept the *Gospel* chronology that Jesus died on Friday afternoon. That would mean he had to be buried before the Sabbath began at sundown. There would be no time for linen wrappings or anointing the body with spices. The conclusion we may draw is that if Jesus was buried at all, it would have been a hasty affair with the body being thrown into a lime-pit. More likely, like thousands of other victims of Roman crucifixions, his body was dumped by the roadside for the vultures and wild dogs.

Even less credible are the recent attempts to claim that the bones of Jesus and/or his family have been found in ancient ossuaries. We are talking about poor Galileans who perished in obscurity, and the idea that their remains would have been collected, carried one hundred kilometers, and put into stone boxes in a Jerusalem cave is laughable. But it does show that there is a tremendous market for such flim-flam. A tourist told me that he saw vials of original breast milk from the Virgin Mary on sale in a market in Bethlehem in the 1960s.

It was a common belief in the Eastern Mediterranean that the soul stayed with the body until the morning of the third day after death. By this point, serious decay would have set in under the hot Mediterranean sun. Thus Jesus was alleged to have risen precisely at the time when other souls would be departing forever. The claim that Jesus descended into Hell was stolen directly from Adonis-worship, which was prevalent in Syria at the time. In a similar vein, the idea that his death is atonement for human sinfulness was taken directly from Mithraism, and was immediately accepted by Paul and other early Christian writers.

But there are always doubts. In this case two Christians who lived in the second century provide the cavils. Papias, a bishop in Asia Minor about 120 CE had heard of only two *Gospels*, *Mark* and *Matthew*. He had never read them, but suggested that *Mark's* chronology and facts were seriously wrong, and that in his belief, Jesus had died of old age in bed at home. Irenaeus, writing in Rome at roughly the same time also seemed to believe that Jesus may have lived to a ripe old age.

Crucifixion in the ancient world was deeply shameful for friends and family. Even the symbol of the cross was at first avoided by the infant church because of its pagan symbolism and as an unfortunate reminder of Golgotha. By the fourth century CE, though, crosses had begun to appear on doorways, on lintels, on eucharistic bread, on the foreheads of believers, and by the eighth century, we begin to see the Crucifixion portrayed in Christian art. The shameful had become venerable.

From Friday afternoon to Sunday morning is not three days, it's a day and a half. Jewish tradition taught that it took three days for a person to be really dead. Hosts of pagan gods had risen after three days. So why was Jesus' tomb found empty on a Sunday? Again, it's the Mithraic influence trumping both common sense and the Jewish tradition. On what day other than Sunday would the sun-god rise?

The sine que non of Christian belief is, or ought to be, the Resurrection. If Jesus did not rise from the dead, his situation as Son of God and as mediator between God and man is in serious doubt. Educated Christians know that much of the traditional story of Jesus is hokum, and they accept that fact with misgivings. But the attitude to the Resurrection is generally non-negotiable. It is common to hear Christians assert that if the Resurrection were disproven, Christianity would collapse into a collection of parables and holy advice. This of course is untrue, for it ignores the enormous power of the pagan ideas which attached themselves to Christianity, and which we have been discussing. To put it bluntly, the Resurrection story has an almost magnetic appeal to the human mind, whether it happened to Jesus or to one of his pagan rivals.

Frequently, however, a close examination of the known

facts and Gospel accounts are closed off by the claim that "It's a matter of belief" or sometimes "It's a different order of thinking." Fair enough, but surely Christian and non-believer alike deserve an airing of the facts, and a consideration of the probabilities. On no other question of Christian theology is there such a wide gap between what is quietly believed in the pulpit and what is accepted as fact in the pew. Certainly the clergy have learned that theirs is a service industry, and the first rule is not to express their doubts.

Resurrection was not unique to Jesus. There were both Jewish and pagan stories extant in the first century of individuals rising from the dead. Apollonius was alleged to have raised from death the daughter of a Roman senator, and Jesus miraculously raised Lazarus—but neither of these were classified as "resurrections" and no supernatural powers were attributed to the lucky recipients. Harpur argues that resurrection had its roots in Egypt, and that the Biblical character Lazarus was in fact the Egyptian god Osiris, who died and rose annually. It is useful to remember that the Palestine of Jesus' time was close to and heavily influenced by the religious traditions of Egypt, and that much of that connection has remained unexplored to the present day.

The Gospel story of the Resurrection is full of contradictions. Surely the Evangelists might be expected to get the central event of their new religion right, but instead the narrative is incoherent. The *Gospels* more or less agree that Mary Magdalene was the first to discover the empty tomb. The tradition that it was a woman must have been very powerful to have survived the centuries of patriarchal spin that was to follow, and the reader can almost hear the Evangelists' teeth grating to admit it. Although there were several stories at the time that Jesus' body had been stolen by his followers, that seems extremely unlikely. They were too frightened and too disorganized.

If you don't believe there are serious problems with the Gospel accounts, take time out here to read the four versions of the discovery of the empty tomb. Two, or three, or several women saw a young man, or two men, or an angel, either sitting or standing. They were either afraid, or were filled with joy, and they either reported it, or they were terrified and said nothing. Obviously resurrection had not been a part of Jesus' teachings, because absolutely nobody was expecting it.

And who first saw the risen Christ? Paul said it was Peter. Matthew said the women in the garden. Luke said first Peter, then a traveler named Cleopas. John said Mary Magdalene. And where were the disciples? They had gone home to Galilee, said Mark. No, said Luke and John, they were still in Jerusalem. It's all pretty unconvincing, isn't it?

To the history of Christianity it really doesn't matter. The miracle of the Resurrection is not whether or not Jesus conquered death, but the apparent conviction of his followers that he had, and the astonishing changes in their behaviour. The disaster of the Crucifixion was turned into a stunning triumph.

Still, fervidity of belief is not an infallible guide to truth. Yes, early Christians were powerfully convinced of the Resurrection and of the appearance of the risen Lord. But were not the galli of Cybele fervent? They must have believed ferociously to have castrated themselves. Were not the followers of Mithra, of Isis, of Dionysos, of the Magna Mater all fervent? Were all pagans deluded, and all Christians reliable? The Christian position has been that since we triumphed, we must have been right. This is Whig history at its most inexcusable, and it is time that it was challenged.

Did Jesus rise bodily or not? Many of the historians and theologians who examine the Resurrection are unimpressed.

Bultmann and his followers reject the stories as fraudulent, arguing that they came about later, as a result of belief in the Resurrection, and so cannot serve as proof of it. F.W. Beare calls the story "legendary embroidery of the crudest type". Hugh Schonfield, in *The Passover Plot*, sold a large number of books by claiming it was all a hoax. Certainly the empty tomb did not seem to have the same grip on first century people that it does on us. People then were far more impressed by Jesus' miraculous appearances to the disciples. We are more skeptical—we know too much about mass psychology, Hindu fakirs, and flying saucers.

There are solid scriptural reasons to be doubtful. To the unsophisticated reader, all four *Gospels* are equally believable, but to the expert who has spent a lifetime examining the nuances of the Evangelists, this is not the case. Scholars now agree that the *Gospel of Mark*, the oldest and most authoritative, should end after verse 9 of Chapter 16. The verses that follow were not written by Mark. This leaves the oldest *Gospel* absolutely silent on both the Resurrection and the Ascension. *Matthew*, written next, contains only a brief and enigmatic account. *Luke* and *John*, written later still, contain the full-blown Resurrection story. As we saw with the birth-stories, this kind of embroidery often had a way of happening in first century Palestine. And so the disturbing empty tomb of Mark soon became the familiar and reassuring story of transcendent life after death.

In the Hebrew tradition, Jews expected a Messiah who would deliver them from the Romans. Throughout their history they had rejected the idea of immortality, but the Greek influence was everywhere. The dead Patroklos had appeared to Achilles, Samuel had appeared to Saul, Scipio the Elder to his grandson, and so now Jesus appeared to his disciples. With the story of the empty tomb, his followers began to develop and embroider the notion that he was still alive. They did not claim that this event was unique.

But the myth-making apparatus was hard at work. There is no description of the risen Christ in the *Gospel of Mark*, written some forty years after the Crucifixion, but by the time of the later *Gospels*, Jesus appeared and disappeared, ate fish and walked through walls, and asked Thomas to put a hand in his wounded side. It was safe to write about it now. The eyewitnesses were dead, the disciples had become heroes, the embarrassing details had been forgotten or pushed aside.

Justin Martyr, one of the most abrasive Christian apologists of the second century, argued that Christianity was true because Jesus' death and Resurrection fulfilled the *Old Testament* prophecies, not that the Gospel stories were true. The difference in emphasis seems slight, but is quite profound. Justin apparently saw the Evangelists as supplying props, not providing essential Truth. An interesting exercise is to read Gospel accounts of the words of Jesus spoken after the Resurrection—they deal with power, authority and leadership—and they are very different in tone from the kinds of things he said before his death.

Jesus' return to earth ended with his bodily ascension into heaven. This was a predictable end, since it had already been claimed to have happened to Adonis, Buddha, Dionysos, Elijah, Enoch, Heracles, Hyacinth, Isaiah, Krishna, Mithra, Moses and Zoroaster. As Christianity grew, the superstitions thickened, and the scoffers were silenced. As late as 1950, Pope Pius XII declared it an article of faith for Roman Catholics that not only Jesus but the Virgin Mary too had been bodily transported up to heaven.

Occasional commentators, from Origen in the third century to John Shelby Spong today have argued that many events of Jesus' life may have been not literally, but only allegorically true, intended to illustrate who Jesus was. Spong calls it a "highly stylized interpretive portrait", perhaps like a late Picasso. This, he says, "does not make the *Gospels*' interpretation wrong". No, but if everything in the *Gospels* stands for something else, it soon becomes so arcane and confusing that it is of no consequence in the ordinary person's life. We may not want total literalism from the *Gospels*, but some factual bedrock does seem to be required.

Over the past two decades there has been a scholarly flurry tracing *Gospel* stories and events back to their roots in Hebrew Scripture. This is exactly where Christian and Jewish theologians have been trained to look, and the search has been richly rewarded. But as of yet few similar searches seem to have been made of the great pagan systems of the Near East. Perhaps it is less jarring to suggest that a Jesus legend is a reworking of a story about the prophet Ezekiel than one about Dionysos.

Certainly we are entitled to wonder how many of these stories and events were lifted from paganism by one or another of the warring factions that emerged after Jesus' death in an attempt to bolster their authority. The battle was protracted and bitter, and it is to this factional strife that we now turn.

13

THE INFANT CHURCH

*"I like your Christ. I do not like your Christians.
Your Christians are so unlike your Christ."*

Mahatma Gandhi

It is now clear to all but the most obdurate that Jesus did not see himself starting a new religion, or as anything but a Jew, albeit not a mainstream one. His followers were just one little group among many at the time. At first, after his death, they attended their local synagogues, but their unusual notions probably made them unwelcome, and increasingly they began to set up their own meetings, frequently in private homes. The split was probably a reluctant one for the Jesus congregation, for that meant they lost the exemptions to civic duties which Jews enjoyed, and more seriously, they were in danger of losing the connection to Jewish tradition and history. For the infant church to have any credibility at all, it needed either to produce a body of sacred scripture, or to appropriate Jewish scriptures. Christianity did both. Under attack by religious enemies, it rooted its founder firmly in history—even if, as we have seen, the history was frequently false.

From the viewpoint of Jews at the time, these Christians represented a real threat to the purity of their religion. Under attack by Greek ideas and Roman armies, the Jews were developing, following thinkers such as Hillel, a new form of Pharisaism which was to allow Judaism to survive centuries of oppression. This new group with its talk of a crucified Messiah was not welcome in the Jewish community. You were either a Jew or you were not. Christians were not.

The first crisis came early. Stephen, one of Jesus' early followers, attacked Jewish traditionalists as being rebellious against Yahweh. Unsurprisingly, he was harassed while preaching and converting, and he complained loudly about the behaviour of these conservative Jewish officials. But the authorities predictably turned on him, and he was executed by stoning on orders of the Sanhedrin.

Followers of Jesus, for their part, also contributed to the widening rift. The apocryphal *Gospel of Peter*, probably written originally about 40 CE, set the pattern: it blamed the Jews for the death of Jesus. In the next few decades, Jesus' life and teachings were recast to make him look unJewish. He was said to have quarreled with the Pharisees, with his neighbours, with his family. He was no longer the enemy of Rome, now he was portrayed as a friend to centurions. His teachings were de-emphasized in favour of the story of his death and resurrection. This "repositioning" is probably the reason so many of his teachings are confusing on questions such as whether to observe the Law, or whether to pay taxes. With time, the anti-Jewish hostility grew more shrill, and once the Empire became officially Christian, it turned downright deadly.

But there were some who tried to ride both horses—we know them as the Ebionites, and they tried to be good Jews who also followed the teachings of Jesus. They are not mentioned in the *New Testament*. They may have been mainly relatives and neighbours of Jesus, and were probably the original Christians. They added their *Gospel of the Hebrews* to the Jewish canon, but it has since been destroyed or lost. They held that Jesus was the mortal son of Mary and Joseph who had been elevated to the title of Son of God through his personal righteousness. They revered the Jewish Law, and despised Paul and the Hellenizing ideas which he championed. But Paul's version was the future, and the Ebionites survived only as a tiny group in rural Galilee until the seventh century—an interesting artifact of what might have been.

The first spiritual leader of the Ebionites was one of the most fascinating characters in our story—the brother of Jesus known as James the Just. The *Gospel of Thomas* has a disciple ask Jesus who is to be his successor, and the answer is that it should be his brother James. It can no longer be argued that Jesus was an only child. Even the archconservative theologian John Meier admits that Jesus was one of a large family: James, Joseph, Simon, Judas, two unnamed sisters, and perhaps more. It may even be that James was older than Jesus: Epipanius, a Bishop of Constantia in the fourth century, claimed James was Joseph's first-born. Paul, who met and was chastised by James, described him as "the brother of the Lord". But there are other possibilities. Jesus' brothers may have been half-brothers, children of Joseph by an earlier marriage. That explanation appealed to Origen, but shortly thereafter the impeccably orthodox Jerome first suggested that James was merely a cousin. This came as a relief to the myth-makers, who were now free to advocate the idea that Mary was a virgin when she bore Jesus, and remained a virgin ever after. But for us the likelihood is that it was a blended family, and that the father of Jesus was not Joseph—otherwise he would never have been referred to as the "son of Mary".

Jesus' preaching put a strain on family relationships. His

brothers tried to get him to stop, then tried to restrain him as being insane. Jesus rejected and avoided them. Even his mother felt his wrath: he refers to her only as "woman" and he was rude to her at the wedding feast of Cana—but that event was so clearly a stolen Dionysian story that we can dismiss its existence altogether.

It is a truly astonishing situation: what we know about Jesus is almost nothing, but he must have existed because his brother did. It is reasonable to assume that Jesus and James shared important beliefs and attitudes. James himself was clearly an important and powerful personality. The historian Josephus gives far more attention to James than to Jesus. Certainly his public career was much longer. James earned the nickname "The Just" because of his unswerving piety - evidently his knees were calloused "like a camel's" from long hours of prayer on the stone floors of the Temple. He wore only seamless linen, he was a vegetarian, he drank no wine, his hair was uncut, and he refused to bathe. His antisocial persona was magnified by his bitter hostility toward the rich and the powerful. He was described by Josephus as a Nazorean—we may assume he was a Nazirite. He probably was honoured by the citizens of Jerusalem as much for his eccentricities as for his piety—much as we regard members of the Old Order Amish.

James had the leadership of the little flock thrust upon him because the belief at the time was that Messiah was a hereditary title. James is described as having inflexible and orthodox views, and after the Crucifixion, he preached that his brother had been the Messiah, but he bristled at any suggestion that Jesus had been the Son of God. Within the growing Christian movement, he was clearly the boss. The critical role played by James has been consistently downplayed so as not to outshine his brother, and also because he stoutly opposed Paul and the Hellenistic wing of the new religion.

James survived Jesus by some thirty years, and became a well-known figure in Jerusalem, where he was admired by the Pharisees. In fact, it is difficult to reconcile the almost cavalier attitude to the Law shown by Jesus with the rigourous and legalistic beliefs attributed to his brother. There are several explanations, but the most likely is that someone has tampered with the sources to discredit James and the Jewish Christians.

Meanwhile the situation with the Sadducees and the Romans was very tense, so that Nazoreans (and their look-alikes the early Christians) were the subject of official interest. In 44 CE Agrippa, king of Judea, cracked down and had the hair of several prominent Nazoreans shorn, then he arrested the "apostles" Peter and James, and had James (and maybe Peter) killed. But James the Just was untouched, so he probably was either too prominent, or too popular.

His luck ran out a few years later. In 62 CE, he fell afoul of the high priest Ananus, who secured a hasty (and apparently illegal) conviction by the Sanhedrin. James was killed, either by stoning, or by being thrown off Temple Mount and then being stoned. The public outrage was such that Ananus was deposed as high priest. There may well have been some interfamily rivalry. It is probably not a coincidence that Ananus was the brother-in-law of Caiaphas, the high priest at the time of Jesus' crucifixion.

After the death of Jesus, events moved faster than a conservative such as James the Just would have liked. After an initial flurry of conversions in Palestine, it became apparent that the real future of the new religion lay outside the Jewish heartland, with the rapid conversion of Greek pagans and godfearers. Many of the followers of Jesus migrated to the city of Antioch, and fell under the influence of the followers of Adonis. Here was another fertility god who had died a cruel death, gone to Hades, and rose triumphantly during the spring equinox. The parallels were so obvious that many began to think that Jesus had been sent to all peoples, not just to the Jews. But there were issues involved in converting these pagans—specifically, dietary restrictions and circumcision. The conversions went ahead anyway until the alarm bells went off back in Jerusalem.

A meeting was called—the so-called Council of Jerusalem. James and Peter represented the Galilean party, Paul and Barnabas were former Jews who had been converting pagans in Antioch, and Titus was a converted pagan. However, James was the brother of Jesus, he clearly had the authority, and he insisted that converted Jews must continue to observe the entire Jewish Law. Paul and the others went home unhappy. But the elephant in the room, the issue that apparently wasn't raised in the presence of James, was the divinity of Jesus. Who could have known that with a few years the Romans would destroy Jerusalem? Who could predict that the party of James would be reduced to a few rural Ebionites, led first by James' nephew Symeon, and then by other blood relatives of Jesus? Who could foresee that Paul's version of Greek paganism, covered by the thinnest veneer of Jesus' life, would conquer the Roman Empire?

The year 70 CE, as years go, has never really received the respect it deserves in world history. The destruction of Jerusalem shattered historical Judaism, radically changed both the direction and prospects of nascent Christianity, profoundly altered the religious history of the Empire and hence the West, and by opening new trade and military adventures to the East, gave birth to a set of grudges in the Middle East whose results we still see today. And yet, despite the extraordinary violence and tension of the times, the *New Testament* omits all mention of it.

Not so the historian Josephus. He gives us the background to the war. He has story after story of preachers and charlatans, rebels and revolutionaries, of Roman reaction and frequent overreaction. Generally, if it was just talk, the authorities tolerated it, but open subversion or anti-Roman activity led to violent reprisals. At the time of Jesus, the Pharisees were the most popular party in Palestine, but by 66 CE, the Zealots dominated, and most Jews had come to support the armed struggle against Rome. Hellenized Jews across the Empire must have watched in horror as their homeland slipped into war.

Once the fighting began, the result was a foregone conclusion. In 69 CE, the Roman general Vespasian besieged Jerusalem with 60,000 legionaries. After five months of famine, the city fell, Roman troops swarmed in, and headed for the Temple. It was desecrated and destroyed, and the city itself was demolished. And demolished along with it was the Jewish state.

An uncounted number of Jews fled the bloodshed for other parts of the Empire, and like other refugees of other times and places, they headed for the shelter and anonymity of large cities. They took their religion with them, and Judaism became a decidedly unpopular minority urban religion all across the Empire. It was a Judaism that stressed ritual purity, strict dietary observances, and moral behaviour, and it helped Jews survive for two thousand years as an ethnic minority under remarkably hostile conditions.

But the impact on the young religion of Jesus was far more profound. First, it was plain that further resistance to Roman power was unthinkable, and Christianity set about to make nice with the Empire. All traces of its rebellious beginnings were removed. Its connections with those perfidious Jews were severed. Christians were now told to see themselves as the new Chosen People. A series of sacred books were produced in the generation after the war, and all of them were profoundly affected by the Lessons of the Year 70, but the event itself was not to be discussed in writing by a Christian for almost 300 years.

Second, the theological shift was almost instantaneous. The Jerusalem Church was finished, done in either by the Roman legions, or by the will of God. Christianity was no longer Jewish, it was now Greek. Forget the Galilean peasant. This was a religion for the whole imperial world—with a divine savior-god, a virgin birth, a resurrection, a Eucharist, and all the other trappings of a Graeco-Roman mystery religion. Those few who had known Jesus personally were now silenced, either by age, war or death.

And our story changes. Until now, we have been looking at historical people and historical events, sometimes shadowy to be sure, but now we turn to the far more nebulous world of those anonymous writers and propagandists who have shaped and controlled our perceptions of Jesus and his time.

14

INTRODUCTION TO THE GOSPELS

"I should not believe the Gospels except as moved by the authority of the Catholic Church."

St. Augustine

God didn't write the *Gospels*, nor did he dictate them. They were the product of four people, probably men, real names unknown, locations unknown, who felt pressed to write a coherent narrative explaining what Jesus' life had meant. They were written outside Palestine, in Greek, to describe events which none of them witnessed. They are not biographies, although it is hard not to read them as such. For many believers, the four *Gospels* are one. There have been innumerable attempts to iron out the contradictions and difficulties: modern efforts range from *The Good News Bible* which modernizes the language, to the Hollywood epic *The Passion of the Christ*.

The *New Testament* is always a best seller, but it makes difficult reading. We carry, as part of our cultural baggage, and often without realizing it, a vast amount of information about the life of Jesus. Most readers who delve into the *New Testament* read the *Gospels* sequentially, and don't see a problem. If you actually sit down and read the *Gospel of Mark*, for example, you usually don't notice the parts which are missing, because your memory fills in the cracks. But if the reader takes a particular incident and compares the four accounts, serious contradictions almost always arise.

Close comparison of written documents is the bread and butter skill of historians. Every nuance is examined, every discrepancy studied as to what it might mean, or what it might imply. As the scholars have set about their work analyzing the early Christian writings, it has become clear that each Evangelist had a definite viewpoint, and that to substantiate it, he selected evidence very carefully. Sometimes we sympathize, and other times we think that the writer stepped beyond the bounds of what we can accept. By comparison, virtually no attention has been paid to the pagan writings of the time. The cumulative effect has been to make Jesus stand out in bold relief as an even more remarkable man than he already was.

Why are there four *Gospels*? Irenaeus writing about 180 CE said there had to be four: there were four winds, four corners to the universe, and four pillars holding up the sky. Well, maybe. Probably there were four communities of believers, each with different priorities and ideas whose Gospel met the exacting standards of survival. Were there more? Oh, yes. Some scholars assert there were as many as eighty. All these others, said Irenaeus, were blasphemous, illegitimate and demonic. Some probably were. But let us be clear. Writers composed new *Gospels* because they weren't happy with the available ones. So, for example, if Luke had a copy of *Mark* and *Matthew* beside him as he wrote, he knew exactly what he was doing when he diverged from them. It was not an accident. He was unhappy with their versions of Jesus and he thought he could improve on them.

Estimates by historians of the Eastern Roman Empire suggest only 2% of adult males were literate. Most Christians were poor, so rates among Christians may well have been even lower. Texts were prohibitively expensive—one sheet of papyrus cost most of a day's wage. One guess is that by the year 100 CE, there were only about fifty Christian men who could read Biblical texts and write fluently. So Paul, Mark and Luke were very, very unusual. Given the skill with which the Evangelists (and especially Luke) tailored evidence, and the sophisticated literary devices Mark used, the authors of the four *Gospels* would be candidates for a Hellenistic chapter of MENSA. The vast majority of early Christian believers could never have read and probably did not understand the sophisticated texts which were the basis of their beliefs.

Thus the beliefs of early Christians were controlled by a very tiny and very elite group of men. They were probably much, much smarter than you and me. When they included pagan stories, recounted dubious miracles, and invented impossible quotes, they knew beyond a doubt that they were misleading the reader.

At present the *Gospels* cannot be dated with accuracy. J.A.Robinson thought they were all written before 70 CE. A few stray scholars think the *Gospel of John* came first. But as non-experts, we will adopt the current consensus: Jesus died about 28 CE, *Mark* was written 72-78, *Matthew* about 80, *Luke* and *Acts* 80-90, and *John* 95-105. For us, the important point is that none of these men could possibly have been eyewitnesses to the events they are describing. If, for example, we accept John's claim that he was an early witness to the Resurrection, we are also left to believe that he waited until he was roughly 100 before he wrote it down. Events of Jesus' childhood would have been as remote to him as the Boer War is to us. The belief that the Evangelists were eyewitnesses, or even talked to eyewitnesses, has now been abandoned by serious scholars.

It seems probable that for the first century of its existence the infant church used oral histories rather than written texts in its meetings—perhaps there were no texts available, or the rate of illiteracy made it difficult to find them, or they were impractical to use. But if there were several dozen written "gospels" floating about, it seems likely that some of them contained material that was unacceptable, such as the writings of Marcion and some of the Gnostics. So it was that about 150 CE, there emerged general agreement on *Matthew, Mark, Luke* and *John*. Two further points need to be made: first, these four were a calculated collection, not some random sample; and second, many of the alterations, additions and deletions to the original works which so aggravate the modern reader were made before these books were, well, accepted as *Gospel*. That is understandable if we remember that they were not intended as sacred works—indeed, they became increasingly regarded as divinely inspired with the passage of time.

The final selection of the Christian *Bible* is attributed to St. Jerome in 383 CE. He selected some 27 books for reading by Christians, including that truly weird mélange of pop Mithraism known as *Revelation*. From then on, this list of 27 was regarded as being of divine origin, and given the presumptuous (to Jews, at least) title of *The New Testament*.

As is the case with much else from that time, there is a critical lack of information concerning the situations under which the four *Gospels* were written. In defence of the Evangelists, however, we should bear in mind that they could not project ahead to a world in which millions of people held each of their words to be infallible. They would have followed the tradition of other ancient writers of putting suitable words and speeches into the mouth of their hero. Perhaps the most famous of these "creations" was the historian Thucydides' version of Pericles' funeral oration for the Athenian dead of the Peloponnesian War. Part of a young man's education was to memorize proverbs, maxims, and bon mots. When writing, the rule of thumb seemed to be that if the saying fit the character of a person, it could be attributed to them. There was a good deal of philosophy, biography, propaganda, prophecy, miracle stories, and even some history being written at the time, and it is only reasonable to expect that, given the dearth of factual material known about Jesus, a significant amount of other material would show up in the *Gospels*. In summary then, the Gospel authors lacked a modern critical sense—but it's hard to condemn them, for so do innumerable modern people.

So we have a conundrum. On one hand, the Evangelists were operating pretty much in darkness, and have been portrayed for two millennia as "doing their best". On the other hand, we have pretty good evidence that some of the darkness was of their own making—there were quite a few things they did not want to discuss, and did not want us to know.

We need to understand that the *Gospels* were written to edify believers—the Evangelists were quite up front about it—and to be honest they have edified a lot of believers for a very long time. They were each an attempt to publicize Paul's vision of the risen Christ whose death redeemed the world. Jesus' words, his deeds, even his location all were secondary to the main point. Further, the excessive cost of parchment meant that these accounts would be short. So explanatory content and proper chronology are missing. The resulting conclusion may not be pleasant for believers, but a lot of gospel content should be classified as just pious claptrap.

What was known of the actual life of Jesus was both embarrassing and politically dangerous. The books we know as the *Gospels* and *Acts* were intended to sanitize and obscure what happened. But as twentieth century Soviet apparatchiks discovered, total cover-ups of historical events are very difficult. Modern scholars pick at the seams, peer through the cracks, revel in inconsistency. For example, when the *Gospels* report the same event, and the wording is almost exact, scholars suspect that somebody is copying, either from one another or an earlier lost document. Thus several apparent testimonies may in fact be but one, and thus far less convincing.

Intensive study of the *Gospels* has made certain things clear. First, the four accounts abound in contradiction. Choose a significant incident—Jesus' birth, the voice from the heavens when he was baptized, his first meeting with Peter and the other fishermen, the attack on the moneychangers, the arrest, the trial, the empty tomb—in every case one or more of the Evangelists must be seriously wrong. Take a moment and read *Matthew 27*, then *Mark 15*, *Luke 24* and *John 19*, and try to decipher who the women are who mourned for Jesus. It is to be expected that four Evangelists would vary in details one from another. We don't expect uniformity in biographies of Stalin or Churchill. But then, nobody bases their lives or the fate of their eternal souls on the career of Stalin or Churchill. Any discrepancy in the *Gospels* immediately poses a serious difficulty. Christians have always proceeded on the assumption that the *Gospels* were reliable. The closer we look, the more ill-founded this confidence becomes.

Bart Ehrman, in his book *Misquoting Jesus* gives us an insider's look into the problem of accuracy in the *New Testament*, and it isn't a pretty one. No copy of a *Gospel* from earlier than 200 CE survives—so we are dealing with copies of copies of copies. Much of the copying from this early period was done by amateurs, and there were plenty of mistakes: inadvertent omissions, unintended additions, repeated words, spelling.

Evenwheretherewerenospacesbetweenwordsandnopunctuation. In addition, sometimes copyists changed the text intentionally—to eliminate contradictions, to avoid giving scriptural authority to their enemies, or to clear up confusion. John's story of the woman taken in adultery, and the last twelve verses of *Mark* are both rather long (and significant) forgeries, added by someone else later.

The problem has been understood for centuries. As early as 1707, scholars had identified a staggering 30 000 examples of variations in *New Testament* manuscripts. The list is now much longer: somewhere over 200 000 variations—more than the number of words in the *New Testament*. It's supremely ironic: a divinely inspired book with thousands upon thousands of disputed and erroneous passages. In any case, we can safely say that discovering what the Evangelists actually wrote seems completely impossible, unless there is a miraculous new find.

In addition, the *Gospels* are not good sources for the life of Jesus. The Evangelists saw events as reflected by the Resurrection ("the unearthly glare of Easter"). Consequently they were written to edify the reader, or as *John 20:10* admits, as deliberate propaganda. The Evangelists knew what they believed, and they looked for complementary evidence to support it. All that had survived of the historical Jesus was a few sayings and some disconnected events, so that Mark in particular had the task of inventing settings for these sayings, and making Jesus' life coherent. No wonder we find so much pagan legend woven into the texts. Jesus had to be shorn of the dangerous political elements, and dressed up for the respectable people of the Empire. Let us be clear on the implications of this for modern Christians: from the time of the *Gospels* on, the historical Jesus has never been crucial to the religion—it was the Son of God, with all his imported pagan imagery and idealism, that has mattered.

With an increasingly strong grip on the syntax of ancient Greek grammar, historians are able to identify "seams" where new material was grafted on to the old. When these additions and changes are studied as a group, patterns emerge, and these patterns were not accidental or random, they were deliberate and focused. Shockingly, many scholars now maintain that most of the important clams for Jesus were invented after his death: many of the miracles, his divinity, the passion and crucifixion and resurrection, and the appearances to the disciples. It's a pretty comprehensive list, and without it, there isn't much left of Christianity. On the other side, much information was intentionally left out, and this is far harder to reconstruct. Jesus was frequently accused of magic. How and when were the *Gospels* edited to remove the most dangerous accusations? We will never know.

So the *Gospels* tell us what a small group of people thought in the generation after Jesus died. To put it another way, the *Gospels* are a key to understanding the needs of the early church. And the key need of the early church was to provide a theological rationale from the existing Hebrew Scriptures to justify the new beliefs. Christian thinkers ransacked Jewish tradition looking for prefigurements of Jesus, and of course they found them by the dozen.

One of the most fascinating suggestions of how this happened was promoted by Michael Goulder, an English scholar. Like a lot of others, Goulder was convinced that the chronology of Jesus' career made no apparent sense—until he overlaid on it the liturgy of the Jewish year and its five great festivals: Pentecost, New Year, Tabernacles, Dedication and

Passover. To simplify a complex argument—Goulder suggests that the *Gospel* account of the public ministry of Jesus was organized as it was by the need to have liturgical readings in an annual cycle, based on a Christian copying of the Jewish year. The Christians had been expelled from the synagogues, and now the new religion needed a framework, and sacred readings. Where else to turn but to Hebrew Scripture? What other pattern but the Jewish year? His position is a convincing one, and it has the ring of truth. But if he is right, and he probably is, it means we no longer have any idea at all of what Jesus did, or when. Did the Sermon on the Mount precede the loaves and fishes? Did he attack the moneychangers before he met Peter? We now have no clue. Even worse is the strong suspicion that the Evangelists, and especially Mark, may have invented incidents and dialogue because they were needed to fit into the liturgical theme. So we don't know the order, and now we don't know whether it happened at all.

In summary, then, only the very naïve can regard any of the *Gospels* as any kind of historical record. (In the case of the *Gospel of John*, readers should be very, very wary.) Early Christians did not regard them as history. They felt free to adjust, elaborate, and change them since the function they served was to provide a myth. With careful observation we can see the myth growing before our eyes. The Evangelists provided a powerful story, and world-conquering theology, but they wrote with far more attention to the politics of the day and to the Hebrew Scriptures than to the life and teachings of the Galilean Jesus.

15

THE FOUR GOSPELS

Just because it's in print doesn't mean it's the Gospel.
Michael Jackson

Untold gallons of theological ink have been spent in distinguishing the purposes of the first three Gospels. In 1790, the German J.J. Griesbach noted the many resemblances between the first two *Gospels*, and suggested that the *Gospel of Matthew* was written first, and that Mark copied him. This is roundly rejected today, and virtually everyone agrees *Mark* came first—somewhere around the year 75 CE, and that Matthew copied from him. They also agree that Mark probably had both written and oral sources to guide him, but these have long been lost. Whatever these sources were, they seemed to have had nothing whatever to do with the written works of Paul. Mark's work is highly political: it was imperative not to blame the Romans for the death of Jesus, and to eliminate any suggestion of hostility to the Empire. Further, none of the Evangelists were eyewitnesses to the events they describe. Christian tradition holds that *Mark* was written in Rome, probably because the author bends over backward to accommodate the imperial power, and also because this *Gospel* is aimed squarely at pagan converts to the new religion. Still, modern scholars think Rome is unlikely, and that the Syrian city of Antioch is the better bet. *Mark* contains a number of glaring errors in the geography of Palestine, and no companion of Jesus—in fact, no Galilean—would have let these simple mistakes go unchallenged. Many of the placenames seem to have been added later, by someone else.

The *Gospel of Mark* is the earliest, the shortest, and the crudest of the four. At least forty years had elapsed since the Crucifixion, and a lot had changed: there was a new political reality (accommodation to the Roman Empire was now de rigeur), a new geographical setting (the great Hellenistic cities), and a new product to sell (the pagan god-man as saviour of the world).

The *Gospel of Mark* had two aims: to absolve the Romans of any responsibility, and to portray Jesus as a great healer and miracle worker. Mark's real enthusiasm was for Jesus the healer. Of the 661 verses of his *Gospel*, 209 deal with miracles. Jesus was portrayed as being in a life-or-death struggle with Satan for the fate of the world. To Mark, it was this healing and miraculous powers that made Jesus' life so significant.

On the other hand, Mark's portrait of Pontius Pilate as a vacilating and indecisive administrator who is bullied by the mob of Jerusalem Jews is totally at odds with what we know of the man. Mark wants us to believe that this tough, seasoned and insensitive Roman would, under pressure from the crowd, let the accused murderer Barabbas go free at Passover. Hardly. Mark reports that the presiding centurion, presumably the veteran head of a crucifixion squad, watched Jesus breathe his last, and then commented that this was truly the Son of God. Hardly. Mark's version of the Passion and Crucifixion was a wholesale whitewash of Roman power and responsibility, and he began the tradition of blaming the Jews, which the other Evangelists were to amplify.

Earlier I described Mark's *Gospel* as being crude. Nowhere is this more clear than in his treatment of the relations of Jesus and his family. Mark says a number of things that a more polished writer such as Luke would never dream of letting slip. For example, in Chapter 3, he reports that Jesus' family believed him to be insane. Surely if Mary had given birth to the Son of God, and it had been announced to her by an angel, she would quickly have scotched any talk of Jesus being mentally deranged.

So too with Jesus' occupation. Mark calls him a carpenter. In first century Galilee, that term did not carry the honourable connotation it does to us. Instead, it implied that he was a landless labourer, whose social standing was even below that of a peasant. He was not a skilled woodworker, agreed Eusibius, but a maker of "yokes and gates". Matthew, not so socially naïve as Mark, quickly amended that—Jesus was now said to be not a carpenter, but the carpenter's son. This claim had an added benefit... now Jesus had a father.

The ending of Mark's *Gospel* is almost universally agreed to be someone else's late addition, because the vocabulary and style differ from the rest of the work. In fact, even the *New Revised Standard Version* raises a red flag, and warns that verses 9–20 of Chapter 16 are probably not authentic. The original version of *Mark* ends with women looking at the empty tomb, and, remarkably, there is no claim of a resurrection. One can see why some second century believer would think it might be of benefit to add a few verses. Of course, there were thousands of manuscripts and lots of *Gospels*, and they were all copied by hand, so simple human error would provide lots of variation in wording. But we are talking here about changes which are both large scale and intentional.

Not really convinced yet? Then you need to consider the fragment of Gospel known as *Secret Mark*. It was found in a letter written by Clement of Alexandria, a respected and well-informed Christian writer of the late second century. Clement said that Jesus raised a young man from the dead in Bethany:

> "And the young man, looking at Jesus, loved him and began to beseech him that he might be with him. And after six days Jesus gave him an order; and when the evening had come, the young man went to him with a linen cloth over his naked body. And he remained with him that night, because Jesus taught him the mystery of the kingdom of God."

It should be obvious why this fragment was not included in the main text of *Mark*. Its very existence puts modern evangelicals into orbit. Either this passage implies a homoerotic relationship, or it implies that this was an initiation, involving secret truths that were not for common worshippers such as us. Clement also refers to the main text of Mark's *Gospel*, and says that Mark omitted some of Jesus' activities, especially the secret ones, and included only those "most useful for increasing the faith of those who were being instructed". In other words, we are not getting the real story. In Clement's view, the first *Gospel* was blatant propaganda.

There is further evidence of secret teachings in Chapter 8. Jesus fed four thousand followers with seven loaves and a few fish, and the leftovers came to seven basketfuls. On a separate occasion, he fed five thousand with five loaves and had twelve baskets of leftovers. In verses 18–21, he is clearly frustrated with his disciples for not understanding the numerological significance of these numbers. Whatever the secret teachings about these numbers were, they have long been lost. Like the disciples, we don't get it either. But these hidden meanings were, to Jesus, an important part of his message.

Overall then, *Mark* defined the tone for what was to follow. The other Evangelists differed occasionally in chronology and location, and each clearly had a different focus, but it certainly seems that when they sat down to write, they had a copy of the *Gospel of Mark* close to hand.

The author of *Matthew* set out to produce a Gospel that was more acceptable for a Jewish Christian audience, and so it is more theologically sophisticated. He used his copy of *Mark*, and part of his purpose was spin control, correcting some of Mark's obvious gaffes. Matthew's *Gospel* seems to have been amended far less than those of John or Mark. It may well be a product of one of those thousands of Jews and Jewish Christians who fled to Alexandria during and after the Roman siege of Jerusalem, and was probably written 80-90 CE. Matthew's story of the Holy Family's flight into Egypt to escape the murderous wrath of Herod is clearly invented, but it would have been a tale with deep resonance for a community of refugees who had just experienced a similar flight.

More than any other *Gospel*, *Matthew* is loaded down with *Old Testament* prefigurements, prophecies, and references. The readers were expected to be somewhat familiar with these. Jesus was the new Moses. The Twelve Apostles were the Twelve Tribes. The Sermon on the Mount echoed the commandments on Mt. Sinai. Jesus had come to fulfill Scriptural law. *Matthew's* treatment of the Jewish Law is ambiguous at best. He claims enormous respect for the *Torah*, and has Jesus say that not one jot or tittle may be changed.

But a quick read of Chapter 5 has Jesus saying over and over "You have heard it said...(in the Law) ...but I say ..." followed by advice that contradicts the Law. Matthew is writing for a tough and critical audience, and he is trying very hard to make the new religion seem to be the old one.

His use of Jewish texts is frequently suspect. Did David, Isaiah, and Jeremiah actually prophesy specific events in the life of Jesus, or was the account of Jesus' life tailored to fit what they had said? Similarly, it would be fascinating to know how much of *Matthew* was accepted as literally true by the readers of his time, and how much would have been seen as symbolic or coded.

The birth and childhood of Jesus had been totally ignored by *Mark*, but there must have been some significant criticism of Jesus' family background, probably that he was illegitimate, because *Matthew* takes great pains to establish a long Jewish lineage for Jesus, back as far as King David himself. *Matthew* also is the first to mention Joseph, and a lot of modern commentators think the Evangelist invented him in order to remove the taint of scandal from Jesus' birth. Matthew found in the *Book of Isaiah* the quote which he rendered in Greek as "Behold, a virgin shall conceive" (which in Hebrew was actually "Behold, a young woman shall conceive"). As we have seen, the Greeks were quite familiar with the claim of a virgin birth, and so despite the long genealogy, Joseph was shunted aside as biological parent in favour of God Himself.

Similarly, it now seems that Matthew was not averse to making up material which he then attributed to Jesus. Meier thinks Matthew invented several of the beatitudes. Spong says Matthew wrote most of the Sermon on the Mount. Grant wonders why Jesus kept warning his disciples not to talk about the miracles, and further wonders if maybe that was because they didn't happen. Of the four *Gospels*, only *Matthew* discussed Herod's mass infanticide. If it had happened, the historian Josephus would have been only too happy to tell us, but he is silent. The Golden Rule cited in *Matthew* was first formulated by Confucius, and later by the Rabbi Hillel.

Matthew also apparently decided to expand on the Resurrection story. Remember, Mark had ended his *Gospel* with the highly dubious story of Jesus' burial, and the discovery by the women of the empty tomb. Matthew apparently found that a bit hollow, so he added some telling details—Jesus appeared to and spoke to the women, and set up a meeting with his disciples back in the safety of the Galilean hills. Matthew adds that the Roman guards who saw all this were bribed by the Jews to keep quiet about it. None of this seems very convincing to the modern reader.

In summary, *Matthew* has to be read carefully if we are interested in what really happened. He had read *Mark*, and realized that damage control was in order, especially with those Christians who came from a Jewish background. Despite his flaws, however, Matthew was probably the most reliable of the Evangelists, especially when contrasted with the smooth propaganda of Luke.

The *Gospel of Luke* was written about sixty years after the Crucifixion. In a world with almost no written records, and short lifespans, that represented three full generations. There is general agreement that the author of *Luke* was educated and well-travelled, and he probably had access to many documents now lost. Certainly he had access to *Mark* and to *Matthew*. There are suggestions that the *Gospel of Luke* was altered by later hands to better fit with the more famous *Gospel of Matthew*. Luke himself may have disagreed with those changes. On a number of occasions, Matthew changed the wording of *Mark* to better suit his conservative Jewish audience. Luke invariably sided with Mark and against Matthew, using the less Jewish version. He saw his target audience as those Christians who had recently converted from paganism, and he makes this clear throughout the work.

Like Matthew, however, Luke wrote to convince readers that Jesus fulfilled all the promises of the *Torah*—that he was indeed the Messiah. His writing shows heavy influence from the *Book of Deuteronomy*. It is reflected in those stories which are unique to him. He too makes occasional references to the prophets, but the reader feels his heart was not really in it.

Luke was certainly no fan of the traditionalist James the Just, because his hero was Paul. He was convinced that Paul had understood Jesus, whereas the other disciples had not. In Luke's hands, the Apostles, and especially Peter, were made to look stupid and even cowardly. They were unworthy of the Messiah. Luke pushes them off to the side to make room for the star—Paul of Tarsus. Of course, even Paul had left the stage some twenty years before Luke wrote, and the fiery apocalypse which both Jesus and Paul had predicted had not arrived. Luke saw his role as smoothing all this out, papering over the problems, producing a coherent chronology, and making early Christians look like solid Roman citizens. He did all this with remarkable elegance. He was a literary genius.

Besides the *Gospel*, Luke was also the author of *The Acts of the Apostles*, which continued the story of Christian origins, especially as carried on by Paul. But before we look at Acts, or even the *Gospel of John*, we need to take a little side trip with historians and theologians as our tour guides. The story goes like this. Both *Matthew* and *Luke* owe a lot of their content to *Mark*, but when all these *Gospels* are taken apart and closely compared, it becomes plain that those segments in *Matthew* and *Luke* which are not associated with *Mark* are also very similar. In fact, they are so alike in content and wording that German scholars decided that Matthew and Luke must have been using yet another source, which they dubbed "*Q.*"

A scholastic cottage industry has sprung up attempting to verify and reconstruct the *"Q" Gospel*. This document was in existence shortly after the time of Jesus, probably 45-55 CE, and seems to have been widely circulated. There may have been oral and written variants, and some are convinced that they can discern an evolution in ideas—stages in the development of *Q*. It is full of aphorisms, sayings and advice, as well as apocalyptic and prophetic admonitions about the imminent end of the world.

Why does all this matter? Because major parts of what we consider Christianity are just not there: no baptism, no "Son of Man", no claims of divinity, no apostles, no conflict with authority, no Last Supper, no trial, no Crucifixion, no Resurrection. The first believers, those who used *Q*, apparently did not need the Redeemer of Paul or the miracle worker of *Mark*. They were satisfied with the ethical sayings of Jesus. It just doesn't seem very likely that all this is an accident.

Well then, just what was in *Q*? It probably was not a chronology of Jesus' life, but rather a disconnected series of short sayings and teachings. It shows more interest in Jesus' words than in his deeds, leading the skeptic to wonder how many of the deeds recounted in the other four *Gospels* were real. Jesus the teacher offers wisdom and spiritual guidance—we are told to feed the hungry, and Jesus the prophet preaches the Kingdom of God and announces the imminent end of the world, although even this may only have been in the later version of *Q*. *Matthew*, *Luke* and even *Mark* all used *Q*, but once *Mark* appeared, the *Q Gospel* faded into obscurity. It bears mentioning that these earliest followers of Jesus were not Christians. They did not see Jesus as the Messiah, so he was not the Christ.

Q shows that the Jesus movement was heavily involved in mythmaking: it kept adding layers and sayings to the words and deeds of Jesus. This may be hard to accept, but it means that words continued to be ascribed to Jesus for many years after his death. Moreover, these words became more forceful and imperative as the social tensions mounted.

The *Q Gospel* would have been theological dynamite if anyone had ever found a copy. None has ever surfaced. Most traditional Christians who have heard of it have ignored its implications. Some deny it ever existed. The notion that Jesus was not persecuted, nor tried, nor crucified, and therefore did not rise from the dead, was not to be contemplated. The very idea that the heroic early Christians, maybe the Evangelists, made all this up, was unthinkable. So it was back to business as usual for a while...until the discovery of the *Gospel of Thomas*.

The fourth of the mainstream *Gospels*, both in time and in Biblical sequence, was attributed to "John". The *Gospel of John* is significantly different from the three "synoptic" *Gospels*. In broad terms, liberal Christians have preferred the synoptics, and evangelicals prefer *John*. Its beginning is well-known, a fragment of Greek (probably Mithraic) poetry which starts

> "In the beginning was the Word and the Word was with God and the Word was God. He was in the beginning with God; all things were made through Him, and without Him was not anything

made that was made. In Him was life, and the life was the light of men. The light shines in the darkness, and the darkness has not overcome it…"

This section is very familiar to most of us: it is believed by millions and understood by no one. "Word" is a very inexact translation for the Greek term Logos, which might better be rendered as Reason. So the fourth *Gospel* is the story of Reason coming to earth in human form, and living in Galilee among people who rejected this divine truth. The concept of Logos was unknown to the Jews, it was a Mithraic idea. Mithra was "the Light of the World", and Mitha's followers were "the Children of Light". The Logos pre-existed the earth, and as a mediator between the High God and his creation, was divine.

There was no question at all that in *John*, Jesus was the Son of God. The real question seemed to be "Was he human?" Jesus is referred to in *John* by a series of terms and analogies: the Vine, the Light, the Life, The Way, the Good Shepherd, and so on. Most of these were pagan terms used to describe Mithras, Horus, or Dionysos. *John* adopted the pagan dichotomy so prevalent at the time: life was a cosmic struggle between good and evil, between light and dark, between the oppressed minority and the big bad world. Thus *John* went much further than the other *Gospels* in incorporating Greek pagan ideas into mainstream Christianity. These ideas had nothing at all to do with the original teachings of Jesus, but they were wildly popular and they were unstoppable. *John's* message was appealing to many new Christians, and his *Gospel* and its paradoxical message seemed to overcome initial suspicions and spread quickly. Many scholars are convinced that the *Gospel of John*, in its current form, has been heavily edited to make it less pagan, and that all of Chapter 21 is the work of someone else.

The *Gospel of John*, then, is even less biographical than the other three. It is, for the historian, completely untrustworthy. As Weddig Fricke says, it is completely out of the question that any saying of Jesus found in *John* was ever said by him. Marcus Borg, as a professional Christian theologian, prefers to dance around it, and words it more delicately: the contrast between *John* and the others is so great that "one of them must be non-historical". For example, John put the attack on the money-changers in the Temple at the beginning of Jesus' ministry, the others put it near the end. If *John* is right, then to some degree Jesus' message of peace was in doubt from the very beginning.

Early churchmen were not big fans of *John*: his theology made him suspect for most of the second century. His portrayal of Jesus was too superhuman, too pagan, too calculated. However, Origen, the third century intellectual and "Father of the Church", was a great admirer of *John*. When he was pressed on *John*'s reliability, he is reported to have said that while *John* may not have always told the truth literally, he always told the truth spiritually. This sounds quite profound, but it really means that *John* tells the reader what the reader wants to hear. Incidentally, Origen castrated himself (certainly the only 'Father of the Church' in that category) and later was accused of heresy. So perhaps we should not lean on him too heavily.

Because the *Gospel of John* was written so late, we should expect to see a more sophisticated development of theological ideas, and so we do. *Mark* and then *Matthew* have Jesus' last words as "My God, my God, why have you forsaken me?" *Luke* quotes him as saying "Father, into thy hands I commend my spirit" and *John* alters this to a triumphant "It is finished!"

In a similar fashion, there are far fewer miracles. Jesus was no humble carpenter here; he undergoes no baptism of repentance, and has no religious crisis. We should assume that the charges of magical practices leveled against Jesus over the intervening time led *John* to limit the episodes of miraculous healing. In fact, *John* shows very little interest in the Galilean years, and does not mention the Sermon on the Mount at all.

The fourth *Gospel* is unique in that it alone mentions the character known as "The Beloved Disciple" (sometimes rendered more racily as "the disciple whom Jesus loved."). The earlier *Gospels* had established Jesus' inner group as consisting of Peter, and the brothers James and John the sons of Zebedee. The Beloved Disciple character was invented by John to represent his own views, and to lend credence to his Gospel, because *John 21* makes it clear that the unnamed Beloved Disciple was in fact John the Gospel writer himself. This Beloved Disciple kept popping up at key moments: leaning on Jesus at the Last Supper, standing with the women of Jerusalem at the foot of the cross, and racing Peter to the empty tomb on Easter. The Beloved Disciple even took Mary into his home and cared for her after Jesus' death, despite the fact that, as we have seen, Mary had several surviving biological sons. To further boost the prestige of the Beloved Disciple, the chief of the apostles, Peter, was portrayed as a thick-headed bumbler, a first century Dagwood Bumstead. But if John the Evangelist personally witnessed the career of Jesus, and this *Gospel* was produced later than the others, John must have been very old when he took up writing. Legend has it that he composed his *Gospel* while living in a cave overlooking the sea on the Aegean island of Patmos. It had a great view, but one would not think it was otherwise a very good location for a centenarian.

Finally, John was the only Evangelist to claim that a belief in Jesus was essential to salvation. Jesus, the Son of God, was sent to the world to save it, and if we mortals believe in him, we will not perish, instead we will have eternal life. On the face of it, this statement is astounding: no belief—no salvation. Goodbye Jews and pagans. Of all the concepts in the *Bible*, this is the most arrogant, and has turned out to be the most damaging for the world. It probably was not intended as anti-semitic, but over the past two millennia it has been used by Christians against a wide variety of foes, with often fatal results. Forcible conversions, pogroms, the Crusades, and the Inquisition all can trace their dubious inheritance to the *Gospel of John*. For two decades, no televised American sporting event was complete without the appearance on camera of a rainbow-wigged gentleman bearing a sign urging us to consult *John 3:16*. Christianity went on to adopt some very strange concepts: the Virgin Birth, the Ascension, the Immaculate Conception, the Trinity, the Nicene Creed, transubstantiation, and more. And the *Gospel of John* was right there, providing the God-given authority for all this rigid belief.

So what was the purpose of the *Gospel of John*? The latest theory, advanced by the Gnostic scholar Elaine Pagels, is that John may have been written as a rebuttal to the *Gospel of Thomas*. The apocryphal work known as *Thomas* suggested that a person should seek to know God by looking into themselves, and their own spark of divinity. This was too much for John, and too much apparently for most believers. John may in fact have thought that the disciple known as Doubting Thomas authored that gospel, for he clearly disapproves of him. We will later look more closely at *Thomas*, but for now it needs to be stressed that the *Gospel of John* took Christianity down one road, the road that led to literalism and a militant orthodoxy, when in reality several other roads were available.

At first glance, then, early Christianity seems to be well-documented. In addition to the Gospels, there is a series of letters by Paul, one of the earliest converts. The *Acts of the Apostles* ought to be the icing on the cake—an account of the founding of the earliest Christian communities. But on examination, it turns out to be very unreliable for the same reason the *Gospels* were—it was all edited and tailored by anonymous hands to fit the needs of the time. Most experts believe the author of *Luke* also wrote *Acts* shortly thereafter, with the intent that it should be read alongside the *Gospels* at public services. Some authorities date it much later.

The public acrimony between the Christians in Antioch spearheaded by Paul and those in Jerusalem led by Peter and James the Just must have been well known. *Luke* set out to minimize the rivalry, and to pretend that the conflict had been settled in Paul's favour. After the destruction of Jerusalem, only Paul's faction was left standing, so *Acts*, and Christian history ever since, can claim it was the will of God. Whatever is, is right.

For sheer mystery and the suggestion of skullduggery, there is nothing in the *New Testament* to compare to the story of Ananias and Sapphira as recounted in *Acts 4* and 5. The surviving disciples, presumably mindful of Jesus' warnings that the world was about to end, adopted a communal approach to property. They lived by begging from the more prosperous, as Jesus had. Anyone who owned land or a house was to sell it and give the proceeds to the apostles. A believer named Ananias conspired with his wife Sapphira to give only some of the proceeds of their property sale to Peter. Peter asked where the rest of the money was, and accused Ananias of lying. Ananais immediately fell down dead. He was hastily buried—so hastily, in fact, that nobody thought to tell his wife. When she appeared, she was immediately grilled by Peter as to the sale price, but she stuck by her husband's version, and she too fell down and died.

Readers have had a lot of difficulty with this incident. What are the chances of two identical sudden deaths? Was there foul play involved? If the early church believed so strongly in communal sharing, why is this the only mention of it? Why did the practice disappear so quickly? *Acts 5:11* says, "And great fear seized the whole church and all who heard of these things." Yes, indeed.

While the first half of *Acts* deals with how Jesus' followers coped with his death, the key Jerusalem Christians disappear without a trace about half way through. We know from other sources that James the Just and James the son of Zebedee died or were murdered as a result of Sadducee intrigues. The fates of Peter and of Mary the mother of Jesus are less certain. Tradition claims that Peter went to Rome, but in all likelihood he perished in Jerusalem, either as a victim of the uprising of 44 CE, or in the Jewish War of 66-70 if he had lived that long. All this was of little interest to the author of *Acts*, for his focus was on Paul. In fact, there are eerie parallels between the *Gospels*' life of Jesus, and *Luke's* account of the life of Paul: the crowds of new converts, the unpleasant journey to Jerusalem, the enmity of the Jewish mobs, false accusations, trials, heroic faith, and so on. Maybe it's all just coincidence—but given the skill and smoothness with which *Luke* manipulated Hebrew sources, we ought not put a lot of trust that all the events described in *Acts* ever happened. And so it is to Paul, the Hellenizing hero of the early church, to whom we now turn.

16

PAUL:
THE INVENTION OF A NEW GREEK RELIGION

"Saul, Saul, why do you persecute me?"

Acts 9:4

Saul of Tarsus, known to succeeding generations as St. Paul, was the most remarkable man of a very remarkable age. He was certainly no Adonis. He was described as being short with crooked legs, and having a stocky body, thin hair but bushy eyebrows, and a hooked nose. All in all, his description resembles that other famous "gadfly on the body of the state", Socrates of Athens. The imagination of Paul transformed a minor political event, namely the death of Jesus, into one of cosmic religious significance. Paul did not convert to Christianity. He couldn't. It didn't exist. Paul invented it. His Christ did not come from the Jesus of history, but was instead an amalgam of Greek saviour-gods. Nevertheless, Paul carried on his life in the unshakable belief that Christ was alive and acting through him…much in the style of a Hindu avatar.

His conversion on the road to Damascus probably came within five years of Jesus' death. He began to evangelize immediately, preaching about the resurrected Jesus whom he thought he had met. Paul was by the standards of the day a prolific letter writer. Of the *Epistles* credited to him, we now believe some were genuinely his work, some probably were dictated to a secretary, some were forgeries, and others were lost. He also was the alleged author of a letter to the Roman writer Seneca, and a third letter to the Corinthians, but these are rejected as forgeries. Most of his written work seems to date from 45-60 CE, and thus it predates all the *Gospels*, and his writing came well before the Jewish War which flared up in 66 CE. The earliest actual copies of Paul's writings date to about 200 CE, some 150 years after he wrote them. As with other ancient works, we need to be aware of the vast scope for both copying errors and more intentional changes to the texts.

He was from a family of Pharisees who lived in Tarsus, a city in what is now southeastern Turkey. Tarsus was a centre of education and philosophy, and the Greek geographer Strabo claimed that it rivaled Athens and Alexandria for learning. It was a hotbed of Mithraic culture, and Paul, whether knowingly or not, absorbed much of it—far more of it than did his contemporary Apollonius. Ostensibly a Jew, Paul was in reality a Greek through and through: his ideas were deeply infused with Platonism, Mithraism, and Dionysianism. Paul decided to be a rabbi, and so he moved to Jerusalem about the year 30 CE to study under the great Jewish thinker Gamaliel.

But Paul was a man of strong opinions, and was constantly attracted to controversy, and possibly to violence. He was soon employed by the high priest as a member of the Temple guard. So it was that he became involved in the efforts by the Sadducees to stamp out these new and dangerous ideas promoted by the followers of Jesus. He attended the stoning of Stephen, the first Christian martyr. Some think he supervised it, some think he held the coats of those who threw the stones. Whatever his role, he was deeply compromised: twenty years later prominent people in Jerusalem were still angry at his collaboration with the high priest and with the Romans. But if he was involved in the death of Stephen, is it possible he could also have been a participant in the death of Jesus just a few years before? Did he actually know Jesus, and find it inadvisable to mention it?

Jesus had been dead only a few years, the persecution of Christians by Jewish authorities continued apace, and so Paul was sent by the Jerusalem authorities to Damascus to enforce Jewish orthodoxy there. While on the road, he heard a voice, saw a bright light, and was knocked to the ground by a force that he was convinced was Jesus. Paul converted instantly from prosecutor to advocate. This kind of event strikes us as odd, but in the religious hysteria of the first century, meeting a god on the road was not all that unusual. What was unusual was Paul's force of character.

Paul was able to change his beliefs instantly, but not his personality. He continued on to Damascus, and began to preach there, but his listeners were infuriated, and he had to flee. It was a pattern that was repeated over and over. He provoked riots in Ephesus. He spent time in prison. He was scourged five times. He was beaten with sticks three times. He was attacked with stones. There were scuffles, arrests, escapes, angry citizens. Paul had appointed himself the instrument of an angry God, threatening punishment to a corrupt world. His listeners were horrified, and you would be too. Paul, the religious genius, was really, really offensive.

Modern Jewish scholars are relatively less impressed by Paul than traditional Christian theologians have been. When they look at the events of the time, they put particular stress on the degree to which Paul was despised by the Jerusalem Christians. He was extremely unpopular with Jews as well.

Some have suggested that the Teacher of Righteousness cited in the *Dead Sea Scrolls* is in fact James the Just; and the Spouter of Lies is no other than Paul. Paul evidently did not believe he needed the approval of James or Peter, because his personal vision of Christ was sufficient. It has now become clear that the purpose of many of his letters was to undermine the authority of James, the brother of Jesus.

The end seemed to come during an ill-advised return to Jerusalem when Paul appeared in the Temple and caused a riot. He was being beaten, but was rescued and then arrested by Roman officials. The imperial authorities had had enough, and Paul had been abandoned by his fellow-Christians, so he was bundled off to Rome for trial. Probably he was the first Christian to appear before the Emperor. Paul's end is unknown. Pious Christian stories suggest that he was tried, but talked his way to an acquittal. Perhaps he was martyred. We have no evidence, so we just don't know. Tantalizingly, Luke dedicates the *Acts of the Apostles* to "most excellent Theophilus", who was likely a highly placed Roman official who knew of Paul's fate. One wonders what Paul's final thoughts were. His views provoked riots and official wrath, but as a Roman citizen and political conservative, he believed Roman institutions would go on forever. Was he at all able to foresee the disaster that was about to befall Jerusalem?

It was left to Luke in the *Acts of the Apostles* to clean up this mess. Luke dutifully presented Paul as tolerant and sensible, the spokesman for a peaceful movement, while knowing he was nothing of the kind. Luke was working mightily to make Christianity respectable. It is a measure of his genius that he succeeded, but we need to recognize that it was a triumph of the propagandist's art.

Paul's *Epistles* are astonishing for their lack of detail about Jesus' life. Certainly the absence of historical references to the founder of his religion should set off alarm bells in the minds of most people. He had lived in Jerusalem either during the Crucifixion, or shortly afterward. He knew Jesus' brother. He met Peter, both in Jerusalem and Antioch. So he was familiar with the neighbourhood, the people, the politics, and with the theology. He knew important aspects of Jesus' life. There are two possibilities, and both have disturbing implications for believers. One is that, at the time Paul wrote, much of what the *Gospels* claim had not been made up yet. The second is that Paul didn't care at all. Both are true.

It is what Paul doesn't say that is most remarkable. In his letters, roughly 100 pages in length, Paul never mentions Jesus' birth, his miracles, his friends, John the Baptist, Judas, Nazareth, the Sermon on the Mount, the Lord's Prayer, the Passion, or the clashes with the Romans. Clearly he had not heard the Bethlehem story: Jesus was "born of a woman" (unnamed), and "descended from David according to the flesh." In describing himself in the *Gospels*, Jesus used the term Son of Man 70 times. Paul didn't use it once. Paul used the name Jesus 15 times, and the term Christ 378 times.

To Paul, Jesus was not a person, but an idea: a pre-existent supernatural being (straight out of Mithraic theology like the Logos of John), who had been sent into the world to save it. The human part of Jesus was weak, and his career was obscure—he was hardly human at all—so why should we care about his birth? The important thing was that the evil supernatural powers which dominated the cosmos were responsible for Jesus' death. Certainly not the Romans.

But Jesus had risen and conquered death, and a major proof of this was that he had appeared to Paul on the road to Damascus. As time passed, Paul's ego grew, and soon he was claiming, on the basis of that mystical experience, to have authority equal to that of Peter and the other apostles. James the Just tried to rein him in, but Paul was irrepressible. Still, it forces modern believers to confront some hard questions. If the teachings and life of Jesus didn't matter to Paul, should they matter to us? Are Christians still willing to countenance the radical change in the direction of their religion that resulted from whatever happened on the road to Damascus? The plain fact is that the historical Jesus was now irrelevant. The only parts of his life that mattered to Paul were his death, Resurrection and Ascension—and we have seen how factually dubious they were. No wonder James the Just, in hearing Paul's theories, lost his cool.

Paul's lack of information about the biography of his Saviour is matched by his apparent ignorance of what Jesus taught. It is unlikely he was acquainted with the Lord's Prayer. He does not refer to the teachings of Jesus to authenticate his own views. Possibly he was embarrassed by Jesus' deep Jewishness, or perhaps by Jesus' adoption of the anti-authoritarian lifestyle of the Cynics, hence Paul thought it better to omit the details.

Paul argued that salvation had been offered, and that the Jews had declined. Now it was to be offered to Gentiles. (Why are they always called Gentiles, rather than pagans?) The Jews had lost their position as Chosen People. No need for a convert to undergo circumcision or dietary inconvenience: a baptism of water, easily understood by both Jew and pagan, would now suffice. Paul had assimilated Jesus into a dramatic pagan myth, and thereby expanded a minor Jewish sect into a world religion. In his writings, it was all there: Mithraism, Dionysian pessimism, Gnosticism, sacramentalism, magic, even polytheism (see *1 Cor 8:5*), and it was all accessible and written in Koine Greek.

One of Paul's doctrines, his pessimistic view of the nature of man, requires additional comment. Jesus had said nothing about such ideas as Original Sin or the Fall of Adam. Nor had the great Hebrew prophets held such a dim view of humanity. But the *Epistle to the Romans* outlines Paul's theories: all humans are sinners, and Christ had to die to save us. This Orphic dogma is so much a part of modern culture that it is difficult for us to see what a barbaric idea it really is. The German philosopher Nietzsche was right in calling Paul "a morbid crank". Paul succeeded in overlaying the simple ethics of Jesus with a universal gloom. Without Christ, he said, we are doomed to punishment for something we didn't do. In the centuries that followed, this distrust of human willpower was to become the dominant view of humanity in the West.

And this is the crunch. Christians since Paul have been committed to his approach. Some early followers of Jesus, such as Montanus, claimed direct revelation from God, but these claims were roundly rejected. Nevertheless, Paul's revelation has been accepted as totally reliable. Because his *Epistles* were so early, and so widely disseminated, other *New Testament* works were probably written or amended to mesh with his views. Jesus, the man in whose name these ideas were advanced, has been reduced to a shadowy figure peering over Paul's shoulder, presumably beaming approval.

When people look at the worship of Dionysos, Horus, Mithra and others, they tend to dismiss them as viable religions because they were mythological in character. Christianity has felt superior to them, because it claimed to be historically based. That claim is fraudulent, and we can now see that it has been fraudulent since the very beginning. Had it not been for the energy and fierceness of Paul, Christianity would not exist- probably not even the *Gospels* would have survived. But the religion of Jesus has paid a terrible price for its success.

Despite the soothing version of events in the *Acts of the Apostles*, there rapidly developed mutual hostility between the two branches of the early church. Paul's letters attacked unnamed rivals who preach "another Jesus". These rivals were in fact Jesus' surviving friends and family. The Jerusalem branch of the infant church was smaller, fiercely Jewish, and had more authority. It was led by James the brother of Jesus, by Peter, Jesus' chief lieutenant, and by someone named Cephas (which possibly was another alias for Simon Peter.) James in particular was not pleased with the news he heard from the city of Antioch. He sent "certain individuals" to Antioch and ordered Paul and Barnabas to report to Jerusalem.

Paul had earlier tried his hand at converting Jews, but had little luck. Most Jews were not buying the idea of a failed criminal as the Messiah. So Paul had turned to the conversion of Greek pagans, where he began to have phenomenal success. However, there was a serious problem—in fact, two problems. If the converts were to obey the Jewish Law, they had to obey the Jewish dietary restrictions, and that meant in particular not eating meat from animals that had been sacrificed at pagan altars. This was the chief source of cheap protein for the poor in the great cities, and so its loss was a considerable hardship.

Even more serious was the Law's demand that men be circumcised. Few adult men were interested in this kind of voluntary pain to their private parts. Worse, in a circumcision, the Jewish official (the mohel) cut off the outer foreskin with a metal knife, then ripped the inner lining with a thumbnail and index finger, and finally had to take the penis into his mouth to suck the blood (of which there was a lot) from the wound. No wonder pagan men were reluctant. The homophobic Paul, who made his views clear in both

Romans and *1 Corinthians*, decided that his religion could do without it. James the Just thought otherwise.

The Council of Jerusalem was probably less glamourous than its description in *Acts 15*. Paul and Barnabas put their case, and Peter also spoke, and then James the Just announced how it would be. He was willing to let converted pagans go uncircumcised; but there would be no compromise on the dietary question. The parting was apparently not amicable. James and the Jerusalem party did not trust Paul and Barnabas, for they not only sent oral instructions with them back to Antioch, but also a letter to ensure that their will was made known. But we are getting Paul's version, and only some of that. Given his personality, we know that he would have been very angry. Is it possible that the chastisement at the hands of James the Just was one of the reasons Paul made no comments on the life of Jesus?

But within a generation the Jewish War and the destruction of Jerusalem changed everything. It became imperative for Christians to cut all ties with the treasonous Jews. Jesus was born a Jew, true, but it was now important to show that he wasn't really one of them. He was to be seen as a loyal citizen of the Empire, not a rebel. Christian theology was turned on its head. The doctrines which had been condemned in Jerusalem were now in the ascendant. The party of Paul was triumphant, and the ideas of James the Just were consigned to obscurity.

Of the 27 books of the *New Testament*, 4 are *Gospels*, and the rest are letters, mostly by Paul. Paul's views dominate the *New Testament*, and therefore dominate Christianity. Paul's *Epistles* make difficult reading today, and must have been even more so when they were written, before the *Gospels* existed to provide a framework. Of the 13 Pauline letters, only 7 are now deemed authentic. The first *Epistle* to the

Thessalonians is considered the oldest Christian written work, dating to about 50 CE. The inauthentic 6 are jointly known as the Pastorals (because we wouldn't want to admit the *Bible* contains divinely inspired forgeries), and they tend to deal with church organization, and to rail against heretics, especially Gnostics.

In fairness, it should be pointed out that other books of the *New Testament*, much like the *Epistles* of Paul, also seem ignorant of the life and the teachings of Jesus. They too stress theology, and are light on the biographical details of the founder of their religion. Maybe looking at the big picture was the literary style of the time.

In addition to winning the battle over circumcision and diet, Paul's approach to Christianity was successful in another area—he made it a religion of city folk. Jesus had been a country boy. The sophisticates of Jerusalem made fun of his friends' Galilean background and accent. His preaching had been far more successful in the countryside and its villages than it was in Jerusalem. Jesus' stories and parables had rural themes: sowing crops, pulling weeds, the harvest.

Paul, on the other hand, was traveled, experienced, urban, fully at home in the Greek world. He was a Roman citizen, and proud of it. He loved cities, especially the big seaports of the eastern Mediterranean. He claimed to be a tentmaker. His connections with the great Temple may have been useful. Estimates are that the priests in Jerusalem were killing approximately 20,000 sheep a year on behalf of worshippers. A recent biography of Paul by A.N.Wilson suggests that Paul may have traded in sheepskins, or sewed the tanned skins together into large tents, which would then be sold to the Roman army.

Paul was familiar with the great pagan religions. He came from Tarsus, the Mithraic center of the region. He spent a lot of time in Antioch, the home of Adonis. He preached and converted in Corinth, a city dominated by the worship of Dionysos. He seemed to be less successful in Ephesus, the home of Cybele and Attis. He did not spend time in the countryside—at least he doesn't speak of it. As a result, Paul's new religion was a pastiche of pagan ideas, ideas which proved popular in the great Hellenistic cities of the Empire. Christianity became urban, closely tied to the Graeco-Roman view of the world. Paul didn't so much convert Romans into Christians, instead he made Christians into Romans.

To what degree then was Paul a pagan? Certainly we can say with Harpur that the Christ of Paul, whoever he was, was not Jesus of Nazareth. Paul's religion was a multiethnic mix of Greek and Jewish ideas, with the Greek predominating. It was the pagan side that initiated the idea of ecstatic conversion and personal transformation. Paul also used the language of the mystery religions, although this has been slow in coming to light because of bad (maybe intentionally bad) translations from the Greek. In *I Corinthians*, Paul complains that his converts were attending both Christian services and pagan rites indiscriminately. Probably they were very similar. We also know that some believers in both Corinth and Galatia were very upset with his ideas, but we don't know the specifics of their grievances. The letters of Paul are full of complaints about "false teachers," whose success forced Paul to write back and intervene. Backsliders, Judaizers, Gnostics, mystics—they all thought they were the heirs of Jesus, and Paul told them all that they were wrong.

A number of modern commentators have looked at Paul as a Gnostic. We will consider Gnostic beliefs in some detail later, but for now let us define a Gnostic as one who has had a transcendental experience resulting in secret knowledge. By this definition, Paul was a Gnostic, and so were most other early Christians. So for that matter was Jesus. Some of Paul's writing is clearly Gnostic: he said he was taken up to the third heaven and had a secret vision. He believed that a divine saviour came to earth from a pre-existence in heaven to save mankind from demonic forces, and then returned to heaven. He was uninterested in external rules, one of the sure marks of the Gnostic. On the other hand, many of the *Epistles* attributed to him attack Gnostic beliefs, but as we have seen, he probably wasn't the author of those letters. Later Gnostics included Paul as one of their number, claiming secret teachings from him. Even Clement, an early bishop of Rome, attacked Paul as a heretic because of his ideas, and because he thought the conversion on the road to Damascus was suspicious and unreliable.

Paul's dim view of women is well known. Women were neither to preach nor to teach. Sex, even within marriage, was deeply suspicious. Physical desire was regrettable, virginity was best, marriage was for weaklings. If you must marry, live as celibately as possible. Ehrman protests that Paul probably didn't write the most misogynistic sections of *1 Corinthians*, but it hardly matters.

Women were the mainstay of the early church, as they are of the church today. In the early years they were easier to convert than men because they didn't face the difficult issue of circumcision. They played a prominent part in the early growth of Christianity. They were frequently among the persecuted because of their public defiance. But as the church grew, it became ever more sexist. Mary Magdalene went from close companion to whore, and the role of ordinary women in church affairs was drastically reduced. Not all of this was Paul's fault, of course. After all, it doesn't seem that either Jesus or James the Just had married. It was an age when asceticism was sweeping through all the Eastern cults, and virginity, whether in the service of Apollo, Cybele, or Christ, was the new measure of sanctity. Women were especially restricted from becoming priestesses, so as not to become unsuitable role models for young girls. Women were welcome, but they had their place. Certainly part of the reason for the triumph of Christianity over more egalitarian sects such as that of Isis, was the resolute masculinity of the Christian sect.

The most fundamental of all Paul's beliefs was that the world was about to end. Jesus' return was imminent. Paul told the Thessalonians that it would happen in the lifetime of his listeners. Later he backed off a bit, saying several conditions had to be met. The same claims had been made in the *Gospels* and attributed to Jesus, so we should assume these notions were commonly held at the time, and were a bit overheated. But the imminent end of the world had an impact on the way Paul advised people to live. Every person should be willingly subject to the governing authorities. Slaves should obey their masters. Women should be silent and submissive.

Apocalyptic beliefs do not appeal to the learned or the comfortable—they have too much to lose. They do appeal to the poor, the dispossessed, the marginalized. Paul noticed that: he remarked in *I Corinthians* that "...not many wise...not many noble..." were to be found in his churches. But time changes things. With the growth of Christianity came comfort and power, and the frantic warnings of Jesus and Paul that the world was about to end got pushed off to a rear pew. The big churches prefer not to discuss it any more, but these admonitions, updated for our century, remain a powerful focal point for smaller, fiercer denominations.

In summary, Paul was convinced that he had experienced the reality of Jesus on the road to Damascus, although he refused to discuss the details of his conversion. He further believed that he spoke for God. When challenged, he pointed to the growing number of converts as proof that his version was correct. He had seized control of a fuzzy-minded cult, and provided a sophisticated rationale for Jesus' life and death. In the process, he had introduced a host of new ideas with no basis in the *Gospels*, or in Jesus' teachings. And he was well aware of it:

> " But if through falsehood God's truthfulness abounds to His glory, why am I still being condemned as a sinner? And why not do evil that good may come? " (*Rom 3:7-8*)

This is an intensely repugnant philosophy; more at home in Stalinist Russia than in a religious text. If it were the common attitude, we may well speculate on how much truth-stretching went on among the other authors of the *New Testament*. For Paul was one of those passionate people who argue vehemently in favour of something, and the next time you meet them they argue just as fiercely against. Our time has seen these men of the spirit come and go—some do good, such as Paul, some do evil, such as Jim Jones—but we have hopefully learned not to trust these self-appointed spokesmen for God.

Paul was sure that his authority was equal to that of Jesus' friends and family. His conviction was so strong that he claimed (in *Phil 1:18*) that even lying is a legitimate means of converting recruits. He angered many and converted many. He dragged in every popular pagan idea that was compatible, and some that weren't compatible. But he won the day, and he has been the darling of Christian theology ever since. He founded church after church in city after city, and provided a set of letters which have provided moral guidance to millions. He was impassioned, energetic, and deeply neurotic. And he, not the historical Jesus, was the true founder of Christianity. What is true of the New York Yankees is also true of Christian theology—nothing succeeds like success.

17

THE APOCRYPHA AND THE GNOSTICS

"Happy is he who is able to apprehend the true causes of things."

Virgil

By now it should have become clear that the growth of early Christianity was not the well-ordered march toward the Heavenly City that is frequently presented. There were deep divisions, and plenty of opinions. Many of these opinions made their way into writing well before Christianity had any uniformity of belief, but like the canonical books, they each laid claim to some sort of tie with Jesus or to his close disciples. Eventually the Church Fathers (if there even was such a group) decided on what was acceptable, and what was not. Two millennia later we may question their choices, but they agreed on a *New Testament* of twenty-seven works, and the rest were variously ignored, defamed, or destroyed. These have come to be known as the *Apocrypha*, and to them we now turn.

There were a great many of them written, but today only fragments of many of them exist. Some such as *Q* and the parts of the *Gospel of Peter* may have been very early. Crossan says *Peter* may date to the 40s. (Naturally, others vigorously dispute that date. It may also be that *Peter* was written early, and then underwent very heavy revising in the second century.). Just as we need to look at the great rivals of Christianity to see it in perspective, so we must not focus only on the accepted books of the New Testament. The apocryphal gospels, epistles, and other writings form an important part of the fabric of the early church. Meier says the apocryphal sources are of no use for learning about Jesus, that they serve only to show superheated second century Christian imaginations at work. Of course, the same might be said by a jaundiced reader about *Matthew, Mark, Luke* and *John*. So we will blithely proceed in the assumption that Meier is wrong, and that the Apocrypha might offer some insight into the teachings of Jesus, teachings that have been abandoned over the intervening centuries.

The Apocrypha are a motley collection. *The Infancy Gospel of Thomas* shows the child Jesus as obnoxious, bratty and dangerous. *The Apocalypse of Peter* says Jesus was laughing while being crucified. The *Egerton Gospel* is named after a financial fund. In the *Gospel of Peter*, the Sadducees realize too late that they made a mistake. The *Gospel of Mary Magdalene* depicts her as a key disciple of Jesus to whom he entrusted secret teachings. That Gospel was soon denounced as heresy, but it was too late to stop Dan Brown and *The Da Vinci Code*.

All the experts have their favourites, depending on which one they got a grant to work on, but the key ones according to Crossan are *Peter* (discovered in 1887), the *Secret Gospel of Mark* (1958), the *Egerton Gospel* (1934), and the big new kid on the block, the *Gospel of Thomas* (1945). In the year 367 CE, Athanasius Bishop of Alexandria, listed 22 books for the *Old Testament* and 27 for the *New Testament*—a list that looks a lot like the *Bible* of today. He then ordered any religious writings which were not on his list to be burned. Somebody, and Elaine Pagels thinks it was probably the monks at the monastery of St. Pachomius in Upper Egypt, gathered a number of these unwelcome books, sealed them in a huge jar, and buried the jar in a hillside. In 1945 they were discovered—eleven complete books and parts of two others—some 1000 pages in all, including the complete *Gospel of Thomas*. This was the famous Nag Hammadi library, also called the *Gnostic Gospels*, and frequently confused with the *Dead Sea Scrolls*.

The *Gospel of Thomas* has in recent years made great strides in credibility since its discovery sixty years ago. Robert Funk, as lead writer of the Jesus Seminar, published *The Five Gospels: The Search for the Authentic Words of Jesus*. This is a remarkable step. For the first time in nineteen hundred years serious thinkers are placing *Thomas* on an equal footing with the big four. But *Thomas* is not the same as the other four: it is a "sayings gospel", a collection of the stories and teachings of Jesus without a narrative line. Its existence had been suspected since the nineteenth century, when fragments of it were found in a garbage dump in Oxyrhynchus, Egypt. Its discovery as a full gospel at Nag Hammadi, and especially its Gnostic content, has led to predictable reactions by conservative scholars, who have fallen over themselves to see who can discredit it most by dating it the latest. Johnson says it dates to 150 CE, Witherington agrees, Habemas says as late as 200, and Meier tries to avoid discussing it altogether by calling it derivative.

But the current thinking seems to be that the *Gospel of Thomas* is early, very early, at least as early as Q. There is no real evidence that *Thomas* is dependent on the other *Gospels*; in fact, the sayings in *Thomas* come across as "more pungent and original". This is a shocker—it means that *Thomas* may in fact be the most, not the least, reliable *Gospel*.

Who was the author of *Thomas*? Was he really the doubting disciple who, according to *John*, had to see and touch Jesus' scars before he would believe? *John* refers to him as "the twin", but was he Jesus' physical twin? Was he the twin of someone else? Did he represent a mystical, daemonic, earthbound force which would be the polar opposite of Jesus, the spiritualized Logos? Was this all part of the secret teaching? We cannot currently be sure. It is tantalizing to contrast the Jesus of *Thomas*—itinerant, mystical, poor—with the Jesus of *John*—triumphant, certain, divine. Did *John* write his *Gospel* to counteract the teachings of *Thomas*? Elaine Pagels thinks so. Was the *Gospel of Thomas* well known? Clement of Rome, writing about 96 CE, does not refer to any of the current written Gospels, but uses a lot of *Thomas*-like phraseology referring frequently to "what the Lord said." In all honesty, we still know very little. The *Gospel of Thomas* was probably typical of other stories which were extant in early Christian communities and are now lost, and its similarities to Q are very strong indeed.

The *Gospel of Thomas* is closer to Q than anything else we have, but it is not the elusive Q: 28% of *Thomas* is in Q, 30% of *Thomas* is in *Mark*, but only 9% of *Thomas* is in *John*. *Thomas* had its roots in the very earliest Jesus movement, but the scary apocalyptic messages of Q are absent. The most relevant point is that, like Q, it has no Passion, no Crucifixion, and therefore no Resurrection. To the earliest followers of Jesus, the significance of his message lay in his teaching, and apparently the death, resurrection, and ascension into heaven were tacked on later, under the Hellenizing influence of Paul. For the Christian church which has tried to base its legitimacy on historical fact, this is a crushing conclusion. Since no copy of Q has been found, it could be (and generally has been) ignored by the Christian community, but the *Gospel of Thomas* is different – it is the proverbial skunk at the Sunday school picnic.

> "These are the secret words which the living Jesus spoke, and which the twin, Judas Thomas, wrote down…"

As with other secret codes, the content of *The Gospel of Thomas* is cryptic, enigmatic, and probably metaphoric. Jesus' message is both hopeful and difficult: his followers must find the Way for themselves. Jesus is not a Saviour, Jesus is not a Messiah. He came to tell us that there is a divine light within each person, and that we each have the power to overcome the evils of the present age. But this self-discovery is not easy: learning to see within ourselves and for ourselves requires effort and discipline. The Kingdom of God is here, spread upon the earth, but people do not see it. Not everyone has the necessary focus:

> "Businessmen and merchants will not enter the places of My Father."

This kind of bluntness would not do for a popular religion—it was as unacceptable for the commercial classes then as it is with those same people today. Most people want simple and practical religious advice such as they received from the *Gospel of John*: just believe Jesus was the Messiah, and you will be saved. It's easy. By contrast, what bishop or church official could ever feel comfortable with Thomas' admonition that we can save ourselves only by looking within?

The religious aphorisms ascribed to Jesus in the *Gospel of Thomas* must seem eerily familiar to anyone who has even a cursory knowledge of the great Eastern religions. Hinduism, long before Jesus, taught that the key to understanding the true nature of reality lay in the recognition of the divine spark (the Atman) present within you, as well as in all other things. Similarly, when *Thomas* has Jesus say "Be passersby", the message is that we need to become detached from the affairs of the world—which was the key teaching of the Buddha.

Is there any chance, then, that Jesus could have been influenced in his key ideas by unknown teachers from the great Eastern traditions? As it turns out, yes, there is. Research has begun to show that sea trade in the ancient world was much more common than had been earlier imagined. In particular, there was frequent contact between the ports of western India and those of Egypt. The evidence is slight, but it seems on balance that Buddhist teachers were living in Alexandria in Jesus' day. Would they ever have traveled and taught in Palestine? We don't know, but it's a tantalizing idea. Similarly, the contacts may have gone the other way. Maybe Apollonius of Tyana was not the only religious seeker from the Eastern Mediterranean to go east in search of knowledge.

Finally, a tiny Christian community on the Malabar Coast of India traces its origins to long-ago missionary conversions by none other than Judas Thomas, the twin. An apocryphical story suggests that Thomas was reluctant to go as a missionary to India, but that he was tricked by Jesus, and then sold by him as a slave to a king of India. Evidence either for or against is missing, but it rounds out our story rather nicely. Tradition there has Jesus saying:

> "Life is a bridge: cross over, but build no house upon it."

The quote is a quintessential mixture of the best of East and West.

In summary, *Thomas* has posed an unpleasant and difficult problem for traditional Christians. If the historians are right about the dating, it (along with *Q*) casts much of the life of Jesus in doubt- no virgin birth, no miracles, no Saviour, no Resurrection—just puzzling parables, and the advice that the Kingdom of God is within you, if only you could learn to see.

If we were to heed *Thomas*, we might begin to look at a very different version of Christianity. Two centuries ago, the American philosopher and President, Thomas Jefferson, produced a life of Jesus stripped of any miraculous events. The focus was only on his teachings and ethics, and it reads as a stern challenge to its readers to become better people. And that is also the message of the *Gospel of Thomas*—be a better person in a better world, and do not rely on institutions to do it for you.

"Buddha", a Sanskrit word meaning "enlightened one", is certainly not far from the Greek term "Gnostic", or "knowing one". Because most Gnostic writing dated to the period immediately after Jesus, it was formerly accepted that Gnosticism did not exist before Christianity. It now has been traced back to 150 BCE, when educated Jews began to move away from a strictly tribal notion of Yahweh to a more abstract vision of a universal God. Despite a number of new discoveries, and a flurry of work from the scholars, Gnosticism still remains pretty much a mystery—the most intimidating school of theology in the history of Western civilization. Clearly this new development was being shaped by a variety of forces: Persian dualism, Greek philosophy, and the Essene movement. The Supreme Deity was beyond description, but like the Hindu Brahman, it was the mind of the universe and therefore was present in all things.

This concept profoundly affected the way Gnostics perceived the world and themselves. They believed the present world was the creation of rebellious forces, which had temporarily defeated and dismembered the One. We individuals are fragments of the One trapped in material bodies. The material world was to Gnostics, as it is to Hindus, an illusion masking a more important truth.

The secret knowledge possessed by all Gnostics was that the individual's true self is of divine origin, and that some day a divine messenger would come to earth to awaken us from our ignorance, and redeem us from this unnatural state. For Christian Gnostics, that messenger was Jesus the Christ.

The world to a Gnostic was an evil place. Now it is not at all clear that this was Jesus' view, but it was the dominant theme of many Jewish and Greek thinkers, and so Christianity and Gnosticism soon picked it up. The question was, how could a supremely good God, unknown and unknowable, have created such a stinking mess? It was impossible that he did so directly. He must have used intermediaries who botched the job.

Gnosticism soon became a philosophy of revolt, of deep alienation from worldly mores, and of indignation at the injustices of life. Because suffering and the ordeals of daily life are not part of the divine plan, they must be a result of error and ignorance...a material cancer which has attached itself to the ethereal particles of the hyperworld. The human body was part of the material world, and so it was both the source of evil and the prison of the soul. If the soul could only be freed, it would ascend into the Empyrian, its natural home, where it would join God.

The first requirement for salvation, then, was not good works, not correct belief, but gnosis, the knowledge of the true state of the world and its relationship to God. Things were not what they seemed: religious rituals, historical events, even daily life itself was infused with hidden meanings and deep symbolism. The material life of Jesus, indeed his whole historical reality, was thus of minor interest, and to some degree a distraction. Having a body exposed Jesus to sinfulness and pain. This was incompatible with the divine nature of the Logos. So to many Gnostics, Jesus was just as mythical as Osiris was to their neighbours. He was an allegory that encoded secret teachings.

This is all very alien to the modern mind, and merely to consider it is difficult. It has led the Americans Freke and Gandy, for example, to posit the notion that the entire life of Jesus is nothing but a carefully constructed code to teach obscure spiritual truths to Gnostic initiates. Maybe none of it really happened. Maybe it's all an allegory for something else, and we have lost the key. But that doesn't really help us, because nobody can go very far down this road without getting seriously lost.

Gnostics went on to deny the authority of the official church, since true authority does not lie in apostolic succession, for example, but in knowledge and understanding. This emphasis on personal revelation was common to religions of the time, and even Paul is full of it. For example, in both *I Cor 2:7* and *II Cor 12:4*, Paul claims to be privy to secret knowledge which he not free to divulge. All Gnostics, then, were simply claiming for themselves the same divine authority which official Christianity had granted to Paul. Likewise, it was the writings of Paul, especially in his interpretation of the life of Jesus in the form of a redeemer-myth, which really kicked Gnostic speculation into high gear.

As Gnostic thinkers tried to reduce Christian ideas into a logical system, things began to get complicated, and the wider the circle spread, the more confusing it all became. Soon the simplicity of worship which characterized early Christianity was replaced by sacraments, symbolism, and other allegorical trappings of Greek paganism. Gnostic speculation became impossibly intertwined with Christianity. It was the Gnostics who first argued that bread and wine were really the body and blood of Christ. It was the Gnostics who felt they needed incense and statuary, who made baptism into an elaborate initiation rite, who insisted that Jesus was the Logos who is the intermediary between God and the universe.

Faith was a useful first step. Gnostics didn't deny the story presented in the *Gospels*, because it was helpful in attracting initiates. However, only the simple and unenlightened were unable to go deeper. For the critical part was to move on—to experience The Truth directly. To most Gnostics, simple faith in Christ, without mystical experience, was shallow and useless. Resurrection, for example, was a spiritual experience, and these profound spiritual experiences were possible and could just as easily happen to you as they had to Paul.

The idea of Christ as allegory is generally inimical to the modern mind, but the ancients took to it like ducks to water. Gnostics found numerological symbolism everywhere, and it is now clear that those parts of Jesus' teachings connected to Pythagoreanism have been eliminated or obscured by later editors, and that the symbolic numerology has also virtually disappeared after the anti-Gnostic purgings. But it was certainly widespread at the time, especially among the mathematically inclined in Egypt. Much of the Gnostic thought was centred in Alexandria, where, after the destruction of Jerusalem, so many Jews and early followers of Jesus had sought refuge. The enemies of the Gnostics, by contrast, seemed to be centred in Rome, good old, practical, political Rome, where a professional and hierarchical priesthood became entrenched.

Without a central authority to guide them, some Gnostics, convinced of the rightness of their religious insights, went well off the beaten track. The Docetists denied that Jesus was ever human, and totally rejected the *Old Testament*. Valentinians denied that Jesus had been human, Corinthians thought he was only a myth, Ophites worshipped snakes. The *Gospel of the Egyptians* objected to sex, on the grounds that it might lead to procreation. The Montanists spoke in tongues. Marcionites taught that women and men were equal. In the *Gospel of Philip*, Jesus makes it plain that he loves Mary Magdalen by kissing her on the mouth on several occasions. The notion of a sexual Jesus was far too extreme for most orthodox Christians—then and now.

But some Gnostics went much further, especially the sect known as the Carpocratians. They built on what now seems to be a dubious tradition—that Jesus loved wine, women and food, and seemed to feel that since they were among the enlightened, the common bonds of behaviour did not apply to them. They opposed marriage, the family, the church, and authority in general. They set out to commit every sexual sin possible. Men could be assured of salvation by having sex 730 times (365 x 2, of course) with Christian women. At their religious meetings the lamps were extinguished, and an orgy ensued, as believers sought salvation, or whatever.

It got worse. Some groups mixed male sperm, female menstrual blood and lentils to make their eucharist. Epiphanius, who spent time in Egypt and claimed to know many Gnostics, gave the Oscar for religious weirdness to the Phibionites, who prayed naked, engaged in promiscuous sex after their communion feasts, and apparently taught that if a child were conceived, it had to be aborted and eaten, so they recommended coitus interruptus. A recent and sympathetic commentator has suggested that they were trying to come to terms with their fear of death. Well, maybe.

No wonder that orthodox Christians, then and now, attacked Gnostics as agents of the devil. Father Raymond Brown, a respected *New Testament* scholar, dismisses Gnostic thought as the "rubbish of the second century". He follows in the footsteps of Irenaeus, Bishop of Lyon about 180 CE, who likewise denounced them as "an abyss of madness and blasphemy". The Gnostics of Irenaeus' acquaintance must have been cut from milder cloth. The sins he accuses them of committing are quite tame: going to animal fights, attending pagan feasts, offering food to idols. Irenaeus was convinced that a lot of Gnostic revelation was either delusional or demonic. Fair enough. But what strikes the modern reader about the work of Irenaeus is the vehemence with which he attacked the role of women. Clearly Gnostics gave women more positions of leadership, and both Irenaeus and his contemporary Tertullian were appalled. In Gnostic services, women not only participated, but sometimes they led prayers and baptized. For the mainline church, this would not do.

One of the greatest of the Gnostics, Simon Magus, had close connections with the circle of Jesus—he was friends with several of the chief disciples. Both Simon and his teacher Dositheus seem to have been disciples of John the Baptist. Simon was a particular favourite of the Baptist, and had he not been in Egypt at the time, Simon might have taken over leadership of the movement on John's death. Simon traveled the roads of Samaria and Judaea accompanied by Helen, a former prostitute. His career as a miracle worker was parallel to that of Jesus, but it came a generation later and included more extravagant claims. He too was The Redeemer of the

World. Simon taught that Yahweh was cruel and harsh, and therefore not the true God. He, Simon, was the true Logos, the sun, the supreme power. Helen was the moon, Athena, Sophia. One legend had him dying in an attempt to impress Nero by flying a demon-powered chariot in the skies over Rome. Another legend had him promise that if he were buried alive he would rise again on the third day. He was, he didn't. A more reliable story has Simon attempting to buy some of Peter's miraculous powers, but Peter indignantly refused, and called Simon the father of all heresies and a thorn in the side. But ideas are free, and Simon seems to have used his friendship with Philip and John to borrow some tricks.

Simon taught that all men are the same – we are all part of the "great power in heaven". He was described by his followers as "Christ" and the "Son of Man". But few today have heard of him. It is one of the ironies of our story that Simon Magus was condemned for attempting to subvert the message of Jesus, while Paul was canonized for doing exactly the same thing.

A second major figure of the Gnostic school was the second century ascetic Marcion. Marcion was very anti-Semitic, which made his choices of Gospel rather problematic. He rejected *Matthew* and *Mark* out of hand, and he apparently was unacquainted with the *Gospel of John*. But he loved *Luke* and the *Epistles* of Paul. Marcion felt that for Christ to be human (and Jewish!) was inconceivably degrading. In fact, Jesus had been a sort of supernatural phantom who had only seemed to die on the cross. That meant that the Gospel accounts of Jesus' suffering and death were false—undoubtedly Jewish inventions. Marcion's version would have completely eliminated the historical Jesus had not the more orthodox view prevailed.

The Mecca for Gnostics was, of course, the Egyptian city of Alexandria. As the port city where East meets West, it had been the hotbed of religious eclecticism since its founding. Alexandrian Christianity had not gone through the internal struggle over Jewish Law that had convulsed Antioch and Rome. Gnosticism evolved here under the influence of a prominent thinker named Valentinius, who himself was influenced by Pythagoras. According to Valentinius, Jesus had been so strong both mentally and physically that food did not become corrupted in his body. Thus he was free to eat and drink, but never needed to defecate.

Another branch of Gnostics, the Ophites, apparently existed in both Egypt and Asia Minor. They taught that Jesus was an angelic messenger from the Supreme Being with a plan of redemption for mankind. Only those who had been initiated into their rituals of snake worship could count on automatic entry into Heaven. Ophite initiates had to memorize the diagram of the seven heavens with their seven planetary rulers, and the guardians at the seven gates (Michael, Gabriel and Raphael are three whose names are familiar). While Jesus had been the Son of Man in his generation, the entire cult of Ophites were now the Son of Man—Jesus' divinity was now diffused among the members, but their godliness was produced as thought, not as mortal flesh.

But by the end of the fourth century, Gnosticism had relapsed into magic, and orthodox Christianity had reacted to it by becoming literalist, disciplined, and more ascetic. Gnosticism enjoyed a revival in the East in a modified form as Manicheanism. Manicheans survived for centuries, although they were heartily detested by both Christian and Moslem, and they were harried from place to place. They suffered heavy-handed attempts to convert them such as the

Albigensian Crusade and the Dominican Inquisition. Some descendants of the Gnostics, the Mandaeans, still survive in southwest Iraq.

Gnosticism, then, was the four-lane bridge over which pagan ideas streamed into Christianity and took it over. Paul's *Epistles* are rife with it. Bultmann is convinced that the evangelist John was a Gnostic before he became a Christian. It appealed to the learned, the wealthy, the highly placed. When these people converted to Christianity, Gnosticism came along too.

It needs to be stressed that we cannot really be sure what the Gnostics believed. The term includes an extreme diversity of views. Most of their general works were destroyed, and only some of the very arcane literature from the inner circles has been found. They embraced metaphysical speculation, which was to the Mediterranean world what the scientific method is to us. We insist that all areas of knowledge conform to scientific precepts as much as possible, so we ought to allow the same latitude to those ancient thinkers who stressed elaborate metaphysical assumptions. Besides, we really haven't come that far. The fastest growing branch of Christianity is that group of churches which, like the Gnostics, ignores historical context and searches Scriptural passages looking for hidden meanings and modern day applications.

Whether it was their excesses, or their egalitarianism, or their failure to win sympathizers in Rome, the Gnostics were doomed as a mainstream Christian force by the middle of the third century. But their speculations forced orthodox Christians to refine their opinions, and turned the new religion into a tightly knit organization able to fight off such speculation. The literalist bishops took charge, and gave a narrow authoritarian tone to Christianity. All *Gospels*, even the approved ones, were scoured and cleaned of almost every reference to secret teachings and initiations. The four approved *Gospels* were not to be seen as allegory, but as fact. The "apostolic succession", a list of Bishops of Rome going all the way back to Peter was invented and disseminated. This was to convince the wavering that the teachings of the bishops were original and dated back to Palestine. The *Gospels* were to be regarded as the personal testimonials of Jesus' close disciples. And of course, the literalists cheerfully burned everything Gnostic that they could find. A truly major loss was the 24 volume work by the Egyptian Gnostic theologian Basilides called *The Exegetica*, which was a detailed Gnostic commentary on the *Gospels*. If we had a copy, it might help to rescue Gnostic ideology from the rubbish bin to which Fr. Brown has so cavalierly assigned it.

And so the literalists triumphed, and Christianity took on the shape we know. The church became structured, disciplined, and centred in Rome. Christians have abandoned the idea that we all share in the stuff of divinity. Nor do Christians have to solve their own problems; there exists a professional and hierarchical clergy to provide the correct answers.

Increasingly though, modern scholars wonder whether this was the triumph of truth, or rather the victory of practicality and politics. For we now know that much of Jesus' message was secret. His parables, for instance, are not at all clear, and he revealed their true meaning in private to those close to him. It was not only Jesus. The Gnostic Valentinius said that his teacher, Theudas, was initiated into "secret doctrines" by none other than Paul. Mystical insights, secret truths, encoded stories—whatever the historical Jesus believed, it certainly fell into the mainstream of Mediterranean mystery religions, and it would be far, far different from what is so confidently preached from church pulpits today.

Gnosticism was the most dangerous foe orthodox Christianity ever faced. It was defeated only by a strict definition of doctrine, by ruthless excommunications, and ultimately by swallowing large and indigestible chunks of Gnostic ideology. The stomach pains have troubled Christianity to this day.

18

THE GROWTH OF THE NEW RELIGION

"Jesus proclaimed the Kingdom of God, but it was the Church that came."

Alfred Loisy

"I didn't have implants. I just had a growth spurt."

Britney Spears

It is reasonable to think of the term "Jesus Christ" as an oxymoron. It was an idea that was gradually constructed over a period of time. Meier, ever the reliable traditionalist, claims that people used it to distinguish the divine Jesus from the others, since Palestine had so many figures with that name. (There is no question that if first century Palestinian parents had used more imagination when naming their babies, our task would be much easier. There did seem to be a shortage of names, and hence lots of confusion about various characters named Jesus, Mary, John, Judas, Simon and James.)

However, when Mark, writing in Greek, translated the Hebrew term Messiah as "Christos", he set the pattern. The actual word seems to have been born as an Egyptian term to describe the god Horus, but its usage to describe Jesus began in Antioch in what is now Syria, and it was early—well before the destruction of Jerusalem in 70 CE. It drew on the local Adonis tradition of a divine Son of God who came to earth. The key idea was that he died as a sacrifice for us. This appealed to people, and it overwhelmed any imported stories of Jesus the itinerant Galilean teacher. As a result, the Christ movement was to be about drama, martyrdom, death and resurrection, not rural parables.

Christianity, to people of these Hellenistic cities, was an exotic new cult combining the wisdom of the mystery religions with the veneer of age provided by its Jewish heritage. It said the Son of God had been here recently. He had died for you. And besides, the new cult was easy and cheap to join. As time went by, Jesus became less and less Jewish, more and more divine. The Jewishness of Jesus, his family and his friends was downplayed and frequently denied. It is significant that, once the movement left Palestine, it made few Jewish converts. Christian churches were filled with former pagans who knew little or nothing of the traditions or history of the Jews. Concepts such as Redeemer of the World, and the Saviour of Mankind were free to sprout and grow unchecked. Even Paul had not gone so far as to actually call Jesus "God". But now the juggernaut was rolling, and the brakes were off.

This rapid growth certainly suggested a deep spiritual hunger in the peoples of the Empire, and it was not a phenomenon peculiar to Christianity. (Interestingly, Buddhism was making great gains in the East at precisely the same time, and also embraced high ethical principles.) Crossan has pointed out that the murdered Julius Caesar, like Jesus, was also worshipped after death. He was officially declared by the Roman Senate to be divine in 42 BCE, and so that made his adopted son Augustus the "Son of God". If it was happening in the Roman Senate, it was happening everywhere. Christianity was well positioned to benefit from the deep psychological needs of its time.

As part of its accommodation with the world, the early church enthusiastically embraced Koine Greek. There were at least nine major languages being used in the Empire, but Greek was most common. So following the leads of worshippers of Isis, Cybele and Mithra, early Christians gave a pass to Hebrew/Aramaic, and took up the language of commerce. In addition, Christians early on adopted the book form (the "codex") for their sacred scriptures rather than the scroll, as being easier to use. And it was a religion of the Book—for centuries it had no central temple, and no great public celebrations, and Christian writings were full of heavy theology, intended for Christian readers, and not necessarily intended as explanations of their doctrine to pagans.

What little we know of the growth of the new church in the Empire does not come from Roman sources. For the first three centuries of our era, Roman writers made only a dozen or so references to the fledging church—all of them brief and derogatory. Of course, there may have been other references which were lost or destroyed, especially if they were long and derogatory. But then, why should a serious pagan writer have paid particular attention to just another passing Eastern enthusiasm?

It does seem as though Christianity moved to Rome very early, largely because the city had as many as 50 000 Jews. It was a great period of multiculturalism and cross-fertilization, and people, perhaps for the first time, felt free to actually choose a religion other than the one they were born into. For example, we know that the great synagogues of the Empire set aside special seating for the "God-fearers", worshippers who sympathized with Jewish morality and history, but who, for dietary or other reasons, were not considered Jews. So the market for potential converts was there. The Christian church in Rome began early, but to the chagrin of many current tourist guides, it was founded by an unknown missionary, and not by either Peter or Paul.

A half century passed before there was any surviving mention of Christians in Roman writing. About 112 CE, Pliny the Younger, governor of an area now part of Turkey, wrote back to the Emperor Trajan to ask what to do about the spreading Christian superstition. The historian Suetonius, writing about 115 CE, mentions that Jews were expelled from Rome about 49 CE after a continuous series of disturbances instigated by "Chrestus". Further, he says, followers of Chrestus were implicated in the great fire of Rome in 64 CE, and some were punished by the emperor Nero, who was probably looking for someone to blame. Tacitus, another Roman writer, had no love for Nero and less for Christianity. He said Christians were "hated for their abominations" and the new religion was a "pernicious superstition". In a part of his work now lost (surprise, surprise!), he apparently tied early Christians to the Zealots who fought to defend Jerusalem in 70 CE. He further said that Christians were singled out by Nero "not so much on the charge of arson as because of (their) hatred of the human race". However, Tacitus felt that Nero went too far in his tortures, using crucifixion, wild dogs, lions and even burning some Christians alive.

But Christianity was on the upswing, and as it grew, it attracted more attention, not all of it positive. Christians were perceived as atheists, because of their refusal to worship the emperor. They were referred to as a plague, or a contagion. The Empire should get rid of them before the gods, offended, sent a real plague. They were a tiny, odd, and antisocial sect, and besides that, they were mostly poor. Converting to Christianity was a difficult choice, and it was hard on both the convert and the family of the converted as well. So it is no surprise that there was a lot of backsliding. Since the Empire had a lot of religions, many of them roughly similar, most people probably felt free to try out various creeds. Christianity would have seemed to be just one among many.

As the Christian church set out to convert the peoples of the Roman Empire, its main weapon was not, as modern people might think, a clear moral superiority to paganism, but rather a widespread belief in miracles. A typical example would be the story of the martyrdom of Bishop Polycarp of Smyrna by a pagan mob in 155 CE. They tried to set him alight, but when fire wouldn't burn him, he was stabbed. From his severed veins flew a dove, and enough blood to quench the fire, whereupon many attending pagans recognized a miracle, changed their minds, and converted instantly to Christianity. Well, maybe. This kind of event was recounted over and over in Christian writings. Whether or not something like it actually happened is of less importance than the fact that it was reported and apparently widely believed by Christians at the time.

But most people converted to the new religion for understandable but mundane motives. They hoped for a miraculous cure for their illness. They wanted to be freed from bad dreams, or obsessions, or anxiety attacks. Perhaps their owners or employers or landowners converted, and they thought it wise to follow suit. They wanted the blessings promised by Christian missionaries. They could see the material benefits of belonging to a large and charitably-minded organization. In addition, the life and death struggle with Gnosticism had made the Church literal-minded, shorn of complex interpretations, and relatively easy to understand for even the dullest of souls.

Christianity offered something for everybody: hope for the poor, subtle theology for the bright, ritual for the bored, moral idealism for the dissolute. This is not to say that Christianity advanced equally on all demographic fronts, for its major gains were among the slaves and working people of the great cities, and these were the same groups that found the other oriental mystery cults so appealing. And there certainly were plenty of slaves to appeal to: Gibbon estimated that there were about twenty million of them in the Empire, mostly in Italy.

Christian preachers soon adapted to this situation. On the one hand, they preached acceptance of the socio-political order (as Paul in *Eph. 6:5* undiplomatically puts it, "Slaves, obey your masters!"). They assumed that the hegemony of the Roman Empire was unchallengeable, the work of God. Gradually Christians came to accept that the Second Coming would not happen in their lifetime. They did not set out to ruffle the feathers of the slaveowning class. In the Empire, slavery was an unquestioned fact of life. Even bishops were known to own pagan slaves, and unlike Jewish slaveowners, Christian proprietors apparently saw little need either to convert or to free their slaves. At the Council of Elvira, the Spanish bishops got tough: they agreed to temporarily ban from communion Christian women who had beaten a slave to death. Clement of Alexandria, about 200 CE, wrote a pamphlet entitled *Which Rich Man Will Be Saved?* containing the now-familiar argument that wealthy Christians need not abandon their possessions, so long as they have the right attitude. Jesus' admonition about the rich man and the eye of the needle was, in the words of Richard Nixon's press secretary, "no longer operative."

On the other, Christians preached that this worldly

inequality would be rectified in heaven. It was a powerful appeal for those millions who felt life was a burden, and who looked forward to the next life. And it was to be the same for all—the rich man would sit between the slave and the artisan. Urban women found Christianity attractive despite its strong male bias, while rural villagers ("pagani") were among the slowest to convert.

Miracles and martyrs had a great impact on the growth of the new faith. Converts were taught that families and society in general were not valuable—in fact, they were demonic. While martyrdom and bravery in the face of death were usually reported second or third-hand, many Christians would have been personal witnesses to ecstatic seizures. In groups of people tense with spiritual expectancy, the emotional fervour of anyone from Oral Roberts to Adolf Hitler can trigger trances, glossolalia, and powerful feelings of spiritual well-being. This has traditionally been attributed to divine intervention, and Christianity has always used the process to make new converts.

The Christian church also provided a strong sense of belonging in an era of depersonalized urban slums and widespread poverty. The ethnic communities of the great cities were drawn to "collegia", charitable support groups which might be based on either occupation or religion. These collegia would provide social assistance when possible, and would have occasional banquets, and at the minimum they paid for a member's burial somewhere better than the pauper's common pit. This social network combining alms and human warmth gave life its meaning for many then, as it would now. Christianity was in the forefront of such organizations because it preserved the Judaic tradition of charity. The infant church went further in actually demanding alms from its members. In *Acts 5* Ananias and his wife Sapphira held back from the church leaders some of the proceeds from a property sale, and were struck dead for their selfishness. This certainly is a far cry from the gospel of acquisitive capitalism preached by some upscale modern clergy, but then, first century Christians were a lot more worried than we are that the world was about to end.

The vaunted moral superiority of early Christians now seems more apparent than real. Naturally, they compared well with the morally lax, but earnest pagans and Jews were as ascetic, as devout, and as charitable as Christians were. Other major religions of the time shared with Christianity an abhorrence of abortion, of infanticide, and of the gladiatorial games. Christian writers boasted of Christian piety and morality, while pagan writers excoriated the same people for being credulous and impious.

So did they live up to their ideals? We don't know. The physician Galen was impressed that Christians cared for the sick during the great measles plague of the third century. He also praised their self discipline, and their sexual morality. In terms of sexual behavior, Christians probably were superior. They hated easy sex: fornication, divorce, homosexuality, adultery, even female flirting. And certainly conversion to Christianity offered the opportunity to change one's life: Justin Martyr bragged of having given up promiscuity, magic, greed, avarice and racism.

While average Christians, like average pagans, struggled to be good people, even in difficult circumstances, the elite who have been styled the Church Fathers seemed to undermine some of that by their practices. They regarded pious fraud as both necessary and good. Many unsympathetic commentators have pointed out the total untrustworthiness of Justin Martyr, Eusibius, Irenaeus, Tertullian, St. Gregory, and a host of others. These writers believed that paganism was evil root and branch, and that fraud and deception were acceptable if it led to greater glory for the Church. They showed no compunction about rewriting history. Many of their fiercest attacks were on the Jews, who, they said, had willfully misunderstood the *Bible* and its message. Abraham and Moses, for example, were not really Jews but proto-Christians. The Jews deserved what they got when God and the Romans joined forces to destroy Jerusalem. These shrill attacks on their enemies probably reached a peak of absurdity with their claims that pagans, under the influence of the devil, had deviously "copied" Christian ritual—before the birth of Jesus—to mislead the Christian faithful.

Christians were thus expected to be totally free of pagan influence, but it's an imperfect world, so backsliding and syncretism were common. Old gods and old rituals don't die easily. The gods Castor and Pollux became Saints Cosmo and Damian; Dionysos was recycled as St. Denis, statues of Jupiter, Apollo and Isis became those of Peter, Paul and the Virgin Mary. Sometimes sainthood was granted rather loosely, as in the case of St. Christopher, who may have been an African giant named Reprebus, may have been a cannibal, or most unusually, was claimed to have had the head of a dog. The emperor Alexander Severus had in his private chapel statues of Abraham, Orpheus, Christ, and Apollonius of Tyana, and he revered them all equally. But for most people, the effect of accepting Christ was the denial of all other gods. This was quite different than moving from the worship of one pagan god to another, for pagans generally did not challenge the existence of rival deities.

The conversion game could work both ways. Some people left the Christianity of their childhood and moved to paganism. We don't hear much about them, of course, because the implication was that paganism was so grotesque that no one would return to it. But some did - the emperor Julian and the philosopher Porphery were notable examples. Again, their motives were probably mixed: they may have been bored, or repelled, or just anti-social misfits...or maybe they were on to something. In any case, the Empire was a time of eclecticism, and no religion was more eclectic than Christianity—it took its ethics from the Jews, its organization from the Romans, and its theology from the Greeks.

We have already seen how rapidly the new religion abandoned its Jewish roots to accommodate the new pagan converts. During the second and third centuries, a more serious attempt was made to reconcile Christian ideas with the logical rigours of Greek thought. Up until about 150 CE, most of the converts had come from social classes with only a passing knowledge of Greek philosophy, but as the religion spread geographically, it also began to move up into the educated classes. Justin Martyr was quite typical when he suggested that demonic control of the world, and hence of our minds, made it impossible to find God rationally. But for every Tertullian who obstinately postured "I believe because it is absurd!" there were many others who had faith in the ultimate rationality of Christian doctrine. A minor debate broke out among Christian writers, for example, over whether pagan moralists such as Socrates might be in heaven. A less edifying discussion in Alexandria erupted over whether believers could continue to have sex after death. The official answer to both, when it came down, was no.

As another example of the growing respectability of philosophy in the church, consider the case of Synesius of Alexandria, a locally famous writer, scholar and teacher. He was offered the post of Bishop, but he declined for three very good reasons: he was a follower of Plato, he thought the Resurrection was nonsense, and he was married.

Nevertheless, the Christian community insisted and eventually prevailed. It would be interesting to know whether he was an exception, or one among many.

The late Empire was a time of increasing formalization in architecture, literature and religion. So we see an increasing systematization of Greek philosophy into Christian doctrine. Christianity became less sentimental, more rigorous, and even a bit more tolerant. In many ways, it's unfortunate that it didn't go further. Had the new religion adopted more Hellenistic broadmindedness, and less Jewish exclusiveness or Roman authoritarianism, many of the later unfortunate consequences of a Christianized society might have been avoided.

In its first two hundred years, then, Christianity had struggled to develop doctrinal agreement, and to centralize authority. Bishops exerted an increasing degree of control: issuing encyclicals, trying to separate true from false doctrine, settling disputes, administering alms for widows and orphans, appointing minor officials—a full range of administrative tasks.

However, by the fourth century, the Christian church had become an autocratic and centralized organization. The conversion of a Palestinian cult into a full blown religion suitable for a mighty empire was nearly complete. Because it claimed to possess absolute truth, its followers were relieved of the responsibility of making their own religious enquiries. It had a sacred book from which most of the dubious sections had been deleted. There was a centralized structure run by the Bishop of Rome. The Mass, the sacraments, and other rituals had definite liturgies and agreed-upon explanations. Above all, orthodoxy was crucial: holding approved opinions had become more important than living a good life. Councils of church leaders met to debate, and then to expel innovators and speculators.

Jesus' admonitions to avoid ritualism and dogmatic hair-splitting had been mislaid in the struggle to conquer the world. The religion of Jesus had indeed become a religion about Jesus—with a full battery of metaphysics, Christology, and arcane practices. We are not looking at the triumph of Christianity, but at the continued triumph of the Roman state, and it religious wing. It is a depressing case study of a religion succeeding not because of its inherent truth, but because it suited the psychic needs of the late Roman Empire. But it needs to be underlined that, had the Church not established such strict orthodoxy, it would not have dominated for two millennia.

Finally, it is one of the ironies of history that an organization which succeeded because it was so flexible in adapting to the mood of the times should be perceived as so out of touch and dogmatic by so many people today.

19

SYMBOLS AND SACRAMENTS

"*A good symbol is a missionary to convince thousands.*"
Emerson

"*How can a man be so stupid as to imagine that which he eats to be a god?*"
Cicero (106-43 BCE)

One notable case in which Greek speculation wormed its way into Christian orthodoxy was the celebrated doctrine of three-persons-in-one-god. The Trinity is not in the *Gospels*, or *Acts*, or the *Epistles* of Paul. In fact, efforts to find it in the *New Testament* are in vain. The idea seems to have been first articulated by Justin Martyr about 150 CE, grew rapidly despite being bitterly disputed, and was adopted as the official church position by the Council of Nicaea in 325 CE. It is an exceptionally difficult doctrine for any religion to adopt, being both unfathomable and useless. Only the most desperate arguments can prevent the notion of the Trinity from relapsing into polytheism.

Where did the idea of the Trinity come from? Another way of asking the question might be "Why is the number three so important?" It may have subconscious roots in the human experience of major events: birth, life, death. The great Austrian psychologist Bruno Bettleheim said our fascination with the number comes from the family triad of father, mother and child. It may simply be that the ancients, for no good reason, thought three was a lucky number. But whatever the explanation you prefer, tripartite divinities have a very long history. Babylon, Persia and Rome all had them, but we can be fairly confident in tracing the Christian Trinity back to classical Hinduism, which had Brahma the creator, Vishnu the incarnate god who lived on earth, and Siva the spirit. The tripartite idea proved popular with the great reformer Buddha, and through his followers, the belief has passed into the West. Aristotle, in the fourth century BCE, said "All things are three...let us use this number in the worship of the gods." His teacher Plato modeled his student's advice by creating a tripartite deity in the *Phaedron*: Agathon (the supreme god or power), Logos (the son of the father made flesh) and Psyche(the spirit or ghost).

Certainly we can say that the Trinity is not an original Christian idea. Moreover, it has nothing whatever to do with the message of Jesus. While we can understand official Christianity adopting appealing pagan ideas, still there is something ludicrous about fourth century bishops, so limited in education and outlook, drawing conclusions about the nature of God which attempted to bind all people for all time. Today we struggle to understand the mentality of those church officials who excommunicated and even burned people who rejected this illogical and curious idea.

If bizarre notions such as three equals one could be adopted by Christian authorities, with how much more gusto they must have taken to more sensible (and pre-Christian) pagan ones such as sun-worship or sacraments such as communion or baptism. Every ancient religion (and most modern ones too) had a solar component. Even Judaism, that most vigilant of beliefs, has at least eight direct references in the Hebrew Scriptures to Yahweh as the sun. The Hellenistic Age was especially keen on solar divinities. Initiates of Isis had to personify the sun in public. Mithraists were direct in adoration of the sun-god. The Roman writers Pliny and Macrobius both claimed that the sun was the real divinity behind the Graeco-Roman pantheon. Christianity could not have avoided solar religion even if it had wanted to, and it is a debatable point whether it wanted to.

Early Christians were accused of being sun-worshippers, and Tertullian took these accusations seriously enough to try to refute them. Second century Christians prayed facing east, in anticipation of the sunrise. Since then, Christian churches have traditionally been built with that same orientation, so the worshippers looking at the high altar are facing east. The timing of midnight mass in Roman Catholicism is sometimes explained as a result of pagan persecution, but in fact it is simply a carryover of Egyptian and Mithraic sun-worship. More solar connections appear in the haloes and curly-haired male statuary of Christian art. Long curly locks on a male statue, whether it be Alexander, Augustus, or Jesus all betray their roots in oriental sun-worship. Even ceremonial objects were of the same origin. The monstrance is a sunburst of gold with the host displayed at the centre. Similarly, the paten, a round metal plate used on the altar during communion services, has its origin in Egyptian rites as a reminder of the constant presence of the sun.

The burning of beeswax candles during Christian worship is especially interesting. Christians rejected their use for centuries as being too glaringly pagan: a Persian pun on the word 'Dabar' which meant both 'The Word' and 'The Bee' reminded Mithraic worshippers that Mithra made all things—including beeswax. The Christian writer Lactantius mocked the use of candles during pagan services in the fourth century, and the Synod of Elvira in 305 CE banned the use of candles in cemeteries. Today funeral services blaze with unnecessary candlelight, and mourners pray for perpetual light to shine upon the deceased, unaware of the pagan origin of their hopes.

The English cleric, Dean Inge, suggested that without sacraments, Christianity would not have conquered Europe. The ancients had long held that, in some mysterious way, the symbol was the same as the object symbolized. A sacrament must be both symbolic and effectual—it must show something, and claim to do something. Despite herculean efforts by generations of theologians to prove otherwise, more and more experts have concluded that Jesus did not institute any sacraments. The current debate is whether any can even be traced back to Paul. Unquestionably sacramentalism was in the air of the time, for the practices of both the Eucharist and Baptism seem to date back to a period before Jesus. When Christians finally became convinced that Jesus was not going to return immediately, the requirements of an ongoing church organization led them to adopt sacramental rites from the other mystery religions. Moreover, Christianity had no lavish outdoor public ceremonies, and compared to the worship of Cybele or Isis, even their private ceremonies were pretty dull. Some type of colourful ritual was needed. By the third century, the new religion had borrowed a number of these rituals: exorcism, unction, the sign of the cross, the kiss of peace. Often these behaviours were done in secret to make a deeper impression—to satisfy religious yearnings, which words alone cannot fulfill.

Pagan water-worship was second only to sun-worship in its antiquity and extent. We have already seen that the

Egyptians believed in the sacred properties of Nile water, and the other civilizations of the ancient world held similar views about their own local rivers, whether it be the Ganges, the Euphrates, or the Jordan. Ritual bathing as part of religious purification can be traced back as far as the third millennium BCE. It existed in the ancient cities of Harappa and Mohenjo-Daro where the pious sprinkled water on their heads and murmured prayers before stepping into the Indus River to bathe. The Christian apologist Tertullian admitted that the rites of the Isiacs, Mithraists, Orphics and Eleusinians were identical to those of his own church, but typically went on to argue that their rites had only an evil influence, whereas Christian ceremonies brought only good.

The Babylonian tradition of baptizing religious converts was the direct ancestor of the rituals of John the Baptist. It used to be supposed that the Baptist's rites were carried on by Christianity, but certain features of the Christian rite now make many people suspect that the early church owed nothing to John—that instead it swallowed the entire Eleusinian Greek baptismal rite holus-bolus. Many Eleusinian temples had sunken tanks in which believers were baptized. Putting fonts of holy water inside the temple doors, and the sprinkling of worshippers by a priest were also common Greek practices. Like the Isiacs and Mithraists, new Christians frequently adopted new names to suit their spiritual transformation: Simon became Peter, Saul became Paul. Paul, having been transformed, set about to provide a Christological explanation for this ancient pagan behavior, and it is an explanation that is still widely accepted today.

While the baptism of a willing adult convert is one thing, the same rite performed on a morally unconscious baby is something else. Again, it was the pagan competition that blazed the way. Long before Christ, the Greeks, the Romans, and the Scandinavians were baptizing and naming children 7-9 days after birth. The baptism was regarded as a symbolic cleansing, and it also made the newborn a legitimate family member and conferred important legal rights on the child. Infants in Hellenistic times were baptized into the Dionysiac rites for fear they would die unsaved in childhood.

At first Christians were reluctant to adopt this policy. They felt that baptism removed all sins, so quite a number of people, including the Emperor Constantine, deferred baptism till old age. If you were baptized early in life, it virtually guaranteed that at some point you would sin, and that created a problem. To allow infant baptism meant a mechanism had to be provided for the forgiveness of any of these post-baptismal sins. Thus the Christian doctrine of penance and the practice of confession evolved simultaneously with the rite of infant baptism. Soon the deathbed baptism was discouraged as showing a lack of faith, and today mainstream Christian churches generally agree that committing an unknowing infant to their specific set of dogmas is perfectly acceptable. And baptism still retains its ancient link with pagan magic. Reciting the proper formula while pouring water over the child's head can guarantee, according to Roman Catholic tradition, that the little soul will be freed from the prospect of insufferable boredom in limbo.

There was quite a debate over offering the sacrament of penance—especially for sexual sins. Confession seemed to offer an easy out for backsliders, and even apostates. But good people, even Christians, sometimes slip, and once again the Church made allowances; that is, it traded some of the high moral ground for popularity.

We have already given considerable attention to communion rites as they were practiced by the major pagan organizations of Hellenistic times; we ought now to examine how the Christian rites evolved in reference to them. Christian communion practices were not always as sanitized and as organized as they are today. And of course the origin of the ritual has its skeptics. John Allegro, in *The Sacred Mushroom and The Cross* has amassed arguments for the position that the original communion meal was a toxic and hallucinogenic mushroom. Unquestionably this species of fungus (amanita muscaria) was consumed in some Greek and Jewish rituals in antiquity, so it would be foolhardy to claim it has no connection to Christianity. But most people part company with Allegro when he claims that Jesus had no real historical existence, but represents only a code name for the mushroom.

On the other side, there is a long human tradition of gods (or men who represent them) being ceremonially eaten. The first century was not that far removed from the time when Carthaginians, Franks, Armenians, Syrians and Boeotians practiced ritual cannibalism of children. Christians were being unwise in talking publicly about secret mysteries, the eating of flesh and the drinking of blood, in an era when this wasn't accepted as just empty talk. Tertullian says, if we can believe him, that human blood was drunk in the worship of the Latarian Jove as late as 200 CE.

It may seem absurd today to devote time to a discussion of whether Christians did in fact ever practice cannibalism, but the fact is that their pagan contemporaries accused them of it over and over again. All around them were religions which practiced animal sacrifice, and urged believers to eat the sacrificed beast. The nineteenth century scholar Edwin Hatch alleged that lambs were occasionally sacrificed on Christian altars. Admittedly human beings are capable of nearly anything, so infant cannibalism cannot be totally discounted, but given Christian views on infant exposure and abortion, it does seem extremely unlikely. However, church fathers answered charges of cannibalism in such evasive ways that the reader is left feeling they are hiding something. One possibility is that the early communion loaf was baked in the form of a child—hence pagan accusations and reluctant Christian responses. This peculiar baking practice must have been persistent, for it was forbidden by Pope Pelagius I in the middle of the sixth century—and why forbid something that doesn't happen?

Both direct and indirect evidence suggests that early Christians avoided the circular host as a communion wafer: it was too pagan and too obviously solar. In the beginning, leavened bread was the norm for communion, since celebrants used people's ordinary loaves, and people took the leftover communion bread home to eat during the week. As the numbers of converts grew, this became uneconomical, and unleavened wafers were substituted as being both more convenient, and cheaper. Magic was part of the appeal of communion. It was common at the time for magicians to put spells on food so as to cause love. Such food was termed "eucharist."

Early Christian tradition in both writing and catacomb painting suggests that the typical eucharistic meal was bread and fish. The wealthy and comfortable ate good food, and quite a wide variety. For the poor, however, there was more boring fare, and much less of it. Most Christians lived in urban tenements called insulae, densely packed, often only one room per family, and so the weekly eucharistic gathering may often have been their only real meal for several days. Sometimes water was used, sometimes water mixed with wine, and if lamb could be found which had not come from a pagan sacrifice, it was eagerly consumed. There is no reason to believe that Christian communion feasts were significantly more pious than those carried on by pagans, and we know that pagan religious meals were often marked by heavy drinking, music, and a generally festive air.

Did early Christians actually believe they were consuming the actual body and blood of Christ? Probably, yes, they did. The theory of transubstantiation (the actual substance changing from bread to flesh, but the appearance remaining the same) was undeveloped until the thirteenth century, but ancient philosophers held that there was a strong but mystical bond between the symbol and the thing symbolized—so strong in fact that the two were perceived as being the same. This explanation has little appeal to modern people.

Paul's *Letter to the Corinthians* sheds some light on the true origin of Christian communion. He was alarmed that the Christians of Corinth apparently saw no difference between their ritual and the local pagan celebration. Other church fathers were to make the stock claim that the pagans had been inspired by the devil to imitate Christian practices, but it is extremely unlikely that as early as Paul's time the pagans were already given to shoddy imitation. The conclusion must be that it was the other way round: the Christian ritual was copied from an existing pagan practice. Scholars are dubious that the Jewish Passover is that source, nor does the Essene sacred meal seem likely. That leaves only the cults of pagan Greece, and in particular the meal of bread and wine shared in memory of Dionysos. It is somehow fitting that the origin of the communion ritual, so common among ancient religions, now seems to have not derived from any narrow tribal cult, but instead is derived from the god who annually provided humanity with wheat, grapes, wine and laughter.

20

SUPERSTITION

"When you believe in things that you don't understand
Then you suffer…"
Stevie Wonder

"Being naïve is not evil, but it can be dangerous. It can and does lead to self-righteousness, and to blind obedience to authority."
Hans Kung

A theme which we have returned to several times is that magic and astrology were vital components of religious belief during the late Roman Empire. The magic of early Christians was primarily in the form of miraculous cures, but the church also found itself also dragged into astrological determinism and compulsive behavior. In religious terms, someone who believes in magic believes that if a ritual is performed perfectly, the supernatural powers are compelled to provide the desired result. That is, the benefit will be derived regardless of the state of mind of either the supplicant or the god. Moreover, the whole of superstition is shot through with fear. Plutarch pointed it out two millennia ago, and it is still true today: the atheist denies the gods, but the superstitious person believes against his will, because he is afraid not to believe.

If we have the power to compel the gods, then it is critical that these powers of compulsion be kept secret. For the priests of the ancient world, living in overwhelmingly illiterate societies, the simplest way to keep these secrets was to write them down, first in their own language, and later in arcane and difficult tongues which only the priests knew. Thus sacred writings, especially ancient ones, came to be seen as powerful and mysterious forces, with every word inspired by the god. In that sense, the evangelical Christian's approach to the *Bible* is fundamentally a magical one.

The conquests of Alexander the Great, and the multicultural mixing which followed, had the effect of unleashing the magicians of Egypt and Mesopotamia on a wider Mediterranean world. This had significant results at a time when superstition played such a large role in the lives of the uneducated. There were important gradations in magical powers. Any common magician had the power of healing. Above him was the magus, who claimed to be Persian, but who often was a Palestinian fraud. The highest level of magic was practiced by the divine man, who really was a god or a demon in disguise.

The attitudes to magic in the Hellenized Empire remind one of the state of voodoo today. It could be used to bring down one's enemies. Romans wrote spells on tablets, then pierced them with nails to bring harm to the person named. Most commonly, though, magic was invoked to help solve health problems. Votive offerings were stone or clay images of some part of the body which needed to be healed. In the Naples region of southern Italy, piles of priapic forms were to be found as late as the nineteenth century. Apparently the problem of erectile dysfunction has been a persistent one.

Names played a major part in magical compulsion. People guarded their real names as carefully as we do our credit card numbers. Calling the true name of a god might compel his help, or it might make him angry—it was wise advice not to use a god's name in vain. Merely mentioning the name of a dead person might disturb his or her spirit, unless you added, "Rest in peace." Litanies, long lists of names, were commonly used in the ancient world, and it was risky to leave any name out. (I can recall as a child in the 1950s reciting the Litany of the Saints—"From the fury of the Northmen, O Lord, deliver us!" When I pointed out that the Northmen had not been a threat for over a thousand years, my religion teacher was quite unappreciative.) In Christianity, numerous healings have been performed using the magical powers associated with the names of Jesus and Mary. Magical compulsion still survives in children's rhymes ("Twinkle, twinkle little star" or "Ladybug, ladybug") The rhyme must be recited when the phenomenon is first noticed to bring about the desired effect.

The last half of the third century CE was a major turning point. The Empire was staggering from economic problems, epidemics, and barbarian attacks. At the same time, and maybe related to it, there seemed to be a loss of faith in the old gods; for example scholars report there was a dramatic drop in the number of prayers and funerary inscriptions. Historians of the written word remark on a sudden rise in credulousness, and a parallel rise in superstition even among the elites over those few decades. And Christianity was there to benefit from the increase in irrational fear. Wonder-working saints replaced the minor pagan gods. Amulets, spells, exorcisms, guardian angels, miraculous cures—the whole battery of supernatural ceremonies was advertised by the Christian preachers as evidence of superiority over paganism. Augustine observed:

"Very rarely, no, never does it happen that someone comes to us with the wish to become a Christian who has not been struck by some fear..."

The major beneficiaries of Christianity's alliance with magic were the priests. It was important that the priest be at least as powerful as the pagan magician, and so the magical aspects of the Christian religion had to be emphasized if it were to compete successfully for converts. Transformation of bread and wine into the body and blood of Christ had a powerful appeal to the third century mind, and gave a tremendous boost to the status of priests who had such power. Non-believers were dismissed before that part of the Mass, lest they discover the priestly secrets. Additionally, priests began to wear distinctive clothing, including the Roman (or dog) collar. This collar was itself the product of rank superstition. Demons were believed to become entangled in knots, and so priests avoided them by wearing the Roman collar.

The highest form of superstition was astrology. It required mathematical skill to cast horoscopes, and to calculate planetary positions, and Greek science had made those skills more readily available throughout the Mediterranean. Astral determinism held that your character was given to you at birth: as your soul traveled downward through the seven heavens toward your body, it picked up characteristics of those heavenly bodies near which it passed. Fate fixed your character. So there was no reason to expect sudden conversions, or radical changes of heart. Only magic could be of use as a remedy against your fate. Astrology governed birth, death, body parts, plants, animals, metals, stone, colour and taste. Many odd numbers were, and still are, considered lucky...folklore is full of the numbers 3, 7 and 9. On the other hand, 13 was extremely unlucky. People were characterized by their leading planetary influence as being mercurial, jovial, martial, saturnine, or lunatic. The belief in astrology was so widespread that Christianity had to come to terms with this psuedo-science. The church taught that fate rules a person until baptism, but after that the power of Christ is sufficient to overcome the effects of the stars. Astrology hung on in popular belief, and as Christianity converted more and more people, the Age of Faith might better be called the Age of Superstition.

No superstition proved more powerful than the belief in demons. Of course, a widespread belief in the existence of demons is accompanied by a widespread belief in demonic possession. It was a dominant theme in Palestine during the time of Jesus, and it was widely spread throughout the Empire over the next two centuries. Thus the main appeal of the new Christian religion was that it offered to deal with this type of mental illness by means of exorcism and miracles. However, miracle healing and the laying on of hands were stock elements of pagan belief as well.

The god Aesculapius in particular was a formidable foe of Jesus. His temples resembled the shrine at modern day Lourdes, with piles of crutches and canes, mute testimony to the miracles done in his name. Even Christians were impressed. Jesus' ultimate victory in this battle of the healer-gods was typical of many such struggles. It was a straight public-relations conflict, and Christian apologists were the masters. Christians argued that their champion possessed all the desirable qualities of his opponent. They cast doubt on their pagan rival, saying that Aesculapius' cures, unlike those of Jesus, wouldn't last. Soon portraits of Christ began to appear in poses that had been typical of Aesculapius. Thereafter, it was all over, and the pagan god was headed for oblivion.

By the fourth century, as Greek philosophy served to put Christian belief on a more rational footing, miracles were becoming more rare. In another attempt to impose orthodoxy and structure, the Church began to discourage them, claiming they were more suitable to the Apostolic Age, when God had played a more direct role in human affairs. There have of course been major revivals of faith healing in the Late Middle Ages, and in twentieth century America. Surveys of religious attitudes continue to show that most Americans, at least, still see miraculous intervention in ordinary life as an almost routine occurrence. So although magic and miracles played an essential part in the victory of Christ over his rivals, it was, and is, a victory of blind faith. The pagan writer Strabo was typical of the intellectuals of his time, and he had as dim a view of humanity as P.T. Barnum:

> "For the mob of women and all the uneducated masses cannot be brought to reverence, piety and faith by the reasoning or the exhortation of the philosopher. There is therefore a need for the instruments of superstition and this cannot be aroused without myths and marvels…"

Almost all prayers are appeals for divine intervention in human affairs. However, true prayer, such as that of Apollonius of Tyana, is that people come to accept the divine will, whatever that may be. By contrast, most prayers are requests for special favours, supplications that the god's will might conform to the will of the person. All religions routinely tell their believers that prayers work, even if the effect is to demean the deity by turning him into what Herbert Muller called a "cosmic bellhop". The image of a god so apparently willing to cancel, suspend or reverse his plans has always sat uncomfortably with thinkers of all religions.

Similarly, the problem of the existence of evil in a world created by a well-meaning god has proven insoluble. The Christian explanation is in fact taken from pagan Stoicism: apparent evil only seems evil because it is not perceived in correct relation to the whole. If, like God, we could only see the Big Picture, we would understand. That explanation didn't satisfy most people then, and it doesn't satisfy people now. As a result, magical appeals to the god have always been used to attempt to exempt the worshipper from even the apparent evil.

No Christian symbol has had a more powerful association with magic than does the cross. A wide variety of pre-Christian cultures had used it as a religious talisman, and its origin cannot be traced to any one religion or society. However, its use in ancient Egypt is well known. It probably began as a Nilometer—a crossbar on a vertical pole used to measure the height of the flood. In a desert country where the flood was life, the cross soon came to symbolize and measure that life. The Egyptian form of the cross, the ankh, is often seen in the hands of the Nile gods. It became the symbol of the sun-god, of life, and of the reproductive powers of the penis. Egyptian women wore it as an ornament around the neck, just as Christian women wear the cross today. The Hebrews, according to tradition, put a Tau cross (the capital T) on their doorposts by order of Moses. This form of cross was also very popular in Mesopotamia where it was a symbol of the saviour-god Tammuz. His lover, the goddess Ishtar, was shown holding a cross in her hand as a symbol of mourning. Buddhist use of the cross also long predates the Christian era.

The cross was also used by the Assyrians, the Chinese, the Etruscans, the Mayas, the Incas, and the Vestal Virgins in Rome. Coins from ancient Asia Minor have been found with a cross on one side, and a lamb on the other. Some Phoenician coins had a cross attached to a string of beads – the prototype of the rosary.

Devout Pharisees continued during the early Christian era to trace a T for Torah on their forehead, breast and shoulders, but when Christians adopted it as the Sign of the Cross, the Jews dropped it instantly and permanently. Soon crosses were widely employed by the Christian community: on doorways, lintels, foreheads, flocks of sheep, eucharistic bread and more.

Just as the cross is very old, with a long history of pagan usage, so is the crucifix. The crucified figure hanging from the tree was hardly original to Christianity, instead it represented whichever of the many pagan saviour-gods was in local favour. The Christian Fathers thus regarded the cross/crucifix with considerable ambivalence: it was a dramatic and powerful image, but it was unquestionably pagan. Minucius Felix, a Christian writing about 210 CE, objected strongly to the crucifix, pointing out that it had been used as a war standard by both the Romans, and the troops of Porus in his campaign against Alexander the Great. But, like most other battles against pagan ideas and symbols, this was a losing cause. When it became apparent that the crucifix was useful both as a magical talisman and a powerful image, its use was redirected to serve a "Christian" purpose.

No area of Christian dogma is more riddled with superstition than the beliefs about the afterlife. All the activities of Heaven—beatific visions of God, choral music, the contemplation of Truth and Beauty—were taken directly from the Orphics and their speculations. Our question here is how the believer was to get to Heaven, and what happened to him/her if that didn't work out. In general, Protestant theology has followed the stern lead of Martin Luther, and argued that a belief in Jesus and his teachings were essential for salvation. Early Christians were a bit more liberal—as witness the debate over whether Socrates was among the saved—but generally agreed that orthodox beliefs were essential.

But the cat had been among the pigeons for years. As early as 300 BCE, Diogenes the Cynic had posed the crucial question: does being baptized mean you will be happy after death, while all the uninitiated are doomed to eternal suffering? To most Christians, deeply enmeshed in magic, the answer was (and is) yes. But why should the innocent suffer? To Greek and Jew alike, the explanation was hereditary guilt. Christians called it Original Sin. It was an unpalatable idea for thinkers because it seemed too arbitrary and unpredictable. It seemed simpler to many to blame an outside force for the evil proclivities of mankind—the Devil.

Pan, the Greek god of terror, was transformed into the Satan of Christianity, but aspects of his character and accoutrements are derived from Seth, Baal, Ahriman, Mithra, and a lot of other retired deities and earth-serpents. From his capital city of Pandemonium, Pan oversaw the realms of Hell. (The actual English word Hell, however, seems to be derived from the Norse Hel, who was the guardian of the land of the dead.) Early Christians believed other gods existed, but they were regarded as evil demons native to Hell. These demons had successfully controlled the world until the birth of Jesus, but now were overawed and cowed by the power of Christ.

Christian preachers set about to make Hell a thoroughly unpleasant place, and by Dante's time in the fourteenth century, Hell was well-mapped and had seven levels.

Unquestionably, this whole construction was yet another fabrication of the pagan Graeco-Roman imagination. The Hebrew tradition had nothing like it. Sheol was simply a realm of nothingness. Gehenna was merely a rubbish fire. The garish "Christian" portrait of monstrous demons, sulfurous smoke and perennial torture would have been instantly rejected by Jesus or James the Just as being unacceptably and obviously pagan. Nevertheless, the graphic descriptions of the fires of Hell provided the faithful with tremendous encouragement to believe in the magical efficacy of the Christian sacraments. Similarly, the Mithraic idea of Purgatory, when it was adopted by Pope Gregory the Great, gave Christians the hope that their prayers could magically release a departed loved one to the happier realms of Paradise.

The tripartite division of the afterlife was so thoroughly pagan and so well known that its adoption by the church caused no stir. Such was not the case with the radical idea of the resurrection of the body. Christianity had adopted with enthusiasm the Orphic teaching that the body contained an immortal soul. But what happened when the body died? The only answer seemed to be that the body would be reunited in the afterlife with that soul. No wonder Christians developed a reputation for being especially reverent around corpses. No wonder martyred Christians had their bodies burned, cut up and scattered by their spiteful pagan persecutors. This belief in the eventual reunion of amputated limbs and destroyed parts has been termed the most incredible doctrine of any major religion. That is probably exaggeration, but it certainly did lead to confusion. Eventually, the church adapted, and began to teach that everyone underwent two judgments, and only after the second would the soul and body be reunited. Of all the tenets of Christianity, this one drew the most sneers and jeers from pagans. But today, in an era of routine heart and kidney transplants, of bionic limbs and blood transfusions, few people give a thought to it.

21

THE VIRGIN MARY AND THE ROLE OF WOMEN

"Mary is the lily in God's garden."

St.Birgitta of Sweden

As it was originally organized in the Greek cities of the Eastern Empire, Christianity was a very masculine religion. In striking contrast to most of their great pagan rivals, Judaism and Christianity had no female deities. Moreover, Christianity has successfully de-emphasized the role played by women in its formation: few people today realize that both *Mark* and *John* mention Mary Magdalene as the first witness to the Resurrection. Despite its male bias, however, Christianity appealed to many women—it was less sexist than Mithraism. Still, both the Trinity and the priesthood, for example, were all male affairs. But the Great Goddess of the Middle East is not so easily defeated. She had flourished since at least 7000 BCE, and after the Christian conquest of the Empire, she emerged again as the Virgin Mary, pretty much unchanged. After all, Mary had the same emotional appeal as Isis or Attis or Adonis—she had lived a human life and she understood suffering. Even her name reveals her as the traditional mother of the hero, for many ancient gods were born of mothers whose names were variants of Mary (Adonis/Myrrha; Buddha/Maya; Krishna/Maritala; Moses/Miriam; Hermes/Maia). Thus we can have no confidence that the mother of Jesus was actually named Mary, or any version of it.

The *New Testament* shows no evidence of Mariology, and makes no comment on her sinlessness. In fact, it says very little about her at all: no Immaculate Conception, no childhood or life, nothing on her death or Assumption. All that was a result of mythmaking which came about long after her time, as Mary's image grew to be the feminine counterweight to Jesus. Oddly, the *Gospel of John* does not refer to her by name. For instance, John lists as witnesses to the Crucifixion "…his mother, and his mother's sister, Mary the wife of Clopas, and Mary Magdalene." This is very unclear: are there three women or four? Why is Mary not named?

In fact, we should disregard the whole story as being fabricated by John. If Jesus was, say, thirty-five years old when he was crucified, and Mary was sixteen when he was born, then that would make her in her early fifties, and her sister would be of similar age. When the average lifespan in Galilee was thirty-five, it is unthinkable that two women of that advanced age would have taken on the two hundred kilometer round trip to Jerusalem on foot, probably with no notice, to witness a crucifixion. (Of course, age may have been no barrier…it wouldn't have been for her husband Joseph. In *The History of Joseph the Carpenter*, he is said to have lived to one hundred and eleven, and to have died with all his teeth.)

For a young Jewish girl of the first century, childbearing was a central life event. Status was achieved by having several children, preferably sons. However, the Christian religion immediately began to spread among the pagans, and they had other ideas—powerful traditions of virgin goddesses such as Artemis/Diana. As the Empire converted to Christianity, the temples of these goddesses, such as the great Temple of Diana at Ephesus, were reconsecrated to the Virgin Mary. The tradition of Mary as virgin began to grow.

Humans have sex, goddesses usually do not. Maybe, speculated some early churchmen, the Virgin Mary never had sex at all. In the second century, *The Proto-Gospel of James* first suggests her perpetual virginity. By the fourth century, Jerome was arguing that it was unthinkable that Mary could have had other children. James and the other siblings were declared to be "cousins" of Jesus. While Mary was recognized as the Mother of God, God was not to have siblings.

By 430 CE, Cyril of Alexandria, well acquainted with the Isis-worship in his city, championed the image of Mary as the all-holy Virgin Mother of God at the Council of Ephesus. By the sixth century the cult was officially approved. But by then the mythmakers had moved on to the question of how the Virgin Mother of God could possibly have had a sinful nature. Soon her sinlessness was extended backward before her birth. Surely the Mother of God must have been immaculately conceived without the human taint of Original Sin. Although Christian thinkers from Bernard of Clairvaux to Thomas Aquinas thought this doctrine was rubbish, it continued to flourish. It existed as part of the Catholic Church for centuries, and in 1854 Pope Pius IX declared it to be an official doctrine.

The Assumption came next. Mary, it was said, was raised body and soul to heaven, where she presumably joined Semele, mother of the divine Dionysos, who had been similarly transported millennia ago. The myth of Mary's ascension is attributed to a deservedly obscure bishop of the second century, but it likely emerged much later, and continued to grow for centuries. The dogma was proclaimed by Pope Pius XII speaking ex cathedra (that is, infallibly) in 1950. A new Feast of the Assumption of the Blessed Virgin was added to the church calendar, to be celebrated each August 13, which just happens to be the day sacred to Artemis, the Virgin Goddess of the Greeks.

Worship of Mary had to tread a fine line. She was far greater than a human woman, but in that increasingly misogynistic age, she could be neither called a goddess, nor worshipped directly. A sect called the Marianites had been condemned for this error in the fifth century. Nevertheless, Mary has been treated as divine by millions of pious Christians, whether or not the theologians approved. Christian art frequently shows the Magi or shepherds worshipping a crowned and jeweled Mary and her infant son, with Mary getting most of the attention. Her cult grew throughout the Middle Ages, particularly her image as the grieving Mater Dolorosa. Few images in the history of mankind carry as much emotional wallop as Michelangelo's Pieta. The late medieval enthusiasm for chivalry and courtly love further contributed to the idealization of Mary: no longer just the submissive wife and devoted mother, she now became the idealized love image for all Christian women.

Mariology had a major setback during the Protestant Reformation when reformers purged her as a pagan intrusion into "pure" Christianity, but it is still very much alive in traditional Catholicism. The popularity of shrines at Fatima and Lourdes show the deep need for a supportive maternal figure. That more recent European event, the appearance of the Virgin of Medjugorje, similarly appeals to the group that Mariology has always courted: working class, anti-intellectual, deeply conservative, apocalyptic, and overwhelmingly female. Mariology, like some other forms of paganism, was unable to enter Christianity by the front door, so it was smuggled in by the unlettered and the disenfranchised.

Of course, the attitude to the Virgin Mary is completely intertwined with the Christian attitude to women and sex. Early Christianity was one of the few societies in human history to have expressed a collective death wish. Virginity, celibacy, monasticism and misogyny had all originated as pagan ideas, but their rigour appealed to Christians, who took them to heart. These values seemed so much more noble than the prosaic virtues of family, children, and continuance of the species.

Certainly the degree of sexual variety in the Roman Empire was wide—maybe too wide: brother-sister marriages among Egyptian royalty, homosexual partnerships in Greece, plenty of domestic sex with slave girls and concubines, eunuchs, Roman aristocratic orgies, adult adoption, easy divorces, pornography, child marriage, and on and on. The Emperor Claudius was considered quite an oddball for only liking adult women. A.N. Wilson said that the idea that the gods would be angry at men for loving boys would have been laughable at the time. Yet that was Paul's position, and it was to become dominant.

The Gospel version of Jesus paints him as treating women respectfully, and according a high place to Mary Magdalen. Paul, deeply steeped in Greek misogyny, was much more harsh. In I *Corinthians* he says"…it is shameful for a woman to speak in church…" and the psuedo-Paul echoed this in *I Timothy* "…I permit no woman to teach or have authority over a man; she is to keep silent…" Probably no other *Bible* verses have caused so much hand-wringing, so many lame explanations, or have been so widely disregarded. But Paul was both immensely influential and ahead of his time, for although his rule was unworkable in practice the general distrust of women became widespread.

The historians agree that women played a large role in the early Church. No priesthood yet existed, and meetings were usually held in a home with the host or hostess in charge. It also seems likely that women were in a decided majority in the first few centuries. There is mention of lots of Christian wives who had pagan husbands, but oddly no Christian husbands with pagan wives. By about 150 CE conservative bishops were separating the sexes during Mass, and by 200 women were banned from public participation in divine worship.

Certainly mainline Christianity was having none of the radicalism being practiced in Gnostic groups. Tertullian and Irenaeus, among others, expressed shock that Gnostics gave leadership positions to women, and even let them baptize! Apocryphal texts such as the *Gospel of Philip*, which claimed that Jesus preferred Mary Magdalen to the other disciples and even kissed her on the mouth, stirred outrage, and were banned.

Most Christians then, as cults often do, saw the world as alien and evil, full of seductions and temptations. They were proud of their puritanical sexual attitudes as a major distinguishing feature of their group. But these attitudes were completely in step with the mystery cults of Isis and Mithra. These pagan sects might require sexual purity—suspending adulterers, and restricting sex within marriage. Their priests might be required to be virgins, or those who had vowed to abstain.

Within Christianity it was agreed that virginity was best. Marriage had been ordained by God only because people were so weak. So marriage was virtually an admission of spiritual failure. Since sex for fun was unacceptable, the procreation of children was the only reason for married people ever to have sex. And who in their right mind would want to bring a child into a world that was about to end? In 251 CE, the plague struck the city of Carthage. Bishop Cyprian told his surprised flock that the plague was good—that it allowed young women to die with their virginity intact.

Augustine, in one of his bursts of self-righteousness, suggested that good people ought to regret ever having sex, and further speculated that married people might be treated as second class citizens in Heaven. Jerome went further. He thought adult virgins ought to avoid baths—their nakedness would doubtless embarrass them. He hoped that attractive Christians ought to deliberately adopt slovenly dress, so as not to distract others with their beauty. Tertullian called women "The gate by which the demon enters." Cosmetics, jewellery and wigs were out. Women were to come to worship veiled, so their hair would not distract men. Most of this misogyny owed nothing to the early Christians of Palestine, of course, but had been taken from the Greeks. The Romans were a bit more liberal: Epictetus, Seneca and Plutarch had seen enough of the world to consider a degree of sexual equality, but their voices were drowned out in the general reaction against women's rights.

There were good social reasons for a woman to maintain her virginity and they might well be masked as piety. Marriage customs of the time often married a thirteen year old girl to a much older husband. A vow of virginity might free a girl from taking a tyrannical husband, from the pain of childbirth, and from the travails of raising a family. Moreover, girls marrying older men meant lots of young widows. Paul advised these widows not to remarry. In any case, within the Christian community there seemed quite a few widows and virgins, and they were responsible for doing much of the charitable work of which the Church was so proud.

The church did provide one example of using sex for a noble purpose. Women who converted to Christianity were told not to have sex with their pagan spouses. We might anticipate that this practice led to a large number of family disruptions, and many hasty conversions of husbands.

A second group that successfully evaded the guardians of dogma were those in the fine arts. The Judaic aversion to statuary disappeared rapidly in the early church, swamped as it was by things pagan. By 200 CE, most of the classic themes of Christian art had already appeared, and Christians were happily converting pagan works into Christian ones. The astrological sign of Pisces the fish for example, was appropriated. Its letters formed an anagram on the divinity of Jesus, and its astrological reference, although totally pagan, suggested that Christianity was the new religion of the new star-age. Likewise, the lamb, despite its connections to Dionysos and Mithra, proved irresistible. The image of the Good Shepherd was a particular favourite. The first god to be shown with a lamb on his shoulders was Hermes, and the phrase "Good Shepherd" was derived from the worship of Apollo. So it is impossible to tell, when a figure of this sort appears from the second or third century, whether the god was Hermes or Apollo or Jesus. Many statues of Osiris were assumed to be those of Jesus, so were other statues of the various sun-gods, and the portrayals of Isis and Horus became the Madonna and Child of Christian tradition.

Were early Christians not dismayed by this obvious parroting of paganism? Did it not bother many of them that their religion was so derivative? No, it didn't, because, to be blunt, the bulk of Christian believers were remarkably vulgar, and deeply anti-intellectual. Religious faith and convictions are always ready to degenerate into credulity and empty opinion, and Christian authorities did not seem alarmed when this occurred. Jesus had taught plain people in a plain language, but by our period, Christianity had become so infused with magic and wide-eyed naïveté that it was indelibly a lower class movement. True, the *New Testament* had been written by and for a more educated crowd, but Christian converts since that time had been overwhelmingly illiterate, and it had made a great impact. Thus the Neoplatonic philosophy and lofty ideals of the *Gospels* and *Epistles* had minimal effect on the majority of believers.

The Koine Greek of the *New Testament* was itself a problem. It was initially useful in exposing Christianity to a wider world, but its uncouth and uneducated phrasing grated on the ears of the cultured. We who are used to the lofty cadences of the *King James Version* have difficulty understanding how serious this obstacle was. But there are over a quarter million inscriptions and letters form this period which have survived, chiefly prayers, business documents, thanksgivings and epitaphs, and it is undeniable that a vast cultural gap separated the average Christian from the literate classes. It is curious that pagan authors who are accepted as learned on social or economic matters are attacked as unthinking bigots when they dismiss Christianity as a bundle of superstitions fit only for peasants. As one example among many, a Syrian bishop near the end of the second century was so convinced of the immediacy of Christ's return that he led his flock out into the desert to meet the Saviour halfway. The results of his millenarian impulses were disastrous of course, just as the results of Jamestown and of Waco have been in our time.

Pagans were first puzzled and then angered by Christian disloyalty to the Emperor. Jews had been exempted from emperor-worship, and had even been permitted to mint their own non-idolatrous coins. But Judaism was seen as a national religion: odd and intolerant, but understandable. Christianity, by contrast, made converts of anyone, had no homeland, and was distinctly international. It was entitled to no exemption. The symbolic act of putting incense into a burner on the Emperor's statue required about the same degree of commitment for them that standing for the national anthem at a ball game does for us. But Christians refused. Moreover, Christians declined to hold public office, avoided military service, and generally behaved in disloyal and unpatriotic ways. This conduct incurred the wrath of ordinary folk far more than of imperial bureaucrats, and it seems clear that most official persecutions of Christians was a result of public demand that something be done.

So there were good reasons why Christianity was unappealing to many pagans. It seemed immoral. It appealed shamelessly to the rabble, to sinners, and even to criminals. People of the Roman Empire were not raised with our belief in equality, and the Christian doctrine of spiritual equality ran opposite to the ideal of the good man as taught by pagan ethicists. In summary, it is perhaps today's Jehovah's Witnesses who are the closest analogy to early Christians. Unintellectual, socially despised, and fiercely committed, the Witnesses seem precisely the kind of people who made up the early church which was to triumph over its pagan rivals.

Whether or not Christianity was responsible for the death of ancient science is a charge which some critics have made, and it is worth examining. Certainly the loss of interest in science coincided generally with the rise of the mystery religions, religions which preferred to explain events in terms of miracles and wonders. It cannot be denied that Christianity was responsible for this tide of anti-intellectualism. As Tertullian said, "Philosophy is the mother of all heresy." And so, by about 300 CE, any Christian who questioned the Resurrection or the Virgin Birth was charged with heresy. But you couldn't question what you didn't know about, and the church busily set about restricting information. At the Fourth Council of Carthage in 398 CE, the attending bishops issued the incredible order that no more secular books were to be read by Christians. In 494, Pope Gelasius issued a decree banning 61 books which he personally disliked, including some epistles and gospels. Not surprisingly, an orgy of book burning followed. Christianity's rejection of scientific medicine proved particularly costly to society when new plagues such as measles swept through the great cities and counted millions of casualties.

But Christianity since its foundation had encountered difficulties in adjusting to an enormous empire in which pagan learning was everywhere. Commerce, education and religion frequently ran together, and the lines were often blurred. For example, the temple of Hadad in Damascus was also the location for the chief market of the city. Porticoes of pagan temples frequently served as classrooms for aspiring physicians and lawyers. Naturally, no Christian could follow callings such as astrologer or magician, or be directly employed by a temple. But Christian religious scruples also outlawed other callings which had considerable contact with pagan learning: professor, teacher, mathematician. Christian children were usually kept out of schools to prevent their becoming polluted by the myths of pagan antiquity. Even seemingly harmless trades such as stonecutter or carpenter were affected, since devout Christians would do no work associated with pagan shrines, and these shrines represented a major source of income for skilled labourers. Generally Christians saw only evil when they looked at the larger society. They were told to avoid the theatre and all public games, but there is some doubt whether that admonition was totally observed. Christians were suspicious of pleasure and fun: music, white bread, shaving, foreign wine, even warm baths. And they seem to have been quite content to throw out philosophy, and its practical handmaidens medicine and mathematics, and to trust themselves to the hands of Christ the Healer.

Christian hostility to classical literature and history was also evident. We can understand their dislike of Homer, Virgil, and other literary giants because of their mention of the gods, and because their works were used as teaching texts in pagan classrooms. But Christianity also put an end to historical writing. Military chronicles, biography, political history, and diplomatic history—all were discouraged and fell into disuse. However, Christianity, as a historical religion, could not totally ignore the past, so two new branches of writing—church history and the lives of the saints—were invented and practiced by Christian writers.

These hammer blows of anti-intellectualism destroyed science for a thousand years. The official story has always been that it was the fault of the Goths, of the Vandals, of the Huns. But the plain fact is that the Age of Ignorance was largely Christianity's doing. We cannot say how much knowledge was lost. An example: many classical Greeks from Pythagoras to Aristotle understood very well that the earth was a sphere. Aristarchus of Samos described the solar system and correctly deduced that the sun was the centre. In the orgy of Christian destruction, only Ptolemy's work on astronomy survived, and Ptolemy held the unprovable notion that the earth was at the centre. Astronomy was stopped dead for ten centuries. Unquestionably, other losses have been even more severe, but we are unaware of them. We will probably never know what we have lost. The assessment made by the Florentine thinkers of the fourteenth century was right: only the revival of pagan Graeco-Roman values reignited the cause of learning in Europe. No wonder scientific hackles go up when evangelical Christians demand that *Genesis* and evolution be given equal time in American classrooms.

22

THE PAGANS STRIKE BACK

"There is no wild beast like an angry theologian."
Emperor Julian

The growth of the new religion did not occur without adverse pagan comment. Much of it was of the mudslinging variety, and in these exchanges the Christians gave as good as they got. There were, for example, those mutual accusations of human sacrifice hurled between Mithraists and Christians. On second thought, it is not quite accurate to say Christianity gave as good as it got—it gave far better than it got. By the end of the fifth century, its pagan rivals had been routed so completely that Europe and the Mediterranean had become, officially at least, a one-religion society. Christians were winners, albeit not gracious or charitable ones.

We need to bear in mind that during this period of rapid growth the Christian Fathers did not have the same attitude to truth that we espouse. Shading the evidence, omitting disgraceful episodes, suppression, and even out and out lies were all common: after all, it was for the greater glory of God. The result of all this is that, as modern historians sit down to read what remains of the religious records of the Roman Empire, they have to put themselves in the place of a devout pagan if they hope to reflect any kind of historical objectivity. Quite frequently, of course, this bias was the unintended result of general ignorance. Even among educated Christian writers were men such as Augustine, who could be amazingly credulous. He claimed he saw Ethiopians

"...without heads, who had two great eyes in their breasts and...people who had but one eye in their foreheads..."

Bear in mind that Augustine was one of the brightest lights in Christian philosophy, a Doctor of the Church. If he could write this kind of drivel, what were the average Christians saying and believing? Obviously their gullibility was irritating to many of their pagan neighbours, and about 180 CE it triggered a reaction from Celsus, a pagan Roman intellectual with a good grip of Jewish and Christian beliefs. He produced *The True Doctrine*, a caustic examination of the origins of Christianity. The book has long since been destroyed by Christians, so we know it only indirectly. But the attack was so biting, so convincing, and so well known that seventy years later the Christian writer Origen, attempting to rebut him, quoted heavily from the original work.

Celsus first teed off on the quality of recruits to the Christian cause:

"Let no educated man enter, no wise man, no prudent man, for such things we deem evil; but whoever is ignorant, whoever is unintelligent, whoever is simple—let him come and be welcome."

Christian converts consisted of:

> "...wool-workers, cobblers, laundry-workers, and the most illiterate and bucolic yokels who would not dare to say anything at all in front of their elders and more intelligent masters..."

And once baptized, the admonition was

> "Do not examine, just believe!"

He also pointed out their tendency to disagree with one another:

> "Christians, it is needless to say, utterly detest each other. They slander each other constantly with the vilest form of abuse..."

He personally knew a few miracle-workers from the Eastern Mediterranean, and he lumped Jesus in with them. They frequently claimed to be divine or "the Son of God", and to have the power to save their followers from the apocalypse to come. Their followers were gullible, taken in by phony miracles and wonders. Christians were, Celsus said, little better than the crazy galli of Cybele.

He was the first thinker to demolish the literal *Genesis* account of creation. He called it shallow and simple-minded. Surely, said Celsus, anyone of intelligence could see that this was all meant as allegory. It's astounding—eighteen centuries have passed since Celsus wrote this, but American political leaders still talk about Adam and Eve as though they existed.

Celsus then proceeded to dissect the life of Jesus and the Church's claim to represent a new Chosen People. He asked that critical question: how reliable are the *Gospels*? And he foreshadowed modern historians with his answer: they are not reliable at all. Jesus' teachings, said Celsus, were a garbled and simplified version of Plato and other Greek thinkers. None of it was new. Probably Jesus had worked as a labourer in Egypt, and so had picked up some Greek ideas, and a little Egyptian magic, before returning to dazzle the ignorant.

It was contradictory to claim that a god could die, if only for three days. Just as absurd was the insistence on the resurrection of the body. Celsus certainly knew enough Greek religion to discern the true origins of many Christian ideas, but at least, he said, the Greeks had not been insolent enough to claim that these absurdities came from God.

The questions he posed were devastating. Why did Jesus, if he was the saviour of the world, come so late in time? Didn't he or his father care about the countless generations long since dead? Was Jesus really the author of the sayings attributed to him? How many times had the *Gospels* been rewritten or edited the better to fit current controversies?

Most damaging of all were Celsus' attacks on Christianity's underbelly: its relationship with Judaism. For the Jews had not disappeared, they were very much in evidence. Christians were trying to claim an antiquity and legitimacy that was not theirs. If Christians were truly the new Chosen People, how could they openly violate Jewish Scripture—God's direct word to the Chosen People? Jesus had clearly declared the Jewish Law must be upheld; yet here were Christians eating pork, ignoring the Sabbath, and walking about uncircumcised. Jesus and John the Baptist were undeniably Jewish, so it must have been their disciples who got off track. As the first serious critic to raise these issues, Celsus made Christianity appear to be illegitimate and discreditable.

Celsus was also distressed at the political stance adopted by the Christian church. Why was it so hostile to civilization?

How could Christians stand by while their society was attacked by barbarians? Why wouldn't they fight? Celsus correctly identified religion as a pillar of society, but his call for a return to the old values was in vain. The lesson of his book is an object lesson to us all: logic and learning are of no effect on the willfully blind.

But Celsus could not have been alone in holding these views. They must have been reasonably well known, or else Origen's book *Contra Celsum* would never have been written, or at least would never have contained so many damaging quotations. Origen himself was more than a little peculiar. He was yet another of those giant intellects that kept popping up in Alexandria's schools. His father had been a Christian martyr, and Origen had followed a lifestyle of extreme asceticism. He refused to wear shoes, for example, and he had castrated himself while still a young man. But he must have sublimated his energies, for he was a prolific author who churned out thousands of pamphlets. In fact, we might suspect him of intellectual hyperactivity, for at one point he employed seven full time scribes to jot down his ideas.

However, his defences against the attacks of Celsus strike the modern reader as weak and inadequate. He denied that there had been any significant revision to the *Gospels*. He declined to answer Celsus' thorny questions about the fate of all those who died before the time of Christ. True, he admitted, Christians refused to actually fight barbarians, but they formed "an army of piety" which prayed for the well being of the Empire. Yes, he agreed, Christians were a bit antisocial:

> "…the people of Christ are hated by all nations, even by those who dwell in the remotest parts of the world."

But Origen's book does make three points which were to be of lasting significance, and two of them were useful insights. The first was that if Christianity is bad, paganism is worse. This claim, which amounts to "...Naah, naah, so's your old man!" has been repeated by many others, always without evidence, for two millennia. Second, he points out that Christianity offers a noble path and hope for all, however much individuals may stray. Third and most interestingly for us, Origen affirmed that it must be understood that parts of the *Bible* are symbolic, and contain layers of meaning. As a minor example, he mentioned the temptation of Jesus by the devil from a mountaintop. Everybody knows, said Celsus, there is no mountain high enough to see all the kingdoms of the world. Of course it is meant allegorically, and so are many, many other examples from the *Gospels*. In many of his other works he explained some of the symbolism in Jewish and Christian tradition, and so he tried to put Christianity on a permanent reasonable foundation.

But not even a stout defender of the faith such as Origen was secure from the cavils of the bishops and theologians. After his death, the Church posthumously declared him a heretic, and much of his work was promptly destroyed or heavily edited. The notion that some (or, horrors! all) of the *Bible* stories might be symbolic was regarded as a particularly mischievous one, and literalist theologians fought a long and ultimately successful running battle against it.

So while Origen is still regarded as a Father of Christianity, (surely the only eunuch to be so designated!) his work in turn infuriated the great pagan philosopher Porphyry. Porphyry was widely acknowledged as a man of staggering erudition, and saw himself as a follower of Plato. His criticism of Christianity was made more formidable by his broad leaning and his powerful and trained intellect, and was given impetus by his encounters with individual Christians. Several generations of Christian apologists struggled in vain to defuse his arguments. Eventually in 448 CE, the Christian emperor Theodosius II invoked the ultimate weapon in the world of ideas, so that virtually nothing of his writing survives.

We know only a few of the many issues which Porphyry raised in the fifteen destroyed volumes, but what little survives indicates that he treated Christianity with a scathing sarcasm rare in his time and unseen in ours. His starting point was a close comparative reading of the four *Gospels*, and a series of objections to their historical reliability. If Jesus is to be regarded as a historical person, said Porphyry, then his life should be examined using the same criteria we would apply to, say, Julius Caesar. While he raised serious questions about the life and teachings of Jesus, he was especially brutal toward Christian believers of his own time, whom he characterized as "confused and vicious." For example, *Mark 16:18* claims that Christian preachers are under God's protection ..."And if they drink any deadly drug, it will hurt them in no way." Fine, said Prophyry, let's give deadly drugs to those aspiring to be priests. That will separate out the charlatans. Porphyry was convinced that a significant number of Christian preachers were con men and bunko artists, out to defraud their gullible listeners. He heaped scorn on the Eucharist: eating a body and drinking blood was cannibalism, and even if it were meant symbolically, who could possibly believe it was the key to eternal life?

Reading the fragments of Porphyry that remain is an eerie experience, since he hits so many notes familiar to the modern reader. He had no patience for *Bible* prophecy, claiming that *Old Testament* prefigurements of Jesus could have applied to anybody anytime. Jesus was born, he suggests, to a young girl named Miriam who had become pregnant as a result of a rape by a Roman soldier. Christian writers had fabricated both the hopelessly tangled genealogy and several events in Jesus' life. The passion story is filled with inconsistencies...somebody is trying to cover up embarrassing events. In fact, Porphyry was the first to examine the many contradictions in the *Gospel* stories, and he pointed to editing and fudging by early Christians as the probable reason. The parables he dismissed as trivial and incomprehensible. He contrasted the careers of Jesus and Apollonius of Tyana, and voted for Apollonius. He thought Jesus was far more deeply involved in anti-Roman politics than the *Gospels* admit, and suggested Jesus deserved to die because he probably was inciting rebellion.

His comments on the early church were equally caustic, and he saw both Peter and Paul as charlatans. He accurately observed that it was not Jesus but his followers who claimed he was divine. He examined the conflict between Paul and the Jerusalem church, and he suggested that Jesus would have been outraged at the changes in ritual and belief promoted by his disciples. He considered that Peter had murdered those resolute anti-communists Ananias and Sapphira. He dismissed Origen's characterization of Christianity as a religion of hope, saying that a religion that offers baseless hopes founded on a false history is of no use to humanity.

It was a powerful and comprehensive attack. What little remains of the fifteen volumes exists only in scattered form, often quoted in a highly negative context by later Christian writers. He clearly had access to sources long since lost—for example, he claims that Tacitus and other reputable Roman writers had accused Christians of participating in orgies, although such claims have long since been excised from their works. In short, had all or most of Porphery's work survived, this book, as well as much other theological criticism would have been made unnecessary.

We have to assume that the biting criticisms voiced by Celsus and Porphyry had a broad base of support among many of the pagans of the Empire. It was apparently easy to dislike the followers of Christ, and many people did so with gusto. On occasion, the Roman state could even be prodded into persecutions. Not all persecutions were the same, of course. Those under the emperors Nero and Marcus Aurelius were relatively mild. But by about 250 CE, Christianity was large enough to be perceived as a serious threat to imperial stability, and the persecutions by Decius and Diocletian were serious: torture, death, slavery, and the gruesome public executions connected with the games and circus.

In the first two centuries, magistrates seem to have reacted with tolerance and forbearance when pressured by lower class pagans to do something about Christianity. Pliny, Suetonius, and Tacitus were all educated Romans, not particularly anti-Christian, who had a fair degree of worldly experience, and they dismissed the new religion as a bundle of harmless superstitions. However, as Porphyry pointed out, Christians took great pride in their unwillingness to compromise. Recent examinations of the trial records of a number of Christian martyrs seem to show that the magistrate was reluctant to pass the death sentence, but was really given no choice by the fiery-eyed Christian defendant. Tertullian tells of a group of Christians in 185 CE who approached a touring Roman governor and asked to be put to death. The governor refused, suggesting they might use ropes or a cliff, and do it themselves.

The persecution by Nero in 64 CE is puzzling, because there could have been very few Christians in Rome at that early date, and to any Roman they would have been indistinguishable from Jews. One suggestion is that Jews initiated the persecution, but this is unlikely. Another is that Christians did indeed start the great fire, but their motives would be a complete mystery, so this too is improbable. Nevertheless, the confusion between Christian and Jew continued for some time. When it became clear that they were separate religions, Christians lost their exemption from emperor-worship, and their troubles began in earnest.

Christians were classified as second only to Epicureans as virulent proponents of atheism. To the pagan of the time, a monotheism which denied the reality of all other gods was atheism, and was downright uncivilized. As Porphyry pointed out, any refusal to take part in the traditional Roman rites insulted both the gods and one's ancestors, and put the whole society at risk. Records indicate that Roman governors usually tried to compromise: would the accused offer incense to the Emperor? No. Would they eat sacrificial meat? No. Would they swear by the Emperor's good fortune? No. Given the superstitious nature of the Romans, and the nearseditious refusal of Christians to join the army, the wonder is that the persecutions were not more common, and more severe.

All in all, historians are convinced that the number of Christian martyrs was exaggerated by the propagandists. Martyrdom for a religious idea was relatively new and unusual—it required a degree of certitude about the afterlife that most religious people of the time did not have. Moreover, the Romans were nothing if not legalistic, so there were few pogroms. Many Christians were farmers in Egypt, Anatolia and North Africa, and Rome depended on them for the grain supply. Mostly their pagan neighbours would have seen these people who lived quietly around them as much like themselves. Certainly we can say that the number of martyrs was far less than the number of Christians who chose to cooperate with official demands. Still, there were martyrs. Most were simply beheaded. The traditional view is that Roman crowds were thrilled by unarmed Christians, especially well-born women, being sent in to their death against gladiators, bulls, leopards and bears.

Whether few or many, martyrs had enormous posthumous respect within the Christian community. Short accounts of their lives and sufferings were published. Often these tended to be standardized and scripted—it was fantasy literature. Bones of the martyrs, and objects associated with their lives were venerated and worshipped. People who died as virgins, it was taught, received sixty times the heavenly blessings of an ordinary person; and martyrs received one hundred times the rewards. We leave to the reader to calculate the celestial benefits for St. Cecilia, St. Agnes or St. Agatha, or the many others who were both virgins and martyrs. Christian adulation for martyrs was getting out of control, and the bishops eventually had to step in to regulate who might be classed as a martyr, and to set up standards for sainthood.

In summary, the idea of martyrdom played an important part in the early church, as did the notion that Christians were constantly being persecuted for their faith. The pious legends that beleaguered Christians were forced to retreat to underground catacombs so they might hold their meetings in safety now seems improbable. Like the Mithraists, and probably influenced by them, Christians seemed to prefer underground worship and underground burial. If security had been a major problem, it is unlikely we would find Christian catacombs that contain so much artwork, or that had been used over such long periods of time.

23

A Tale of Two Emperors

"Might was the measure of Right."

Lucan

"Religion is regarded by the common people as true, by the wise as false, and by rulers as useful."

Seneca

The final remarkable character in our story is the Roman emperor who came to be known as Constantine the Great. The story of his "conversion" at the Battle of Milvian Bridge is a well-known bit of folklore. The story goes that the evening before the fateful battle against his rival Maxentius for control of the imperial throne, Constantine saw a cross in the clouds, and decided that this was an omen. He ordered his troops to paint a cross on their shields and, whether through divine intervention or otherwise, he won the battle. The exact nature of the cross, and its meaning to Constantine at the time, is still disputed. Some think that the conversion had nothing to do with religion, but was yet another of Constantine's cunning political moves.

Late in life Constantine gave a highly embroidered version of these events to the historian Eusebius which included a dream, a heavenly voice, and an appearance by Jesus who (astoundingly) gave him advice on military strategy for the upcoming battle. But neither Constantine nor Eusebius are reliable at all.

Constantine's position as a Christian hero is dubious. His personal life left a lot to be desired. He was exceptionally vain: he required 1000 hairdressers, not to mention the "innumerable" cooks and eunuchs. And he was uncommonly ruthless, even by the low standards of the imperial court at the time. He had hundreds of unarmed Frankish prisoners put to death in a public arena. Nor did he shrink from murder. He murdered a rival, his brother-in-law, and his nephew. When he also murdered his own son, his wife, the daughter of Coel, Duke of Britain (Old King Cole) had the effrontery to criticize him, so he had her locked in her bath and boiled to death. Clearly he was not one to be hindered by mere scruples, for as he wrote to the Patriarch of Alexandria:

> "We have received from Divine Providence the supreme favour of being relieved from all error."

Constantine was raised in the worship of the sun-god, and did not actually convert to Christianity until on his deathbed. Although we cannot speculate with any confidence about his thought process, it seems quite likely that he refrained from calling himself a Christian because he was egoistical enough to believe that he was the Anointed, the New Christ. For example, at his enormously elaborate and expensive public ceremonies, Constantine preferred to be greeted by shouts of "Holy! Holy! Holy!" So both his religious enthusiasm and his moral character remain in considerable doubt. He was clearly far more interested in Christianity as a politically useful force than in its potential for human improvement. Constantine was all too willing to use Christianity for political ends, and the Church, to its shame, was all too willing to cooperate.

Constantine's reign came to mark a watershed in both the creation of central religious authority, and in its enforcement of doctrinal orthodoxy.

Certainly there had been imperial persecutions before Constantine—of Christians, Jews, Dionysiacs, Isiacs, and many others—but they had been undertaken in the interest of civic loyalty. However, after it became the de facto official religion under Constantine, the Christian church rapidly learned to use its position to harass its pagan enemies. Constantine, for his part, tried to use his authority to unite Christianity by bringing heretical sects into line. We really can't talk about "orthodoxy" before the time of Constantine because until then, no side had the political firepower to enforce its view.

The attempt to enforce conformity in Christian doctrine peaked at the Council of Nicaea in 325 CE. Some 300 bishops (including Nicholas of Smyrna, the prototype of Santa Claus), their travel expenses subsidized from the imperial coffers, assembled under the not-so-benevolent eye of the emperor to decide pressing issues of faith. Constantine had already made half-hearted attempts to legislate an end to heretical sects, but there were too many, and the situation was too confusing. Nicaea would remedy all that. On arrival, the bishops promptly piled dozens of petitions against other Christians in Constantine's lap. He burned them all. He had seen enough. He wanted unity.

The Council's very first decision was that no man who had been voluntarily castrated was to be eligible for the Christian priesthood. That out of the way, the bishops turned to other matters. The Church was reorganized into four

Patriarchies (Rome, Antioch, Alexandria, and Jerusalem), later to become six (with Carthage and Constantinople). The date of Easter was set as the first Sunday after the first full moon of spring. Anybody celebrating Easter on any other day was henceforth excommunicated. Mary, it was determined, was indeed the Mother of God. But the most crucial of the several hot-button issues at Nicaea was the divine nature of Jesus.

Jesus was widely accepted as having been both human and divine, but the question was—just how divine? Was he eternal and equal with the Father, or was he a divine being brought into existence by the Father? While today this might seem to be hair-splitting of the highest order, it was serious business in the fourth century. The debate was extremely heated. Arius, an African priest living in Alexandria, had become fed up with the Jewish and pagan theatrical productions in the city poking fun at the Christian doctrine that the Father and the Son were the same age. He proposed, quite sensibly he thought, that the Father should be considered older than the Son. This was taken by his enemies to mean that in some small way Jesus was not equal to the Father. Arius was present at Nicaea, and he had a lot of support for his view, especially in the Eastern part of the Empire. Arius and his followers understood that to give Jesus (and then the Holy Spirit) equal standing with God the Father made rather a hash out of monotheism. The doctrine of the Trinity, Arius pointed out, was intellectual gobbledegook.

But theology was one thing, and politics another. Arius found himself outfoxed by the Patriarch Alexander, who was able to sway many in the assembly, including the gullible and vacillating Bishop Eusebius (the "Father of Church History".) Most importantly, Alexander had the ear of the Emperor

Constantine. The Emperor, whose theological and philosophical knowledge was, to be charitable, limited, came down hard against Arius. Those present at the Council were pressured into agreeing that Jesus was co-eternal and of the same substance as God the Father. Arius and his followers signed on, left Nicaea, later recanted, and were expelled from the Church. Most Christians, both then and now, probably didn't care. Nevertheless, for those who use the Nicene Creed as their basis of belief, the egregious political interference by Constantine has left a very sour taste. We have to assume that at least some of the bishops who officially agreed with Constantine's interpretation of the Trinity and who recited the new Creed beginning "In the beginning was the Word, and the Word was God..." were also aware of *John 14:28*— "The Father is greater than I."

But the pattern had been set. Theological issues would henceforth be settled not by individual conviction, but by councils of bishops, and they would continue, as at Nicaea, to keep a sharp eye on the prevailing political winds. The Nicene Creed, which is still the standard in many Christian churches, was put together with enormous effort. It basis was a statement of belief by the gadfly Tertullian who, ironically, ended his days as a heretic. Constantine pressed the bishops for an official statement of belief, convinced that it would help unite rival Christian groups. And so the Nicene Creed, recited by millions but understood by none, became the touchstone of Christianity. The focus of the imperial religion was now to be about arcane beliefs, and not so much about ethical behaviour.

The earthly rewards for agreeing with Constantine were not long in coming. The Church had been most cooperative in assisting imperial unity, and the price was to be paid by pagans and deviant Christians. After Nicaea, church property which had been confiscated was restored, and bishops were empowered to sit in judgment in civil cases. Priests were given tax exemptions, and unsurprisingly, a host of new men presented themselves for ordination. Ambitious Christians were on the move, and the number of new converts was staggering. Meanwhile the civic-minded pagans, long the bulwark of the Empire, became demoralized and alienated as Constantine began rewarding Christians with high positions. The Church was given the power to censor or suppress any hostile writings, and it did so with ruthless efficiency. Mere possession of written works referring to Jesus as either a magician or a political agitator might expose their owner to the death penalty. Constantine wished to leave his mark, and ordered a new Christian church dedicated to St. Peter to be built on Vatican Hill, and the Church of the Holy Sepulchre to be erected in Jerusalem. Nor were the Jews forgotten. They were forbidden to enter Jerusalem except for one day a year, and no new converts to Judaism were allowed.

Constantine reigned over most of the Empire for three decades, and it marked a significant turning point in the religious life of the Mediterranean and European world. At first there seemed to be a degree of compromise all around. For example, Constantine's coins showed the letters of Christ's name on one side, while the other showed a portrait of the sun-god over the words "Sol Invictus" (the Unconquered Sun), a common pagan phrase. In 321 CE, Sunday was declared a day of rest, an innovation that pleased both pagan and Christian. But within a short time, the situation changed.

Christians were no longer an embattled minority—they were a fervent, growing, and militant majority, and they were not willing to extend to pagans the general tolerance of belief which had been extended to them. Constantine's Christian followers became bolder, and began to destroy some pagan temples where abuses of various kinds were suspected. By the end of his reign, bands of Christians were regularly raiding temples and shrines to strip away and melt down the gold, silver, brass and bronze. Pagan worshippers were quite aware that these raids had the tacit support of the Emperor, and usually remained passive lest harm come to their wives and children. Sometimes the beneficiaries of these forays were individual Christians, and sometimes the coffers of the state. The last half of the fourth century became an especially ugly time of violence, persecution and mob rule in which the Church showed the pagans what real persecution was.

In addition to persecution of individuals, the Church Militant reacted with extreme hostility to any critical writings. Non-Christian books were everywhere destroyed in great bonfires worthy of the Third Reich. Copyists were discouraged from replacing them by the threat of having their hands cut off. The Druidic university town of Bibracte in Burgundy had survived conquest by Julius Caesar, but not the anger of Christian mobs. It was burned to the ground in 389 CE, its 40 000 students scattered, and its library of books—legal, astrological, grammatical, literary, and religious—were all lost forever.

The incidents of violence, and the consequences, were probably even worse at the other end of the Empire. Alexandria was the intellectual capital of the world because its port was the major transit point between the Mediterranean and both the Nile Valley and the East via the Red Sea. City authorities had a policy that any ship carrying a new book had to leave a copy at the Museum Library. As a result, the Great Library of Alexandria housed between 500 000 and 750 000 books on every conceivable topic. It was the equivalent of a large modern university, with faculties of

Mathematics, Astronomy, Literature and Medicine, and some 14 000 students. Disaster struck just before the Christian era—in the siege of Alexandria by the troops of Julius Caesar, the Museum Library caught fire and was destroyed.

The loss was tragic but not total, because some 300 000 additional volumes were held in the Temple of Serapis, or Serapeum. And so during the Christian era, the Serapeum grew and thrived as the centre of learning for pagan and Christian scholars alike. But the brotherhood of scholarship did not extend into the streets of the city. By Constantine's time, pagan and Christian mobs fought pitched battles, often triggered by obscure theological disputes. And in 391 CE, following an exceptionally vehement sermon by Theophilis Bishop of Alexandria, a mob of Christian monks burned the Serapeum to the ground, and murdered many prominent scientists and philosophers. In their frenzy of destruction, their superstitions intimidated them enough to make them pause a moment before going at the great statue of Serapis with their axes.

But some people are slow to get the message. Hypatea, one of the most brilliant women in world history, and her century's leading representative of Neoplatonism, continued to lecture on Greek philosophy even after the Serapeum was destroyed. Hypatea was the daughter of Theon, a noted mathematician of the time. Besides her eloquence and intelligence, she was famous for her beauty and her modesty. Bishop Theophilis' successor, St. Cyril, naturally found her intolerable. Cyril was quite ready to use local monks as muscle, and they were quite brazen, often throwing stones at the governor when he appeared in public. Cyril was in all likelihood the moving force behind the murder of Hypatea. His charge that Hypatea was guilty of sexual impropriety seems ludicrous. Still, a group of monks under his urging dragged her out of her lecture hall. She was stripped naked, then stoned to death with roofing tiles. But this important symbol of feminist scholarship was not to get off that lightly. Her body was literally torn to pieces, then, incredibly, the flesh was scraped off her bones and the whole soggy mess was burned. The message to pagans, feminists, and the educated elite of the Empire could not have been clearer. The new order would not be as tolerant as the old. Learning, feminism, and elitism were all equally unwelcome.

Why did the imperial authorities tolerate this level of violence against pagans? First, it was enforcing a uniformity—which most governments prefer—and the oppression of pagans and heretic Christians was the price to be paid. Secondly, and probably more important, the destruction of so many pagan temples was a financial windfall to both the government and to those who participated in the looting.

It goes without saying that humanity would have benefited enormously had those libraries and temples not been destroyed, or had even a single charred biography of an Isiac or a Dionysiac survived the flames, but the destruction was so complete that we should assume that it went on and on over several generations, with the complicity of most church leaders.

In terms of destruction of information, then, the Christian Church has a lot to answer for. We know about the intentional burning of the Serapeum, and the Druid centers of learning, and much later, the destruction of the great Mayan libraries of Central America. These were all incredibly tragic losses to human culture. So were the smaller losses—the private collections, the architectural treasures, the traditions of oral scholarship. How much has been lost forever? It is fair but sad to say that no other organization in human history has done so much to restrict and destroy knowledge, and it was always done in the name of God.

Christianity's combination of legal and extralegal force and political ascendancy was phenomenally successful. Within 150 years of the accession of Constantine, the religion had grown from about 10% of the population to almost 100%. Heresy as well as paganism was on the run: the last few Montanists locked themselves into their churches, and burned themselves to death rather than fall into the hands of their fellow Christians. The orthodox church had won, and its use of coercion had been so successful that it was to use it again and again in the centuries that followed.

The spectacle is not a pleasant one. Persecution, whether by pagan or Christian, is the reflex side of absolute and unthinking religious conviction. In the late Roman Empire, it is the unmistakable sign of a civilization in decay. Urban people must learn to live with moral uncertainty and clashing beliefs—it is the byproduct of meeting many types of people in the course of the day. The disappearance of tolerance heralded the end of city life as a whole. Edward Gibbon, in his massive *Decline and Fall of the Roman Empire* reluctantly concluded that the triumph of Christianity was the major cause of the fall of Rome. We don't really care much any more, but maybe we should.

Since about the year 400 CE, then, Christianity has been the dominant religious force in the Western world. The ease with which it moved from powerlessness to autocratic control is remarkable. It was now simpler to be a Christian than anything else, and those pagans of timid soul soon flooded into Christian assemblies. Buildings had to be adapted or built to house the growing congregations. In a period of declining real incomes, Christians understandably preferred to avoid the costs of new buildings. (Indeed, the economy of being a Christian and not having to support expensive temples was a further appeal of the new orthodoxy.) Christians embarked on a policy of reconsecrating and using suitable pagan temples, but even larger quarters were needed. Basilicas, the courthouses of the Empire, were pressed into service, and soon that architectural form became the common one for church construction.

Along with the new converts came many of their previous customs: holy water fonts, murals, vested priests, music, relic-worship. Pope Gregory the Great wrote to Augustine of Canterbury, advising him to permit and even encourage "such harmless pagan customs as were capable of a Christian interpretation". Since this frequently meant no more than changing the name of some god to that of a Christian character, we would be right in expecting that the fifth and sixth centuries showed a definite lowering of religious standards in day-to-day practice. Furthermore, the church immediately embarked on the conversion of the various tribes of Germanic barbarians. Barbarians would probably never have converted to the classical paganism of Rome, but Christian missionaries found fertile ground.

Now that Christianity was in control, a shift was required in its attitudes to power. Previously, Christians had avoided occupations which contributed to idolatry, and that had included the army. Now the use of force was deemed to be in defence of the faith, and that was permissible. The imperial virtues of discipline and force were adopted. Not everybody was comfortable with the new regime, but dissidents learned that the simplest solution was to join the monastic movement which swept through the West.

It was not a time for urban life. The population was in decline; there were crop failures, measles epidemics, and serious problems in supplying the great cities with food.

Germanic and Asian barbarian tribes wandered through what remained of the Empire, pillaging as they went. For many people the best option seemed to be to go back to the land, and put oneself under the protection of an overlord, who might provide some small degree of protection against a very uncertain life. In cultural terms, the neglect and antipathy toward intellectual pursuits of these Christian centuries did more damage to the heritage of the ancient world than did the arsonous behavior of the barbarians.

But paganism was too old and too deep to disappear without a whimper. Constantine's nephew Julian (aka Julian The Apostate) was the last person of consequence until Lenin to try to suppress Christianity. Julian had been raised as a Christian in the imperial household, and he was lucky to have survived the bloodbath that followed Constantine's death. The events of his youth, and perhaps his exposure to Constantine, gave him a lifelong dislike for the murderous, plotting Christians of his childhood. He also showed an unusual sensitivity, considering the times:

> "From my earliest years, my mind was so completely swayed by the light which illumines the heavens that not only did I desire to gaze intently at the sun, but whenever I walked abroad in the night season when the firmament was clear and cloudless I abandoned all else without exception and gave myself up to the beauties of the heavens...and yet I call heaven to witness, never had a book on this subject (i.e. astronomy) come into my hands nor did I as yet even know what that science was."

On his accession to the throne in 361CE, he announced

his conversion to paganism, and urged others to do the same. Julian's beliefs combined pagan syncretism with an unwise confrontation of Christians. He was generally a Mithraist, but he also promoted Apollo, Serapis, Cybele, Mars, Helios and Horus. He understood very clearly that if paganism was to flourish, it had to rid itself of primitive and objectionable features, and adopt Greek philosophy. However, he did not seem to understand that the mystery religions had long since become private salvation societies, and that his dream of organizing them into some sort of imperial church was quite impossible.

Moreover, too much of Julian's time and energy was spent in infuriating Christians. He pointed out that *Mark*, *Matthew* and *Luke* had not called Jesus God. While this is accepted today, it was not a good idea for a pagan to try to face down the intolerant and narrow churchmen of his time. Julian argued that the serpent in the garden had been good for humanity, because it had made Adam and Eve morally responsible. He took holy water from pagan temples to the market and sprinkled it on fruit and vegetables, so scrupulous Christians would be forced to eat what they claimed was polluted. Finally, Julian had plans to rebuild the Great Temple of Jerusalem to show that Judaism was alive and well, and that Christians were false in their claims to be the new Chosen People. Julian's plans were never completed. He was killed in a military campaign in Persia, secure in his position as one of the great villains of Christian history.

With the death of Julian, the last real barrier had been removed, and Christianity set about using the machinery of the state against its rivals. Pagans, Jews and heretics were equally pursued. Temples were burned, schools were closed, laws were passed. In 377 CE the Christian prefect of Rome, one Gracchus, used his influence to have a major Mithraic sanctuary destroyed. In 379 CE the Christian Emperor Gratian, on the urging of Ambrose Bishop of Milan, refused the traditional honorific title of Pontifex Maximus because of its pagan associations. In 385 Paetextatus, the Mithraic Father of Fathers and the intellectual and spiritual leader of paganism, died in Rome, opening the way for Christian pontiffs to take over the Vatican. Within 44 years of Constantine's death, the Emperor Theodosius "The Great" made belief in the Nicene Creed compulsory for all subjects of the Empire, and for good measure, banned all assemblies of heretics. Two years later, the Olympic Games were ended...or rather, began a recess of 1503 years. It was legal to be a private pagan until 472, and finally Pope Leo closed that door and ordered the death penalty for those holding "erroneous beliefs."

And so at this melancholy juncture we leave off our tale. Religion, like most other human pursuits, showed very little development in the West over the next thousand years. But the legacy of the ancient pagan gods lived on in "Christian" doctrine, and in the linear sense of time which had developed in late antiquity. This new concept of time was first articulated in Augustine's book *The City of God*, but its major connection with us is through the calendar. It is to this final contribution of paganism that our study now turns.

24

THE CALENDAR

"He who has art and science also has religion."

Goethe

Seasonal festivals, the basis of every calendar, are far older than civilization. Recent and somewhat speculative work on some Neanderthal sites has suggested that these hominids kept track of the phases of the moon, presumably for religious purposes. Even modern people, safely insulated from the vagaries of climate and weather, feel the urge to celebrate the change of seasons. We don't often think of them as seasonal feasts, but they are. Would St. Patrick's Day be celebrated with the same enthusiasm if his birthday fell in mid-January, and his favourite colour were taupe?

In any case, calendars are very old, and up until recently, were usually inaccurate over time. The problem is that the full moon arrives approximately every 28.5 days, and the solar year every 365.25 days. These are not particularly cooperative numbers. By the time of the Babylonians, the problems were understood, but the solutions were not. Babylonian priests began their year with the first full moon after the spring equinox. (Sound familiar? It's the modern Passover, and Easter is the first Sunday afterward.) Of course, if the weather were bad and the royal astronomers could not see the full moon, the beginning of the year was delayed until they could. The priests loved the number twelve, so they devised a twelve month system with thirty days apiece—for a total of 360 days. Every few years, when the error began to become obvious, they added an extra month. For example, the month of Ellul, our September, was normally followed by Tisri, but sometimes by Second Ellul.

Our calendar is derived from the Romans (the "kalends" was the first day of the month) and they originally had ten months, each with 36 days, and they also began the New Year in the spring. They tried to add extra days when needed, but as you might imagine, it became hopelessly confused. King Numa tried using the moon: he devised a lunar calendar of twelve months and 355 days. This made the confusion worse, since it left the Romans with a calendar whose ninth month was named September ("Seventh Month"), whose tenth month was named October ("Eighth Month") and so on. We have perpetuated this illogic, but few people even notice, since few people can translate Latin. Other Roman months were devoted to special gods: Janus the god of doorways, Februs the god of purification, Mars the god of rain and war, April an obscure goddess of opening, Maia goddess of nursing and child care, Juno the queen of heaven. The two months following June were Quintilis and Sextilus. A further reform of unknown date tried to make the calendar fit more closely to the solar year: the beginning of the year was moved to January 1, but the length was wrongly fixed at 366.5 days.

In 46 BCE, as part of a comprehensive package of reforms, Julius Caesar enlisted the help of the Greek astronomer Sosigenes for yet another reform. Poor Sosigenes had to insert a fifteen month year to get things back on track, and then all the credit went to his boss. When Julius was assassinated, his adopted son Augustus decided to perpetually enshrine him by naming the seventh month after him. The Roman Senate, thoroughly impressed, or thoroughly cowed, promptly insisted that the current emperor be honoured too, and that Sextilus be renamed August. Sosigenes' work was admirable…his year of 365.25 days was only 11 minutes too long. This "Julian" calendar served the Western world for centuries, and was used as late as 1917 in Tsarist Russia, by which time the error had piled up to some eleven days.

The Romans had always used the legendary founding of their city as a base point for numbering the years, but this had too many pagan associations for some Christians. In the early fifth century CE, Dionysius Exiguus introduced into Italy the liturgical calendar used by Eastern Christianity, which used Jesus' birth as a base year. It now turns out that Eusebius, the earlier writer on whom he based his calculations, was a few years in error, so that the modern date of the Nativity should probably be 7 BCE. However, in view of the dubious nature of the whole Christmas story, it hardly seems worthwhile to correct the error.

The seven day week has been attributed to both the Egyptians and the peoples of Mesopotamia, with the latter being more likely. The Akkadians, who dominated the valleys of the Tigris and the Euphrates about 2600 BCE observed a seven day week which honoured the sun, the moon, and the five visible planets—the only regular moving objects in the sky. It is likely that the custom was established long before that. Perhaps as a result of their fascination with the sky, Middle Eastern religions came to see the number seven as sacred, and to attribute a special metal, stone, plant and animal to each of the seven sacred celestial bodies.

The names which we use for the days of the week are

derived from a confluence of Roman and Norse mythologies. Obviously the sun and the moon took precedence in the week. Tuesday is for Ti or Mercury. Wednesday is named for the Norse Wotan (or Odin) who was the Roman Jupiter. Thursday is named for Thor or Mars. Friday is sacred to the goddess Freya, the only significant goddess in the Teutonic heaven. Freya's day had previously been devoted to several Mediterranean goddesses: Venus, Ishtar, Bona Dea, and others. Friday also had a tradition of being unlucky. In Jewish tradition, it was the day of the Fall of Adam, of the Great Flood, and of the collapse of Solomon's Temple. Christians naturally assumed this must have been the day of the Crucifixion. Friday also had a long association with the eating of fish. The Syrian goddess Bona Dea was patroness of the fishing industry. For the goddess Venus and the Hindu god Vishnu, the fish was a symbol of fertility. Christians were generally disinterested in fertility. They probably ate fish for the contrary reason—Pythagoras taught that a fish diet helped curb sexual desire.

Saturn's day came last because it is the slowest of the visible planets, being the furthest from the sun. Saturn was a gloomy god, and no wonder: he got to be patron of cold, darkness, obstruction, and death. The Babylonians seem to have been the first to require that people abstain from certain activities on Saturn's day. Their fellow Semites, the Hebrews, adopted their strict code of Sabbath behavior after their forced residence in Babylon. The seventh day of the week was also one of special observance in Egypt; it was dedicated to Amon, and commercial activity was generally suspended on that day.

The change of the Christian holy day from Saturday to Sunday was in part a result of Christian hostility toward its Jewish heritage, and in part a cave-in to solar worship. The

New Testament makes several references to the early church observing the Jewish Sabbath. The Roman writer Pliny mentions that Christians met before dawn "on a certain day of the week", but neglects to tell us which day. No Christian writer before 300 CE tried to give a justification for Sunday observance, presumably they recognized what a weak case it was. It was practiced about 150 CE according to Justin Martyr, but we don't know how widely. Christians abandoned the Sabbath as they did the Law of Moses, and circumcision, and dietary laws—arguing that the Law of Moses had been superseded by the Law of Christ. Today we can be more definite: Sunday services represent the deep infiltration of Mithraism and sun-worship into Christianity. The original Lord of the Lord's Day was Mithra. In 321 CE Constantine issued an imperial edict making Sunday the legal day of rest, but craftily did not specify whether it was to be devoted to Mithra, Apollo, or Jesus. But he was careful not to affect the wheat harvest:

> "Let all judges and all city people and all tradesmen rest upon the Venerable Day of the Sun. Let those dwelling in the country freely and with full liberty attend to the culture of their fields."

Today, when Sunday closing laws are a nostalgic memory in most jurisdictions, we can still be rather fuzzy about our priorities—many are the nominal Christians who sleep through Sunday services, but dutifully spend Sunday afternoon at the beach, absorbing the warm blessings of the god of the sun.

If we examine our present calendar and its holidays, we find numerous remnants of pagan antiquity. New Year, connected as it was to the birthday of the sun, has a long connection with fire festivals—parades, lights, and processions. Since evil spirits gathered in great numbers at New Year, bells, horns and other noisemakers were useful in scaring them off. January 6, the Feast of the Nativity in Easter Orthodox churches, was recognized as the birthday of Jesus by all Christians until the Roman church moved the date back to December 25 to coincide with pagan solar festivals. The Gnostics taught that January 6 was the celebration of Jesus' baptism by John. Western Christians celebrate the Epiphany on that day, often understood as the day the Magi arrived to worship the infant Jesus. So January 6 has long been a big day for Christians. In fact, however, it was the birthday of Dionysos, and the Christian traditions were grafted on to a celebration for the divine infant of the pagan Greeks.

Another interesting date, February 2, falls very near the midway point between the onset of winter and the beginning of spring. It was a day celebrated by the ancient Egyptians with plenty of lamps and candles to honour the Immaculate Virgin, the goddess Neith. The Romans also lit candles to honour both Ceres, the Roman version of Demeter, and Februa, the mother of Mars. The ancient Celts went out on February 2 to look for the first snowdrops in the winter woods. Thus, that date already had a long history when it was co-opted by Christians as the feast of the purification of the Virgin Mary. Then it became Candlemas, a celebration of Jesus being presented to the elders in the Great Temple. In a sort of overflow effect, candles were also prominent in religious ceremonies on February 3, dedicated to St. Blaise, the patron saint of throats. The celebration of Candlemas has declined recently, but festivals of light are resilient: North Americans have recently developed a new non-religious solar festival...Groundhog Day.

Mid-February was traditionally a time for fertility rites. The Roman Lupercalia was quite lewd. Each February 15, priests of Faunus, usually young aristocrats, sacrificed goats (everywhere the symbol of male fertility), skinned the sacrificed animals, smeared blood on their foreheads, and then ran a race around the Palatine Hill dressed in goatskin, while slapping at female bystanders with bloody strips of the hide. This dubious behaviour was intended to ensure female fertility, and to ease the pain of childbirth. As time went on, the celebrations became more rowdy, with plenty of drinking and sex. Marriageable girls put tokens into an urn, young boys drew them out, and they paired off. Eventually this grew to a point where it shocked even the blasé Romans, and so Augustus tried to curb the festival by banning participation by adolescents, but the custom lasted until at least 494 CE. Some time during the Middle Ages, these fertility rites and the red and white colouring became associated with the feast of the martyrdom of St. Valentine one day earlier. The modern lover, buying cards and chocolates out of romantic sentimentality, has little idea of the carnal festivities behind the original Valentine's Day.

March was the first month of the ancient Roman calendar. This accounts for not only the numerous festivals in March, but also the lack of them in January. To any culture in the Northern Hemisphere, March meant growth and life. The ancients believed, consciously or unconsciously, in sympathetic magic: imitation of natural phenomena might speed their onset. The rites of spring are especially rich in jumping, dancing, and wearing green. In general, these festivals were more important in the north of Europe than around the Mediterranean, where the seasonal changes are less noticeable. The first day of a new month was commonly an occasion for some religious ritual or other. In the case of

March, Roman households were expected to extinguish their hearthfires on the last evening of February, and rekindle them under the supervision of the high priest (the Pontifex Maximus) on March 1, their New Year's Day. This ceremony has survived only because Christians grafted it on to their Easter celebrations.

Easter too was an ancient pagan feast day, since covered over by a Christian veneer. Despite those well known Hebrew legends about the institution of Passover by Moses, there is now clear evidence that Passover was a lunar feast of the ancient Canaanites which came just before the spring barley harvest. Passover was to be celebrated on the evening of the first full moon of spring, no matter what day of the week. A firstborn male lamb was slaughtered to ensure a good crop, and to pay homage to the constellation Aries, which at the time dominated the eastern horizon at the spring equinox. Moreover, it was the season when many of the Mediterranean vegetation goddesses such as Cybele, Astarte and Ishtar mourned their dead lovers. Alcohol, sex, weddings and leavened bread were banned. This is the origin of Lent. Some peoples insisted on abstaining from meat during the fast, and so the last few days before Lent became Carnival. (Carne vale = farewell, meat!) The Hebrews took many of these customs with them to Egypt, and encountered an Egyptian spring festival featuring dyed eggs. These eggs were hung in the temples to honour the gods, or they might be exchanged with friends.

When early Christians tried to establish an annual celebration of the Resurrection, they ran into some difficulties. For at least the first two centuries, it was celebrated fourteen days after the first full moon of spring, with no regard for the day of the week. But such was the pressure of popular sunworship in the Western Empire that the Latin churches began postponing the celebration until the following Sunday, while the Eastern churches continued to follow the older tradition for another century. This issue was, like the Trinity, one of the key discussion points at the Council of Nicaea in 325 CE. As with the decision on the Trinity, the majority of bishops sided with the Latin position. The English term Easter is derived from the Norse fertility goddess Eostra, often associated with those other emblems of fecundity, eggs and rabbits. Eostra must be smiling down from Valhalla at the comeback her symbols have made with the aid of modern merchandising techniques.

Because Roman men typically spent much of the summer at war, the Roman calendar had few interesting events between April 1 and October 31. April 1, All Fools' Day, was a last opportunity to celebrate the coming of spring. The feast day of John the Baptist, June 24, replaced a similar midsummer festival dedicated to Adonis. The European peoples had contrary opinions about the month of May. It was certainly not merry to the Romans. The whole month was given a gloomy tone by the Lemuria, the Day of Ghosts, which fell between May 8-15. Families paid tribute to all the dead of their household, for dead relatives could become quite nasty if not given proper respect. It was therefore not a good month for other family events such as marriage. Romans much preferred to marry in the month dedicated to Juno, the protectress of women, family and childbirth. The Celts in the north of Europe were more optimistic about May—May 1 was the feast of Belenus, the Celtic god of fire, sun, and male virility. It was a magical time of year, and Celts born in May were especially lucky. Mayday festivities have enjoyed a certain stability of form since that time—from medieval peasants dancing around their phallic maypole to Soviet soldiers strutting beside their phallic ICBMs.

While Celts and Romans were at odds concerning the supernatural associations of the month of May, they were in full agreement on the melancholy nature of November. Roman families, to a remarkable extent, lived in fear of their dead ancestors. The dead demanded homage, as well as food and drink, several times a year: in February (Parentalia), in May (Lemuria), and again at the beginning of November. As November 1 approached, the souls of the dead grew restless and hungry, and ghosts might appear at the door seeking food. Among the Celts, it was commonly believed that nature slept between November and February; thus October 31 became a fire festival celebrating the end of the natural year. Celtic pagans, and later Celtic Christians, lit bonfires and ignited firewheels to discourage the spirits which roamed the land at this time of year. "Punkies", somewhat like modern jack-o-lanterns, were put outside doorways in Somerset to invite the spirits back into their former homes, and thus allay their vengeance. The English have perpetuated many of the fire rituals as Guy Fawkes Day on November 5, but the customs predate Mr. Fawkes by thousands of years.

Since all of pagan Europe was busy celebrating this autumn festival, the Christian church decided to yield rather than deny its emotional power. November 1 became the Day of the Dead for Christians. This was later split into All Saints' Day on November 1 for the famous dead, and All Souls' Day on November 2 for everyone else. In the eighteenth century, the Gregorian calendar replaced the old Julian version in much of Western Europe, which necessitated an adjustment of some eleven days. The city of London had street disturbances, as people demanded "Give us back out eleven days!" When the Armistice of 1918 was declared, European peoples had another day to remember their dead…a gloomy ritual on the gloomiest day of the gloomiest month of the year.

Confusion within the calendar also lay behind the various dates used for the sun god's birthday in December. For centuries the ancients mistakenly believed that the correct date of the winter solstice was December 24, rather than December 22. And so the first day of the new solar year, the sungod's birthday, if you prefer, was celebrated on December 25. It is remarkable how many people deplore the secularization or commercialization of Christmas as unworthy of its "true meaning", apparently unaware that December 25 was the time for gift giving, revelry and excess for centuries before Jesus. Just as Lent coincides with the waning of the winter food supply, so Christmas plenty may have originally come from an inability to preserve all the food from the autumn harvest.

Birthdays, even divine ones, were not usually celebrated in ancient Mesopotamia, and Egypt seemed to be the first culture to celebrate the winter solstice as we do. According to legend, Osiris was born on December 27, and Horus/Harpocrates on December 23. At the festival, images of the infant saviour Horus were brought out of the inner temple and put on display for the public. Women in particular felt that praying in front of the image of the Baby Horus was useful. Devout Egyptians took the opportunity to place toys and other presents atop the tombs of deceased infants, in the hope of giving them comfort. We have already pointed out that in Palestine, Adonis had been born on December 25 in Bethlehem, and this doubtless influenced their Jewish neighbours. However, Hanukah, the Jewish festival celebrated in December, was quite a minor event—the anniversary of the re-dedication of the Great Temple. If there were no Christmas, it seems unlikely there would be a Hanukah to counterbalance it.

Besides Saturn, Osiris, Horus, Dionysos, Adonis and

Jesus, the seventh god born at this time of year was the Unconquered Sun himself, Mithra. In Rome, his birthday party had come to dwarf the earlier December festival of Saturnalia. Saturn, supposedly the king of ancient Italy during its Golden Age, was celebrated December 17 –23. Saturnalia was a time for high living and indulging in food, drink, gambling and other forms of riotous behavior. Slaves and masters changed places, and a mock king was chosen to preside over the banquets. On December 22, dolls were given to the children. More gifts were distributed on January 1. In about 270 CE, the Emperor Aurelian built a huge temple to the sun in Rome to please his god Mithra. Soon it was Mithra rather than Saturn who was honoured, but the big party went on just the same.

Meanwhile the snowy north had some traditions of its own. The dead of the family were believed to revisit their old homestead on December 24, and it was customary to set a meal for them. Santa's milk and cookies has a long pedigree. The most celebrated seasonal food was the boar's head. This would be of little appeal to our dandified tastes, but the boar represented Schrimnir, the boar of Valhalla, whose flesh feeds all dead heroes. This midwinter remembrance evolved into the festival of Yul. Troops of demons, their arrival announced by bells and horns, might appear to demand food and beer. Celtic and Nordic homes were to be well prepared for visitors, demonic or human, at this time of year.

Christian Christmas celebrations can be dated back to about 185 CE, although it was not official as the Feast of the Nativity until 353. It grew rapidly in popularity, and in 534 the Emperor Justinian forbade all toil on December 25. Eastern Christians were reluctant to celebrate Jesus' birthday on what was so obviously a pagan feast day. They argued for January 6 or April 19 or May 20, but to no avail. The belief that Jesus had been born on the winter solstice was without Scriptural authority, of course, and many people have pointed out that spring was a more likely time. But the sun ruled. Soon the Annunciation was dated to March 25, using Christmas as a base point for calculations. Likewise, the belief that the birth occurred at midnight came from sun worship, and led to the tradition of midnight Mass. Advent, the lent-like pre-Christmas period, was instituted to make the event even more welcome. An apocryphal work of the fifth century introduced the legend that the ox and the ass had spoken at the Nativity. The ox and ass were clearly sacred to Mithra, but the tradition survived in the popular imagination that stable animals converse on Christmas Eve. These obvious and numerous pagan insertions into Christianity seem to have alarmed few people. Pope Leo the Great warned against them in 450 CE, but although the Pope had stopped Attila the Hun, he couldn't stop Christmas.

The Christmas custom of decorating the interior of houses with green vegetation was well established by the time of the Roman Saturnalia, and probably goes back to Egypt. Egyptians had carried green date palms indoors for the winter solstice, although the reason for doing so has long been forgotten. Romans trimmed their trees with trinkets and candies. They also favoured holly—its red berries and white flowers in some way represented masculinity, and to Christians, the prickles and blood-red fruit served as a reminder of Christ's crown of thorns. Romans also cut evergreen boughs and brought them inside for decoration, although again we are not sure why. Perhaps it was an offer of hospitality to the woodland sprites. Maybe the green symbolized life and fertility. In any case Christians found the practice cheerful, and began to copy it. Predictably, Tertullian and other grim church authorities condemned it all as rank idolatry. Far more restraint had to be shown in the use of ivy, since everyone knew it to be the badge of Dionysos. Ivy might be worn as a crown or a wreath, but it was best kept outside the home; hence the origin of the Christmas wreath on the door.

Northern Europeans were willing to be flexible on these matters. Druids, the priests of the Celtic peoples, held mistletoe to be sacred. As a parasite which grows on oak trees, it was quite rare. It was cut with great ceremony by the Archdruid using a golden knife, and preferably a white ox would be sacrificed in thanks. Mistletoe over a doorway was a symbol that old grievances and feuds, ever simmering among Celtic families, were to be forgotten. Sacred objects of outdated religions are usually believed to bring bad luck, and so mistletoe was strictly banned in Christian churches. Just as in Rome, the peoples in Celtic lands decorated trees with fruits and cakes during the winter solstice. When the Christian authorities tried to discourage it, the results were uneven. In France and Spain, the use of evergreen boughs as decoration gradually died out, but in Germany and England, the custom continued to flourish. And at Strasbourg in 1605, we have the first recorded example of a Christmas tree being cut and taken into the house for decoration.

In fact, the history of Christmas is interesting enough to go beyond our normal boundaries to examine it. The earliest tableau of the Nativity was probably in Greccio, Italy in 1224, and may have been the work of Francis of Assisi. It featured actors as Mary and Joseph, and a figure of the Christ-child lay on a straw bed, while a real ox and ass looked on. For the English, mince pies represented the variety of gifts of the Magi. In sixteenth century England, these pies were oblong, and had the infant Jesus outlined on the top crust. That notorious spoilsport, Oliver Cromwell, made them illegal as part of his general campaign against Christmas. All that feasting and celebrating was too close to the pagan Yul to please Puritans, and so the observance of Jesus' birth was banned in Scotland in 1583 and in England by 1649. By the nineteenth century, few people in either Britain or Puritan New England celebrated it...Ebenezer Scrooge was the norm. December 25 was a regular working day in Boston until 1856, and Boston public schools held classes on Christmas Day until 1870.

Next to Jesus, the most important person of the season is St. Nicholas, who began his career as Bishop of Myra in Asia Minor. Few reliable details of his life are known, but he may have been imprisoned by the Emperor, and he probably participated in the Council of Nicaea in 325. Legends about him grew rapidly after his death, particularly his miraculous powers to save children threatened with tragedy. He became one of the major saints of the Middle Ages, and his feast day of December 6 was the occasion for giving gifts to children and the poor. Then he was transformed by the Germans into Father Christmas, and later by the New York Dutch in to that benevolent magician, Santa Claus, and his traditions also migrated to Christmas.

Christmas celebrations have had strong associations with music since the earliest times. Carols were originally pagan round dances connected to vegetation worship. In the Middle Ages, they were popular all year round. The earliest Christmas carol of which we know is a twelfth century Anglo-Norman effort, and like other carols it tries to tell a sacred story to a danceable tune. An effigy of an infant in swaddling clothes was a common sight in German churches, put there so children could dance and sing carols around it. There is good reason to think that both the music and words of the *Boar's Head Carol* were the product of that man of many talents, King Henry VIII. Today, these true carols are few. Pious Christian songs no older than the eighteenth century have taken their place. However, the music is first rate. George Frederick Handel composed the music to *Joy To the World* and *While Shepherds Watched*, and Felix Mendelssohn is responsible for *Hark! The Herald Angels Sing*. Christmas songs are a pretty good indication of what is believed by rank and file Christians, and a few lines from popular ones show that at least at Christmas, the old sun god is still alive and shining:

> "...radiant beams from Thy holy face..."
> "...Son of God, Love's Pure Light..."
> "...In thy dark streets shineth
>   the Everlasting Light..."

25

A Look Ahead

"Paganism died, agreed – like the last stegosaur, or like a coral reef?"
Ramsay MacMillan

"And what rough beast, its hour come round at last Slouches toward Bethlehem to be born?"
W.B. Yeats

Historians of religion have often portrayed Christianity as the latest and best edition of the ancient world-religion which people have followed for millennia. Certainly one might suggest that new conditions call for new beliefs, and the collapse of ancient civilization definitely qualified as new conditions. Nevertheless, it is difficult to justify the idea that Christianity is so superior. Were the ancient pagans really stupid, gullible and misguided when compared to Christians of the same era? Today, a Christian who suggests his religion is superior to Islam, for example, can expect a spirited debate. But a Christian who denigrates Isis-worship is met only with silence. Slowly, of course, this incredible bias is being rectified, in part because we are losing faith not only in the Christian religion, but also in the technological society to which it gave birth. If Christianity is to survive as the greatest of the world-religions, it must become capable of more growth and innovation than it has shown in the last few decades.

For example, Christianity will have to come to terms with its past, and with many of the issues raised here. It has for centuries attempted to present itself as enlightened and rational, but it has a lot of skeletons in the closet. It consciously destroyed its rivals, and their ideals, and much of the evidence that they ever existed. Christianity has always been the spiritual home for many sincere souls who long for spiritual betterment and for social regeneration, but it is arguable whether this group ever made up the majority of believers.

In the light of what we know now, can we continue to concede that the early Christian Fathers should have a lock on Christian doctrine? Can we continue to assume that Jesus' ideas were not permanently derailed by Paul, or by Mithraism, or by the Gnostics? Christianity, it turns out, triumphed because it was popular, not because it was true. Its rapid growth from the moment of its birth took it in many strange directions which its founder would not have liked. Just try to imagine James the Just touring the Vatican, or Jesus' friends contemplating the $660 000 000 paid out by the Diocese of Los Angeles over sexual abuse. It remains to be seen whether these theological issues become serious enough in the future that we could contemplate a new Reformation.

In addition, an unbridgeable gulf is developing on these matters between the scholars and the believers in the pews. There is a profound ignorance concerning the historical background out of which Christianity emerged. The decline of classical studies and the virtual disappearance of ancient history from high schools and even colleges have opened the door to unhistorical and faith-based interpretations of events and beliefs. In addition, society has approached these events from a Christian perspective for so many centuries that the bias will prove almost impossible to eradicate. In years gone by, the ignorance of the uneducated was tempered by respect for the erudition of many Christian antiquarians, amateur philologists, and the like. There have been fanatics, often of the millenarian sort (The Fifth Monarchy Men, the Saints of Munster, Jonestown, Waco) but in general cooler heads have usually prevailed.

Today, the professionals write books that only other professionals can read. The field of popular religion is left to fundamentalist pitch-men, whose command of psychology and propaganda techniques is excellent, but whose historical interest and knowledge approaches nil. To their congregations, who think that "ancient" means before 1970, the alleged sayings and life events of Jesus stand out in much bolder relief that need be.

In the perpetual struggle for control of religion, emotion frequently wins out over reason. It is generally true that religious people believe because they need to. Many believers arrive at their position by God-given conviction, and they are impervious to rationality, and bored by historical enquiry. But suggestion, mass psychology and pathological delusions are all easily and frequently confused with divine grace. Emotions are not a good guide to religious truth, any more than they are an infallible guide to choosing a life partner, or devising a foreign policy.

Certainly humans are creatures of emotion, but they are also the most curious of animals. As I did the research for this book, I was stunned to discover how rare written discussions of this topic have been. Even the great Sir James Frazier shrank from pointing out the obvious – that Christianity is a religion stuffed full of the castoff rags of pagan creeds. Why have there been so few attempts to discover how much of Christianity is really ancient paganism in modern dress? Why have we all been so willing to give the dubious behaviours of early Christians a free pass? The answer for the past fifteen hundred years is that Christianity has been such an overpowering social force that to attack or undermine it has traditionally carried heavy penalties. As the American wit Dave Barry said:

> "The trouble with writing about religion is that you run the risk of offending sincerely religious people, and then they came after you with machetes."

It is a truism that religion is the most conservative of institutions – consider the paroxysms exhibited recently in mainstream churches by the simple demand for sexual equality. Then try to imagine the terror with which the clergy view a Christless world. It ought to make us marginally more sympathetic for those pagans of the early Christian era who loved and trusted their old religion, and resisted leaving it. Certainly there is far more at work here than social pressure. When our religions and our legends give such shape to human society, maybe we cannot bear to think about the consequences of abandoning these comfortable old myths and developing new ones. People go to their religion for solace, so the last thing a Christian congregation wants is a clergyman who publicly airs his doubts about the reality of Jesus. The clergy after all are salesmen, and the modern customer wants a product with a guarantee.

Can we live without faith? Probably not, but we ought to try to live without falsehood. Is this book doing more harm than good? No book can do as much harm as the bad religion

— A Look Ahead —

of Jim Jones or Torquemada. Don't we need Christianity for its morality? No, because remarkably ethical people such as Gandhi can be found who don't share our religious heritage. In short, if this essay is full of errors, they will be exposed by further historical investigations, and they will fade away. On the other hand, if Christianity has no unique content and is only a synthesis of other creeds, it will continue to decline.

But don't expect total collapse anytime soon. In the nineteenth century, a Church of England missionary, Bishop John William Colenso, want to South Africa to convert the Zulus. The Zulus knew nothing about Jesus, but were experts in moving large numbers of people and cattle. They proved conclusively to the Bishop that even cramped together five abreast and omitting their baggage, sheep and cows, the Hebrews in crossing the Red Sea would have formed a column one hundred miles long. Thus the claim of *Exodus* that they completed the passage in one night was manifestly impossible. Bishop Colenso was bowled over, and on his return to England, explained the Zulus' arguments in his book *The Pentateuch Examined*. This long-forgotten volume provoked no fewer than one hundred and forty books in refutation. So we can certainly expect that mainline Christianity will continue to have its ardent defenders who will claim for it originality, superiority, and uniqueness that cannot be sustained by the facts. For the facts are that what we call Christianity is paganism from beginning to end. But the ancient gods are resilient and slippery beings buried deep in the psyches of modern people, and the concepts and rituals related to their worship will continue to be with us for a long time to come.

26

SOURCELIST

Angus, S. *Mystery-Religions and Christianity*. London, John Murray, 1925.

Angus, S. *The Religious Quest of the Graeco-Roman World*. New York, Scribner's, 1929.

Armstrong, Karen. *A History of God: The 4000 Year Quest of Judaism, Christianity and Islam*. New York, Knopf, 1993.

Bammel, Ernst and C.F. Moule (ed.) *Jesus and the Politics of His Day*. Cambridge U.P., 1984.

Beare, F.W. *The Earliest Records of Jesus*. New York, Abingdon Press, 1962.

Bonwick, James. *Egyptian Belief and Modern Thought*. Indian Hills, Colorado, Falcon's Wing Press, 1956 (first published 1890).

Borg, Marcus. *Jesus and Buddha: The Parallel Sayings*. Berkeley, Ulysses Press, 1997.

Boulding, Elise. *The Underside of History: A View of Women Through Time*. Boulder, Colorado, Westview Press, 1976.

Bruce, F.F. *Men and Movements in the Primitive Church*. Exeter, Paternoster Press, 1979.

Budge, E.A. Wallace. *Osiris – the Egyptian Religion of*

Resurrection. New Hyde Park, New York, University Books, 1961. (first published 1911).

Bultmann, Rudolf. *Theology of the New Testament.* (2 vols) New York, Scribner's, 1951.

Burland, Cottie. *Myths of Life and Death.* London, Macmillan, 1974.

Butterfield, Herbert. *The Whig Interpretation of History.* London, Bell, 1931.

Butz, Jeffrey. *The Brother of Jesus and the Lost Teachings of Christianity.* Rochester, Vermont, Inner Traditions, 2005.

Campbell, Joseph. *Masks of God: Occidental Mythology.* New York, Viking, 1964.

Carpenter, Edward. *Pagan and Christian Creeds: Their Origin and Meaning.* New York, Blue Ribbon Books, 1920.

Casson, Lionel. *Travel in the Ancient World.* London, Allen and Unwin, 1974.

Coffin, Tristam. *The Book of Christmas Folklore.* New York, Seabury Press, 1973.

Conteneau, Georges. *Everyday Life in Babylon and Assyria.* London, Edward Arnold, 1954.

Crippen, T,G. *Christmas and Christmas Lore.* Detroit, Gale Research Co., 1971 (first published 1923).

Crossan, John Dominic. *The Birth of Christianity: Discovering What Happened in the Years Immediately After the Execution of Jesus.* San Francisco, Harper, 1998.

Crossan, John D., *The Historical Jesus: The Life of a*

Mediterranean Jewish Peasant. San Francisco, Harper, 1991.

Crossan, John D. *Jesus: A Revolutionary Biography*. San Francisco, Harper, 1994.

Crossan, John D. *Who Killed Jesus?* San Francisco, Harper, 1995.

Cumont, Franz. *The Afterlife in Roman Paganism*. New Haven, Yale U.P., 1922.

Cumont, Franz. *The Mysteries of Mithra*. Chicago, Open Court, 1903.

Cupitt, Don. *The Debate About Christ*. London, SCM Press, 1979.

Danielou, Jean. *The Dead Sea Scrolls and Primitive Christianity*. Baltimore, Helicon, 1958.

Danielou, Jean. *A History of Early Christian Doctrine Before Nicaea* (3 vols). London, Longman and Todd, 1973.

David, Rosalie. *Cult of the Sun: Myth and Magic in Ancient Egypt*. London, JM Dent, 1980.

Deissmann, Adolf. *Light From the Ancient East*. London, Hodden and Stoughton, 1910.

Doane, T.W. *Bible Myths and Their Parallels in Other Religions*. New Hyde Park, N.Y., University Books, 1971 (first published 1882).

Dodds, E.R. *Pagan and Christian in an Age of Anxiety*. Cambridge U.P., 1965.

Durant, Will. *Caesar and Christ*. New York, Simon and Schuster, 1944.

Ehrman, Bart. *Lost Christianities: The Battle for Scriptures and the Faiths We Never Knew.* New York, Oxford, 2003.

Ehrman, Bart. *Misquoting Jesus: The Story Behind Who Changed The Bible and Why.* San Francisco, Harper, 2007.

Evans, Christopher. *Is Holy Scripture Christian?* London, SCM Press, 1971.

Ferguson, John. *Religions of the Roman Empire.* Ithaca, N.Y., Cornell U.P., 1970.

Ferm, Vergilius (ed.) *Forgotten Religions.* New York, Philosophical Library, 1950.

Festugiere, Andre-Jean. *Personal Religion Among the Greeks.* Berkeley, U of California Press, 1960.

Fox, Robin Lane. *Pagans and Christians.* New York, Knopf, 1987.

Fowler, W. Ward. *Religious Experience of the Roman Empire.* New York, Cooper Square, 1971 (first published 1911.)

Freke, Timothy and Peter Gandy. *The Jesus Mysteries: Was the "Original Jesus" a Pagan God?* New York, Harmony, 1999.

Fricke, Weddig. *The Court-Martial of Jesus.* New York, Grove Weidenfeld, 1990.

Furneaux, Rupert. *The Other Side of the Story: The Strange Story of Christianity–The Dark Spot of History.* London, Cassell & Co., 1953.

Fustel de Coulanges, Numa Denis. *The Ancient City.* Garden City, NewYork, Anchor, 1955.

Gibbon, Edward. *The Decline and Fall of the Roman Empire, Vol. 1.* New York, Everyman's Library, Knopf, 1910.

Glover, T.R. *The Conflict of Religions in the Early Roman Empire.* London Methuen, 1909.

Goguel, Maurice. *The Birth of Christianity.* London, Allen and Unwin, 1953.

Gough, Michael. *The Early Christians.* New York, Praeger, 1961.

Grant, Michael. *St. Peter: A Biography.* New York, Scribner, 1994.

Grant, Robert. *Gnosticism: A Sourcebook of Heretical Writings From the Early Christian Period.* New York, Harper and Bros., 1961.

Graves, Kersey. *The World's Sixteen Crucified Saviors.* Boston, Colby and Rich, 1879.

Guepin, J.P. *The Tragic Paradox.* Amsterdam, Adolf Hakkert, 1968.

Habermas, Gary. *Ancient Evidence for the Life of Jesus.* Nashville, Thomas Nelson, 1984.

Hackwood, F.W. *Christ Lore.* London, Eliot Stock, 1902.

Halliday, W.R. *The Pagan Background of Early Christianity.* New York, Cooper Square, 1970.

Hanson, R.P. *Difficulties for Christian Belief.* London, Macmillan, 1967.

Harnack, Adolf. *The Mission and Expansion of Christianity.* New York, Harper Torchbook, 1962 (first published 1904.)

Harpur, Tom. *The Pagan Christ*. Toronto, Thomas Allen, 2004.

Harrowven, Jean. *The Origin of Rhymes, Songs and Sayings*. London, Kaye and Ward, 1977.

Harvey, A.E. *Jesus and the Constraints of History*. Philadelphia, Westminster Press, 1982.

Hatch, Edwin. *The Influence of Greek Ideas on Christianity*. New York, Harper and Row, 1957.

Hays, H.R. *In the Beginning: Early Man and His Gods*. New York, Putnam's 1963.

Heyob, Sharon Kelly. *The Cult of Isis Among Women in the Graeco-Roman World*. Leiden, E.J.Brill, 1975.

Hinnels, John R. (ed.) *Mithraic Studies (2 vols)*. Manchester U.P. 1971.

Hopkins, Keith. *A World Full of Gods: The Strange Triumph of Christianity*. New York, The Free Press, 1999.

Huttman, Maude. *The Establishment of Christianity and the Proscription of Paganism*. New York, AMS Press, 1967.

Hyde, Walter W. *Paganism to Christianity in the Roman Empire*. Philadelphia, U. of Pennsylvania Press, 1946.

James, E.O. *Christian Myth and Ritual*. Cleveland, Meridian Books, 1965.

Johnson, Luke Timothy. *The Real Jesus: The Misguided Quest for the Historical Jesus and the Truth of the Traditional Gospels*. San Francisco, Harper, 1996.

Johnson, Paul. *History of Christianity*. London, Weidenfeld and Nicolson, 1976.

Josephus, Flavius. *The Works of Josephus: Complete and Unabridged* (trans. William Whiston). Peabody, Mass., Hendrickson, 1987.

Keck, Leander. *A Future for the Historical Jesus.* Nashville, Abingdon, 1971.

Kee, Alaistair. *Constantine Versus Christ.* London, SCM Press, 1982.

Kenny, John. "The Christmas Star" in *Rotunda.* Toronto, Royal Ontario Museum, Fall 1982.

Kent, John. *The End of the Line? The Development of Christian Theology in the Last Two Centuries.* Philadelphia, Fortress Press, 1982.

Koestler, Helmut. *Ancient Christian Gospels: Their History and Development.* Philadelphia, Trinity Press, 1992.

Krythe, Maymie. *All About Christmas.* New York, Harper and Row, 1954.

Laeuchli, Samuel (ed) *Mithraism in Ostia.* Evanston, Ill., Northwestern U.P., 1967.

Laing, Gordon. *Survivals of Roman Religion.* New York, Cooper Square, 1963.

Larue, Gerald. *Ancient Myths and Modern Man.* Englewood Cliffs, N.J., Prentice-Hall, 1975.

Legge, Francis. *Forerunners and Rivals of Christianity.* New Hyde Park, N.Y., 1964 (first published 1915.)

Lewis, Abram H. *Paganism Surviving in Christianity.* New York, Putnam's 1892.

Lindsay, Jack. *Men and Gods on the Roman Nile.* New York, Barnes and Noble, 1968.

Mack, Burton. *The Lost Gospel: The Book of Q and Christian Origins.* San Francisco, Harper, 1993.

Mackey, James. *Jesus: The Man and the Myth.* New York, The Paulist Press, 1979.

MacMullen, Ramsay. *Christianity and Paganism in the Fourth to Eighth Centuries.* New Haven, Yale U.P., 1997.

MacMullan, Ramsay. *Christianizing the Roman Empire.* New Haven, Yale U.P., 1984.

MacMullan, Ramsey. *Paganism in the Roman Empire.* New Haven, Yale U.P., 1981.

Malina, Bruce. *The Social World of Jesus and the Gospels.* London, Routledge, 1996.

Mead, G.R.S. *Apollonius of Tyana.* Chicago, Ares Publishers, 1980 (first published 1901.)

Mead, G.R.S. *Fragments of a Faith Forgotten.* (2nd ed.) London, Theosophical Publishing Society, 1906.

Meier, John. *A Marginal Jew: Rethinking the Historical Jesus Vol. 1; The Roots of the Problem and the Person.* New York, Doubleday, 1991.

Meier, John. *A Marginal Jew: Rethinking the Historical Jesus Vol. 2; Mentor, Message and Miracles.* New York, Doubleday, 1994.

Miles, Jack. *God: A Biography.* New York, Knopf, 1995.

Mitton, C.L. *Jesus: The Fact Behind the Faith.* London, Mowbray, 1973.

Momigliano, Arnoldo. *On Pagans, Jews and Christians.* Middletown, Conn., Wesleyan U.P., 1986.

Momigliano, Alfredo. *The Conflict Between Paganism and Christianity in the Fourth Century.* Oxford, Clarendon Press, 1963.

Muller, Herbert. *The Uses of the Past.* New York, New American Library, 1952.

Murray, Gilbert. *Five Stages of Greek Religion.* (3rd ed.) Garden City, N.J., Doubleday, 1951.

Newsom, Carroll. *The Roots of Christianity.* Englewood Cliffs, N.J., Prentice-Hall, 1979.

Nillson, Martin. *The Dionysiac Mysteries of the Hellenistic and Roman Age.* New York, Arno Press, 1975.

Nock, A.D., *Conversion: The Old and the New in Religion From Alexander the Great to Augustine of Hippo.* Oxford, Clarendon, 1933.

Nock, A.D. *Early Gentile Christianity and Its Hellenistic Background.* New York, Harper Torchbooks, 1964.

Nock, A.D. *Essays on Religion in the Ancient World.* Oxford U.P. 1972.

Ogilvie, R.M. *The Romans and Their Gods in the Age of Augustus.* New York, Norton, 1969.

Olson, Carl (ed.) *The Book of the Goddess Past and Present.* New York, Crossroad, 1983.

Otto, Walter. *Dionysos: Myth and Cult.* Bloomington, Ind., Indiana U.P. 1965.

Pagels, Elaine. *Beyond Belief: The Secret Gospel of Thomas.* New York, Vintage, 2003.

Pagels, Elaine. *The Gnostic Gospels.* New York, Vintage, 1981.

Pagels, Elaine. *The Origin of Satan.* New York, Random House, 1995.

Patterson, L. *Mithraism and Christianity: A Study in Comparative Religions.* Cambridge U.P., 1922.

Rahner, Hugo. *Greek Myths and Christian Mystery.* London, Burns and Oates, 1963.

Reece, Erik. "Jesus Without the Miracles" in Harper's December, 2005.

Ridge, Mian (ed.) *Jesus The Unauthorized Version: Ancient Accounts of the Unknown Christ.* New York, New American Library, 2007.

Riley, Gregory. *The River of God: A New History of Christian Origins.* San Francisco, Harper, 2001

Robertson, John M. *Christianity and Mythology.* London, Watts, 1910.

Robertson, John M. *Pagan Christs: Studies in Comparative Hierology* (2nd ed.) London, Watts, 1919.

Schaberg, Jane. *The Illegitimacy of Jesus.* Sheffield, The Academic Press, 1995.

Sloyan, Gerard. *The Crucifixion of Jesus: History, Myth, Faith.* Minneapolis, Fortress Press, 1995.

Smith, Morton. *Jesus the Magician.* San Francisco, Harper and Row, 1978.

Spiedel, Michael. *Mithras-Orion: Greek Hero and Roman Army God*. Leiden, E.J. Brill, 1980.

Spong, John Shelby. *Jesus for the Non-Religious*. San Francisco, Harper, 2007.

Spong, John Shelby. *Liberating the Gospels*. San Francisco, Harper, 1996.

Spong, John Shelby. *This Hebrew Lord: A Bishop's Search for the Authentic Jesus*. San Francisco, Harper, 1993.

Teixidor, Javier. *The Pagan God: Popular Religion in the Graeco-Roman Near East*. Princeton U.P., 1977.

Toynbee, Arnold. *Christianity Among the Religions of the World*. New York, Scribner's, 1957.

Trocme, Etienne. *Jesus As Seen By His Contemporaries*. Philadelphia, Westminster Press, 1973.

Turcan, Robert. *Cults of the Roman Empire*. Cambridge, Mass., Blackwell, 1996.

Vermaseren, Maarten. *Cybele and Attis: The Myth and the Cult*. London, Thames and Hudson, 1977.

Vermaseren, Maarten. *Mithras: The Secret God*. London, Chatto and Windus. 1963.

Vermes, Geza. *Jesus the Jew*. London, Collins, 1973.

Weigall, Arthur. *The Paganism in Our Christianity*. New York, Putnam's, 1928.

Walsh, Michael. *The Triumph of the Meek: Why Early Christianity Succeeded*. San Francisco, Harper and Row, 1986.

Wells, G.A. *Did Jesus Exist?* London, Elek/Pembertin, 1975.

Wells, G.A. *The Historical Evidence for Jesus.* Buffalo, Prometheus Press, 1982.

Wells, James. *Christ and the Heroes of Heathendom.* London, Religious Tract Society, 1886.

Wilken, Robert. *The Christians As the Romans Saw Them.* New Haven, Yale U.P., 1984.

Wilson, A.N. *Paul: The Mind of the Apostle.* New York, Norton, 1997.

Wilson, Ian. *Jesus: The Evidence.* London, Wiedenfeld & Nicolson, 1984.

Witherington, Ben. *The Jesus Quest: The Third Search for the Jew of Nazareth.* Downer's Grove, Ill., Intervarsity Press, 1995.

Witt, R.E. *Isis in the Graeco-Roman World.* London, Thames and Hudson, 1971.

Zugibe, Frederich. *The Cross and the Shroud: A Medical Inquiry into the Crucifixion.* New York, Paragon House, 1988.